Acknowledgments

In the process of creating this book, a number of people have been enormously helpful to me and deserve special acknowledgment. First, I would like to thank my family, particularly my mother, Judith Alderman, and my father, Edward Alderman, for their support and encouragement. Alyson Shaff and Jennifer Diamond helped me tremendously with their perspective, patience, sanity, and friendship. Throughout the course of this project, Patricia Rose lent me incredible amounts of motivation, enthusiasm, insight, and support, which I greatly appreciate. Berlene Rice is in part responsible for the creation of this book, initially helping me to explore and understand this topic. I would also like to acknowledge Lisa Schimmel, who gave me many useful comments at various stages of revisions, and Cathy Reto, who consistently encouraged this endeavor. Finally, I would like to thank the staff of New Harbinger Publications, in particular Kristin Beck, for giving me the opportunity to have this book published, and Leslie Tilley, editor extraordinaire, whose careful and critical attention really made this book what it is.

Table of Contents

Introduction   1
How to Use This Book

PART I   **Understanding Self-Inflicted Violence**   5

1   **What Is Self-Inflicted Violence?**   7
Characteristics of Self-Inflicted Violence • What SIV
Is Not • How Does Self-Inflicted Violence Develop?
• The Course of Self-Inflicted Violence • Who
Typically Engages in Self-Inflicted Violence? • Types
of Self-Inflicted Violence

2   **Why Do People Engage in Self-Inflicted**   29
Violence?
Relief from Feelings • A Method of Coping
• Stopping, Inducing, or Preventing Dissociation
• Euphoric Feelings • Physically Expressing
Pain • Communication • Self-Nurturing
• Self-Punishment • Reenacting Previous Abuse
• Establishing Control

3   **The Nature of Self-Inflicted Violence**   53
Shame and Self-Inflicted Violence • Ritual and
Self-Inflicted Violence • Is Self-Inflicted Violence
Impulsive?

4   The Cycle of Self-Inflicted Violence   69
Thoughts and SIV • Emotions and SIV • Models
of SIV

**5   Self-Inflicted Violence and Other   91
Psychological Factors**
Trauma • Eating Disorders • Substance Abuse
• Suicide • Borderline Personality Disorder
• Dissociative Identity Disorder • Assessing for
Other Factors

PART II   Ending Self-Inflicted Violence   111

**6   Talking to Others About Self-Inflicted   113
Violence**
How SIV Affects Communication with Friends and
Family • Deciding to Begin Therapy

7   Deciding to Stop Self-Inflicted Violence   127
Why Should I Stop? • To Improve Psychological
and Physical Health • When Should I Stop? • How
Do I Stop? • What Do I Do When I Feel Like
Hurting Myself?

8   After Self-Inflicted Violence   157
What You Can Expect • Coming Out and
Empowerment • Healing Through Helping
• Resources

PART III   For Others

9   For Family and Friends   169
What You May Feel • What You May Think
• What to Do and Not Do

10   For the Therapist   183
Types of SIV • Prevalence of SIV • SIV and
Psychotherapy • Specific Psychotherapeutic Issues
• Therapeutic Strategies

References   207

Introduction

As Laura entered her house she slammed the front door behind her. It had been a bad day, a very bad day. She headed straight through the living room, down the hallway to her bedroom. She hadn't had a day like this in quite some time. Things at school had been terrible. She had failed an important biology test, gotten in trouble for being five minutes late to class, and even had a fight with her best friend. To top it all off, she had missed her bus and had to walk the three miles home from school. As Laura locked the door to her room, she was so angry that her whole body was shaking. All she wanted to do was cry, but no tears would come. Her world seemed to be falling apart around her.

Laura knew what she needed to do to feel better. She took a small wood box from under her bed. Carefully lifting its lid, she removed the contents, a single-edged razor blade and a packet of gauze bandages. Sitting on the carpeted floor, gently rocking back and forth, she stared at the silver blade in her hand. She needed to do it, she told herself. It was the only way she could feel better, feel normal again.

Laura felt no pain as she made the first of several cuts on her left forearm. She watched as the blood spilled from the cuts and dripped down her arm. It felt warm and soothing on her cold skin. After cutting herself in three or four places, Laura wiped the blade clean with a piece of gauze and placed it back in its box. She wrapped her wounds tightly with the bandages, only then feeling the hot sting. Although she felt tired and drained, she also felt much better. Cutting herself had worked, just as it always did.

Although to the majority of people, this story might sound bizarre and unlikely, the fact that you have picked up this book indicates you already know that such events occur. You may be aware of this because you know someone—a friend, family member, student, or client—who self-injures. Or you may know from personal experience, because you hurt yourself, as Laura does, to get through bad times.

The point of this story, indeed the point of this book, is that self-inflicted violence (SIV), or deliberate self-injury, is a behavior that helps people cope and survive. It is not a form of craziness or insanity, as it has often been depicted. People who engage in self-injurious behaviors are not nuts, weird, or deranged, but are people like anyone else, just struggling to deal with what life hands out the best way they can.

In writing this book, I had two principal goals: to provide information and education about self-inflicted violence, a topic that has been severely neglected by the mental health field; and to tell people who self-injure that they are not alone. Many people engage in SIV, and someday many others will recognize this fact.

The Scarred Soul presents most, if not all, of what is currently known about self-inflicted violence. Also included are numerous activities and exercises to help you better understand SIV and decrease or end your own use of SIV, and information for those helping others who engage in SIV.

The text is divided into three distinct sections. The first part, "Understanding Self-Inflicted Violence," spans the first five chapters of this book. It is intended to help you explore and better understand basic issues related to self-injury. Topics include the definition of SIV, exploring why and how SIV occurs, and examining the nature of SIV, and related psychological factors. By the time you have finished reading this first section, you should have a good understanding of self-inflicted violence and the role it plays.

Part II, "Ending Self-Inflicted Violence," is composed of chapters 6 through 8, and presents various methods that can be used to decrease self-injurious behaviors. You will also gain a better understanding of what to expect throughout the process of ending SIV. Even if you are not ready to stop hurting yourself, this section should be informative, interesting, and useful.

The third, and final section of this book is entitled "For Others," and is intended for those dealing with people who self-injure. Friends and family, therapists, and concerned others can use this last section to explore their own feelings and their roles in the lives of those who engage in SIV. Friends and family are offered methods for taking better care of both themselves and those who are hurting themselves. Therapists can explore specific issues and strategies, as well as their limitations in working with clients who self-injure.

How to Use This Book

Although this book is written in simple language and often uses metaphors, anecdotes, and humor to convey ideas, it also offers a comprehensive view of SIV. Each chapter has several activities, intended to help you better understand and control the role of SIV in your life. The more effort and care you put into completing them, the more effective and useful they will be. You will need a three-ring binder and paper or a notebook to record your responses in, because you will want to have them all in one place. From time to time you will be asked to refer back to your responses to a previous exercise as part of a new activity, so it will be important for you to have easy access to your journal or notebook. You may even want to keep this book together with your notebook.

Self-inflicted violence is a difficult issue to live with, to talk about, and even to read about. You may find parts of this book to disturbing, disgusting, or depressing. Those reactions are fairly typical. If this book triggers something for you and makes you want to hurt yourself more than usual, put the book down right away and do whatever you need to do to take care of yourself. You may need to talk with a friend, a therapist, or physician. You might want to take a walk or a hot bath or go to the gym. You might even need to call a crisis line or go to a hospital. Whatever you need to do to keep yourself feeling safe and sane, *do it*. This book will still be around when you feel strong enough to explore some of these issues.

Whether you are someone who is engaging in self-inflicted violence, someone helping others who injure themselves, or someone who is just interested in this topic, I hope you find what is presented here to be interesting, educational, and helpful. My goal throughout the entire book is to provide something from which everyone can learn and grow.

Living with self-inflicted violence is not easy—nor is living without it. I hope that someday soon you will feel secure and safe enough and that you have enough resources that you won't need to hurt yourself anymore. Until that time, keep struggling, keep coping, keep surviving, and keep growing, knowing that you already possess what it takes to succeed—strength and courage.

PART I

Understanding
Self-Inflicted Violence

CHAPTER 1

What Is Self-Inflicted Violence?

The term *self-inflicted violence* is best defined as the intentional harm of one's own body without conscious suicidal intent. In simpler terms, self-inflicted violence (SIV) is the act of physically hurting yourself on purpose.

You may have heard self-inflicted violence referred to as self-mutilation. However, the term *self-mutilation* is a bit misleading, in that it implies that you have permanently damaged or altered your body. This is not always the case. Often, self-inflicted violence has an unnoticeable or temporary effect on the body. Hitting or punching yourself is an example of an act that without question is designed to inflict harm; however, there is often no obvious damage to the skin or body. Thus, the more inclusive term *self-inflicted violence* provides a better, more accurate description of the nature of these acts.

Characteristics of Self-Inflicted Violence

Although it may seem like a strange idea at first, SIV is actually a method of sustaining life and coping during an emotionally difficult time. SIV helps some people feel better by giving them a way to physically express and release their tension and emotional pain. For others, SIV produces chemical changes in their bodies that actually make them feel more happy or more peaceful. (Many of the ways in which SIV is used as a method of coping will be discussed in detail in chapter 2.) Thus, self-inflicted violence is used as a way to temporarily feel better.

Several key components help to identify and define self-inflicted violence. First, SIV is an act that is done *to yourself*. If you have a difficult time controlling your temper and strike out at others, while this is violent, it is not *self-inflicted* violence. If you purposefully burn yourself with a cigarette, this is SIV because you are the recipient of your own abuse. You have to do something harmful to yourself for an act to be considered one of self-inflicted violence.

Second, SIV is a behavior done *by yourself*. If you have another person do something that causes you physical pain, such as getting a tattoo or piercing, you are not engaging in SIV. However, if you do something which injures yourself, such as sticking yourself with pins, needles, or nails, you may be performing an act of self-inflicted violence.

Third, for an action to be identified as SIV it must include some type of *physical* violence, such as hitting, cutting, or burning. All sorts of violence exist, many of which are not physical, like stalking, terrorism, verbal abuse, and other emotionally destructive behaviors. You may even act in ways that are emotionally punishing to yourself, such as acting in self-defeating ways or thinking of yourself as lazy, stupid, or ugly. Although these behaviors are likely to be very disturbing, they are not SIV. SIV is physical, although not all acts of SIV cause noticeable physical damage. If you hit yourself very hard, even if it doesn't not produce a bruise or other mark, you are still engaging in SIV. Regardless of the actual physical effect, SIV has to involve some injury or pain to your body.

Fourth, self-inflicted violence is not performed with the intention of killing yourself. For example, two individuals might each cut their own wrists, one performing an act of SIV and the other attempting to commit suicide. As mentioned above, SIV is used as a way to cope and feel better—to sustain life—so actions made in an attempt to end life do not constitute SIV behaviors.

Lastly, SIV is an intentional act: People who engage in SIV hurt themselves on purpose. You probably remember times when you've clumsily hit your thumb with a hammer, dropped something heavy on your foot, or cut yourself while slicing a bagel. These occurrences are not episodes of self-inflicted violence; they are simply accidents. SIV is not accidental, and in many cases it actually follows a planned or ritualistic pattern. People engaging in SIV may use a particular instrument like a special knife, or may only hurt themselves in a specific environment or at a certain time of day. These patterns are in no way coincidental. Like the SIV act itself, they are purposeful and intentional.

Brian is a seventeen-year-old high-school senior who described his SIV actions this way: "When things just get to be too much, you know, and I feel like I'm losing it, I'll cut myself with razor blades. I just roll up my sleeve, grab the razor, and start slicing. It doesn't really hurt, you know. And when I'm done, I feel kind of numb for a while, and things don't seem so bad anymore." While there are many causes, forms, and results of SIV, Brian's actions clearly demonstrate each of the necessary characteristics that define a behavior as SIV.

To summarize, acts of self-inflicted violence are

- Done to oneself

- Performed by oneself

- Physically violent

- Not suicidal

- Intentional and purposeful

The following section will help you begin to determine whether you have engaged in SIV.

Activity 1.1: Do I Practice SIV?

This activity is designed to help you figure out whether you have actually engaged in SIV. For this and most of the other exercises in this book, you will need a notebook or loose leaf binder with paper and something to write with. You will be answering several questions in writing, and then referring to your answers in later activities. Leave space in the margin for notes you may want to add later on.

Spend a few minutes now thinking about the different ways you have hurt yourself. If you have hurt yourself on a number of occasions, this exercise will be more helpful if you can recall a specific incident that is fairly representative or characteristic of the others. Alternatively, if you have hurt yourself at different times in ways that are very different from one another, you may want to answer each of these questions for each of those times.

1. Where were you? Be specific about the location, not just home, school, or work, but the room or space you were in.

2. What time of day was it? Morning, afternoon, evening, night? Was it dark outside or light?

3. What led up to your hurting yourself? What do you remember about what happened or how you felt before you hurt yourself? Write down as much as you can recall about what preceded the incident.

4. Was anyone else involved? Did you hurt someone else or did anyone help you to hurt yourself?

5. Did you hurt yourself on purpose or was it an accident?

6. How did you hurt yourself? That is, what method did you use— hitting, cutting, burning, picking, pulling out hair? You may have your own terms to describe your behaviors. To fully understand

your self-injurious behaviors, it is important to identify the specific terms you use when you think about these activities. For instance, you might think of cutting yourself as *blading* or burning yourself as *roasting*. Be sure to write down the words you use to describe what you do.

7. Was the act physically violent or was it emotionally abusive? Did you actually harm some part of your body, or did you do something that caused you to fail or think less of yourself or others?

8. Did you intend to kill yourself, or was hurting yourself a way of trying to feel better (either emotionally or physically) even though it may have caused pain?

9. Look back over your answers. Did the act or acts you described meet the criteria for SIV? Was it done to your body and by yourself (not someone else)? Was it deliberate (on purpose) and physically violent? Were you using it as a way to cope or feel better (and not as an attempt to die)?

Some other types of activities bear some similarities to SIV, as discussed in the following sections. If you are confused about whether you have practiced SIV, reading those sections should help clarify the issue for you.

If you have determined that you have engaged in SIV activities, don't worry. You probably knew this already. You will find this book helpful to you in a great number of ways. Keep reading!

If you have determined that you have not engaged in SIV, and you are still concerned about some of your behaviors, reading this book may still be useful. However, you may also want to pursue other sources of information or assistance, such as reading other books or consulting a therapist or counselor.

What SIV Is Not

Self-inflicted violence differs from other behaviors that can or may have injurious effects, such as professional tattooing or piercing, drug use, ritualistic mutilations, and plastic surgery. The distinguishing factors between SIV and these other behaviors generally relate to both purpose and means. SIV behaviors can be viewed as methods of coping, generally having the goal of immediate tension relief. This is to say, SIV makes you feel better in the short term—it decreases anxiety, stress, and negative feelings. The way SIV helps you feel better is fairly complex, involving both psychological and physical factors (the specifics of how and why SIV does this are discussed in chapters 2 and 4).

Also, as discussed in the last section, self-inflicted violent behaviors are inflicted by yourself and to yourself.

The following sections further describe some of the fundamental differences between SIV behaviors and other activities that may be self-injurious.

Alteration of Appearance

Alteration of appearance refers to the purposeful and deliberate act of changing the way your body looks. In many ways, alteration is similar to SIV. For instance, both acts may have the goal and effect of making you feel better in some sense. However, differences between SIV and alteration occur both in method and purpose.

Alteration may be more accurately thought of as self-decoration; it is generally performed in an attempt to enhance the body. This is in direct contrast to self-inflicted violence, in which the purpose of the act seldom has anything to do with beautification. When people engage in SIV, the point of their actions is not the effect it has on their physical appearance—as it is in alteration—rather, it is the effect the act has of easing their psychological distress.

A second important distinction between self-inflicted violence and bodily alteration is in the actual method. A key factor of SIV is that it is self-generated. If you engage in SIV, you hurt yourself through your own actions. In contrast, alteration of your appearance is typically performed by *another*—usually someone trained and/or licensed to do so. If you have tattoos or piercings, most likely you obtained these decorations from the (hopefully) steady hand of another. Likewise, for obvious reasons, plastic surgeons seldom practice on themselves. Thus, alteration, in that it is generally not self-inflicted, fails to meet the definition of SIV.

Alteration differs most from self-inflicted violence in terms of the precipitating factors. While alteration usually stems from feelings of dissatisfaction with your body, SIV typically stems from such feelings as isolation and alienation (this will be discussed further in chapter 2). Getting a tattoo, piercing, or breast implants (for example) generally has the goal of making you more noticeable or more attractive—that is, of decreasing aloneness. For that reason, and because the nature of the act requires verbal and physical contact with at least one other person, alteration is inherently social. SIV, on the other hand, not only begins with feelings of isolation, it increases alienation because it is something that you do to yourself, in private, and keep hidden (in most cases) from others.

Piercings (particularly of the ears), tattoos, and plastic surgery are all relatively common occurrences in our society. If you have altered your body in some way, which is likely, it is important to recognize the distinction between alteration and self-inflicted violence.

Ritual Mutilation

Ritual mutilation can best be described as the alteration of one's body in order to fulfill a demand set forth by some societal group. A society, religion, or peer group may require a particular form of mutilation before a person is accepted as an adult or as a member of the group. Ritual mutilation occurs in many contexts and societies and presents itself in many forms, including genital mutilation, branding, scarring of the face and chest, and some forms of tattooing. Religious, cultural, and societal factors all contribute to instances of ritual mutilation.

Ritual mutilation differs from self-inflicted violence, as alteration does, in terms of its purpose and method. The purpose of ritual mutilation typically includes some rite of passage, such as entrance into adulthood or initiation into a group. You may have read stories or seen pictures of teenagers who undergo tattooing or branding in order to join a particular street gang. Recently, the United States Marine Corps began investigating a ritualized hazing practice called blood pinning. In this ritual, "jump wing" pins are beaten into the chests of newly graduated paratroopers by senior members of their unit. The new paratroopers are literally stabbed with these pins and experience great physical pain as a part of their entrance into this elite group.

In contrast to self-inflicted violence, the goal of ritual mutilation is not to change a distressing emotional state. In fact, ritual mutilation often *produces* emotional as well as physical distress. Many people do not undergo ritual mutilation by choice, rather they are forced to participate. Pain from these procedures is typically intense: anesthetics, if used, tend to be inadequate, and conditions are often not sanitary, leading to infection and long-term problems. In some cases, like that of the paratroopers mentioned above, fear and/or other emotional distress is part of the ritual.

Like alteration, ritual mutilation is generally performed by another or in the company of others, as opposed to SIV, which is practiced in private. Also unlike SIV, the results of the ritual mutilation (scars, tattoos, brands) are usually displayed or publicly acknowledged. Individuals who have engaged in ritual mutilation often feel proud of their scars. Scars or injuries resulting from self-inflicted violence, however, are usually hidden, because most individuals who injure themselves feel great shame about the behavior. Shame is, in fact, a major factor in SIV, as will be discussed in chapter 3.

Activity 1.2: SIV or Another Behavior?

For this exercise you will need to refer back to your answers for the preceding activity.

Look back over what you wrote for activity 1.1. Do any of the actions you described now appear to be alteration of appearance, ritual mutilation, or self-destructive behaviors, rather than SIV? If so, make a note of that in the margin beside the description.

If *all* the actions you described qualify as alteration of appearance or ritual mutilation, then it is unlikely that you practice self-inflicted violence. Nonetheless, ritual mutilation—and in some cases alteration of appearance—

have their own emotional and psychological costs, for which you may want to seek help.

If some or all the incidents you recorded qualify as SIV, the next section will help you understand how they came about.

How Does Self-Inflicted Violence Develop?

One of the more interesting phenomena related to self-inflicted violence is its origin. More often than not, the actual course of development is difficult to determine, let alone understand.

Self-inflicted violence is almost always a secretive behavior. People are reluctant to tell others about their self-injurious activities for fear of others' reactions. At best, someone who practices SIV will be seen as weird; at worst, mentally ill. Loss of affection and loss of autonomy are real possibilities, due to misperceptions about SIV and those who engage in these behaviors. So it is for good reason that SIV is typically kept hidden. And because SIV is so well concealed, it remains mysterious just how individuals first learn or conceive of this behavior as an option.

A young woman named Leslie explained how her self-injurious behaviors developed:

> I first started cutting around the beginning of high school. I can't remember specifically the first time I cut. I can't even remember why I wanted to cut or how I learned about cutting. All I knew was that cutting felt good. Or maybe it just made everything else feel less bad. In any case, it helped.

The way Leslie recollects the origins of her self-injurious behavior is common. If you are unable to remember how you got the idea to hurt yourself in the first place, you are not alone. Most people who engage in self-inflicted violence have little or no idea of how they actually began to do so. An overwhelming number of individuals can cite no definitive event. They cannot remember how they learned of SIV, and they state that their self-injurious behaviors "just happened." Particularly if you've been injuring yourself for a long time, you, like Leslie, may not be able to remember the first time you hurt yourself. If so, don't worry, this is normal.

Occasionally, self-inflicted violence develops through a process known as observational learning. *Observational learning* means learning how to perform a behavior by watching someone else do it. Observed behavior that is rewarded or that appears to be rewarding, is more likely to be imitated than behavior that is punished or has negative consequences.

For example, a fairly common current phenomena is for an untrained individual to perform CPR to save a life. When these people are asked how they knew what to do, they say that they had seen it on television:

They observed the procedure and its positive effect, and mimicked how it was done.

Although for most people the chances of witnessing someone performing an act of SIV are small, in some environments the odds are much higher. Observation and learning of SIV behaviors has been noted in both psychiatric hospitals (and similar facilities) and prisons. In these environments, people typically feel intense negative emotions and have little control over their lives. So they may be more likely to engage in SIV in these places than they would in another environment, since the SIV helps them cope with their pain and powerlessness. The lack of privacy in these settings make these behaviors visible to others who are in the same negative situation, and having observed the behavior, they may in turn try SIV as a coping mechanism.

There is also more concrete aspect. People who engage in SIV in institutional settings often receive secondary gains—benefits such as special treatment or attention. If you see someone behave in a way that apparently improves his or her situation, and yours is similar, it makes perfect sense that you would do the same thing in an attempt to improve your situation.

Observational learning, however, accounts for only a small percentage of people who engage in SIV. So it is likely that you have never seen someone else intentionally hurt themself, let alone tried to mimic that behavior. Like many individuals who injure themselves, as well as researchers and clinicians, you may be totally in the dark about how you began to hurt yourself. One of the characteristics that makes self-inflicted violence so interesting and unique is its mysterious origins.

Activity 1.3: How Did I Learn About SIV?

This activity will help you to determine, as much as possible, how you first began hurting yourself. Even if, like many people, you cannot recall specifically how you became aware of SIV, this exercise will still be helpful. By looking at how you discovered that these behaviors helped you in some way, you will be laying the groundwork for learning how to stop hurting yourself.

In your journal, answer the following questions in as much detail as possible.

1. How did you first learn about SIV? Be as specific as you can. Did you see someone else injuring themselves? Did you read about this behavior or see it in a movie or on television? Did someone tell you about SIV? Did you discover it accidentally? Perhaps you unintentionally hurt yourself when you were emotionally upset and you found that it made you feel better.

2. What happened the first time you deliberately hurt yourself? (If you can't remember the first time, describe any specific incident). What was happening before you hurt yourself? What were you

doing, feeling, thinking? How did you injure yourself? How did you feel during and after this incident? Did hurting yourself make you feel better, worse, or both?

3. Why have you continued to use SIV (assuming that you have)? What did it do for you that made you try it again? Did it produce or reduce certain feelings (name those feelings)? How did it help you?

We will revisit your answers to these questions in a later chapter. In the interim, if you recall any additional details about how and why you started to engage in SIV, add them to what you have written in your journal.

Physiological Aspects of SIV

Although it is unclear exactly how people originally learn to hurt themselves, there are several theories about the role of physiology in this process. Your biology, including your particular genetics and the chemicals in your body, affects your feelings, thoughts, physical sensations, and even your behavior. The influence of the body on the mind (and vice versa) has been shown time and time again and has been examined in such areas as alcoholism, heart disease, mental illness, and cancer. Your physiology could influence your desire or need to engage in SIV in several ways. One widely recognized physiological factor that could influence your SIV activities is related to endorphins. Neurotransmitters, including endorphins, are chemicals that carry information through your brain and help you to think, feel, and act. The nervous system contains many types of neurotransmitters (at least fifty), each of which affects you differently. Endorphins are simply one of these chemicals.

Endorphins are natural opiates and are involved with helping you to feel pleasure and control the sensation of pain. Drugs such as morphine work because they mimic the action of endorphins. When your brain releases endorphins you generally feel a pleasurable sensation, similar to that produced by morphine, heroin, opium, and codeine. Endorphins also protect you from experiencing pain. When you injure yourself, your brain is sent a signal that tells it to release endorphins so that you don't feel much pain. Many people who engage in SIV indicate that they feel little, if any, physical pain from their self-injuries.

One theory about the relationship between SIV and physiology suggests that some people engage in SIV because their endorphins aren't functioning properly. According to this theory, these people have a problem maintaining what would be considered a normal level of endorphins in their system—their endorphin levels are too low—and they use SIV to generate additional endorphins. Although this theory seems logical, the limited amount of research that has been done in this area hasn't provided much support.

A second theory about the connection between physiology and SIV postulates addiction to endorphins. It has been shown that SIV can produce endorphins before, during, or after the actual act of self-injury. It has been theorized that some people become so addicted to the feelings produced by the release of endorphins that they purposefully injure themselves in order to produce these chemicals. Although this may sound bizarre, many people who engage in physical exercise—which also produces endorphins—say they do so just for the pleasurable feelings they experience when endorphins are released. Clearly these are powerful chemicals.

Although SIV may seem like an extreme way to produce endorphins, some research supports this theory. One study found that when the effects of the endorphins were blocked (by administrating a drug called naltrexone), so that the release of endorphins was no longer gratifying, the SIV activities of the individuals in the study did, in fact, decrease. Because the chemicals were no longer working in ways that were pleasurable, there was no reason to continue using self-inflicted violence to release them. However, this addiction theory only held true for those people who were injuring themselves frequently and severely. For most people who engage in SIV, this theory has not yet been found to be accurate. Thus, although endorphins are clearly powerful chemicals that efficiently provide pleasure and control pain, they may not be a primary influence on self-injury.

Dopamine, a neurotransmitter that has been linked to psychological health, is also thought to play a role in self-injury. Too much dopamine in the brain is associated with an inability to think clearly and rationally. In some cases, excess dopamine has been thought to be the cause of schizophrenia, a psychological disorder in which the person loses contact with reality. Although it has not actually been proven, some researchers believe that excess dopamine can cause a person to self-injure, but the dynamics of how it might do so have not yet been explored.

Serotonin is another neurotransmitter believed to affect SIV. Serotonin is involved in both sleep and depression. Excess serotonin can cause you to feel sleepy or depressed. Serotonin is eventually converted to melatonin, the same hormone that is touted as a sleep aid and cure for jet lag and you can buy at your local natural foods store or pharmacy. Insufficient amounts of serotonin have been thought to influence self-injury, but again, exact ways in which deficiencies of serotonin are associated with SIV haven't been determined.

As you can see, a great deal of mystery and controversy still surrounds the role of physiology in self-inflicted violence. Although physiology may play a part in influencing SIV, not enough is known to draw any firm conclusions. The origins and development of SIV behaviors are likely to remain a mystery for some time.

The Course of Self-Inflicted Violence

Although the origins of SIV are still obscure, the typical course is better understood. Self-inflicted violence tends to follow a fairly predictable pattern, typically first appearing during adolescence. Adolescence, as you may well remember, is a time of great turbulence and change. Perhaps it is this radical change that creates the need for new and more extreme methods of coping.

The following analogy may help clarify this point. Say you have a car with a small hole in the muffler. You put a piece of duct tape over the hole to control the sound somewhat. So you still hear a bit of noise when you drive, but a lot of the time you just tune it out; it isn't very troublesome. You're able to drive around like this for a long time, with the noise sometimes bothering you and sometimes going unnoticed. This represents your childhood.

However, after a while, you find that the hole has suddenly gotten a lot bigger. You can't control the noise with just a piece of tape, and you are absolutely unable to ignore the sound. It may have even become so bad that your friends, family, or neighbors have started nagging you to do something about your muffler and its obnoxious racket. You have now entered adolescence. The ways you used to cope simply don't take care of your current problems, which are bigger, tougher, and more numerous than anything you had to deal with as a child. You need to find new ways to help you live, and you may have turned to SIV to help you cope with the turmoil of adolescence.

One of the new things adolescents must learn to deal with is the increased need for autonomy and control that accompanies adolescence. Adolescence is the time in life when you start to achieve a real sense of yourself as an independent and autonomous person, capable of making your own choices and decisions. Unfortunately, the adults who up until that point have been deciding things for you don't always see things the same way. When you injure yourself, you are demonstrating (if only to yourself) that you are in complete control of your own body, and in that respect you have autonomy. Everyone has a need to feel in control in some sense. Self-inflicted violence can be one way of asserting control.

Also, as you probably remember, during adolesence social relationships go through tremendous change, often leaving teenagers feeling alienated and isolated. As mentioned earlier, these feelings often lead to episodes of self-injury as a way of coping with the pain.

Most people who self-injure begin by cutting themselves on the arm or leg with a knife, razor blade, or other sharp object. Typically, SIV then moves from an initial act of cutting to a trial of various other forms of wounding, such as burning or hitting, until the person settles on a preferred method. People most commonly use cutting or burning as their preferred SIV activity. Sometimes, however, people choose hitting, nail biting, hair pulling, breaking bones, or interfering with the healing of wounds as their preferred method of self-injury.

The occurrence of self-inflicted violence tends to peak in the early to mid-twenties. Like the adolescent years, the early twenties are a time of great change and conflict in people's lives, and they often present many new responsibilities and roles. During this time, SIV may be used as a coping mechanism to temporarily gain a sense of control over a complex and confusing world and relieve the extreme tension accompanying this age.

Most coping mechanisms, such as crying, sleeping, exercising, shopping, and even SIV lose their effectiveness over time. It is probably for this reason that the occurrence of self-injurious behavior decreases with age. Most individuals stop engaging in SIV by the time they reach their thirties. This decrease in SIV seems to occur independently of any intervention of psychotherapy, medication, or related techniques. This means that, although there are certainly ways to end or reduce your SIV activities earlier—and good reasons for doing so—it appears that inflicting self-harm is something you may well simply outgrow in time.

Note that the information presented above describes the *typical* course of self-inflicted violence; you may find that your pattern is quite different. For instance, you may have started hurting yourself much earlier or later than adolescence. You may initially have hurt yourself by some other means than cutting. You may be over thirty and continuing to hurt yourself. If the course of your self-inflicted violence is much different from what is noted here, you are not alone. The limited amount of information available on SIV may present a skewed picture of the development and course of this behavior. It is very likely that others have had experiences similar to yours.

Activity 1.4: SIV's Course Through My Life

This activity will help you to assess the development of SIV in your life. You may be surprised at the amount of change that has occurred since you first started to injure yourself. You may also be surprised by the length of time you have been engaging in SIV.

In your journal, answer the following questions.

1. How old were you when you first intentionally hurt yourself?

2. How old are you now? How long have you been engaging in SIV?

3. When you first began to engage in SIV, how did you typically go about it? Was there a particular method you used?

4. What methods of injuring yourself have you used since then? What method(s) do you currently use?

5. When the SIV first started, how often would you hurt yourself? Daily? Weekly? Monthly?

6. How often do you hurt yourself now?

7. Have you tried to stop engaging in SIV? If so, when and how many times? How long were you able to refrain from hurting yourself?

8. Have you ever sought psychological help for SIV? What kind (individual, group, inpatient)? How long were you in therapy? How did it affect your SIV activities?

9. Why do you think you returned to SIV?

As with the preceding exercise, we will be using your answers to some of these questions in later activities aimed at stopping SIV. If you recall any further details in the meantime, add them to what you have written in your journal.

Who Typically Engages in Self-Inflicted Violence?

It's difficult to describe a "typical" anything. A "typical" dog, a "typical" rainy day, a "typical" politician—each of these will mean something different to everyone. It is similarly difficulty to create a composite of the "typical" individual who self-injures. However, by assembling the traits commonly found in people who hurt themselves, it is possible to create a portrait of the person who typically engages in self-inflicted violence.

As you read this section, you may find yourself thinking *This isn't me at all* or *This part seems right, but that part is way off.* And you'll be absolutely correct. You won't exactly meet the description of the "typical" person who engages in SIV. However, you will almost certainly find some similarities between yourself and the hypothetical "typical."

Gender

Both men and women intentionally injure themselves. In fact, the proportion of men and women who engage in SIV is roughly equal. However, women are seen more often than men in settings related to psychological services (such as a therapist's office), so in this environment—in the psychological community—the prevalence of self-injury among women appears to be higher than among men. Similarly, prison settings produce a greater number of SIV behaviors among men than among women, most likely because more men are imprisoned than women. Thus, in different settings it can appear as though one gender engages in self-inflicted violence more often than the other. In truth, however, this is not the case in the population as a whole.

Age

As mentioned earlier, SIV typically begins during adolescence. It then escalates or becomes more frequent during the early twenties and decreases or disappears in the thirties.

Substance Abuse

Many individuals who injure themselves also have histories of abuse of such substances as alcohol and drugs. This is not surprising. People often use alcohol or another drug to change their mood or physical state—to feel differently. Self-inflicted violence has a similar goal: It is used to change the person's emotional—and sometimes physical—experience. Substance abuse and self-abuse both serve as methods of coping, in that they help people to get through difficult moments. Both activities can temporarily help alleviate distress and negative feelings. It is probably the similar function of the two behaviors that makes substance abuse a commonly found characteristic among people who engage in SIV.

It is interesting to note that while histories of substance abuse are common in individuals who engage in SIV, rarely will individuals be under the influence of a substance when they engage in deliberately injurious behavior. Perhaps SIV provides such an efficient method of coping that additional coping strategies, such as drugs and alcohol, become unwarranted.

Eating Disorders

The presence of eating disorders, like that of substance abuse, is also common in people who engage in self-inflicted violence. Eating disorders, including anorexia nervosa and bulimia nervosa, seem to provide a way to temporarily alleviate negative or difficult emotions. That is, they have a similar function as self-inflicted violence.

Unlike drugs and alcohol, which generally are not used during an episode of SIV, eating disorders frequently coexist with SIV. The reason for this is quite simple: Eating disorders and their effects can last a long time, whereas the effects of drugs and alcohol wear off fairly quickly. For instance, if you were to have a few beers, the effects of the beer would be gone within a few hours at most. At that time, you might decide that you still feel bad and engage in an act of SIV to try to feel better. However, if you have anorexia nervosa, you are radically underweight, and you are unable to change this condition in a short period of time (such as a few hours or a few days). So if you have anorexia nervosa and you decide to hurt yourself, the two factors, eating disorders and SIV, would occur simultaneously. The topic of eating disorders and their relationship with SIV is discussed more thoroughly in chapter 5.

Poor Mood Regulation

As discussed earlier, self-inflicted violence is one method of regulating your mood or emotions—what psychologists call affect. People who engage in self-injurious behavior often lack the ability to effectively regulate their emotions in other ways. Thus, it makes sense for them to use SIV as a strategy for managing their emotions and affective states. The flip side of this is that people who are better able to manage their moods are generally not motivated to harm themselves. Therefore, it makes a lot of sense that there is a close relationship between self-inflicted violence and poor regulation of mood. This topic will be discussed further in chapters 2 and 4.

History of Abuse

The majority of people who hurt themselves were hurt by others when they were children, suffering physical, sexual, or emotional abuse. A nineteen-year-old college sophomore relates, "I hurt myself so that I can feel the pain of now, of today. I'd rather feel pain from now, that I'm creating, than the pain from my past . . . I was abused pretty bad as a kid." This statement illustrates some of the connections between SIV and abuse. SIV can be a way to replicate the original abuse, to establish control, to provide self-punishment, to express emotional pain, or some combination of several or all of these things.

If you engage in self-inflicted violence, chances are pretty good that you were abused as a child. However, this does not mean that everyone who was traumatized during childhood goes on to injure themselves as adolescents or adults. Child abuse is simply related to self-inflicted violence; it does not cause SIV. The role of trauma in SIV activities will be discussed in more detail in chapter 5.

History of Psychological Treatment

A history of psychological treatment is common among people who injure themselves. The same feelings or experiences that lead people to engage in SIV also lead them to seek other answers, such as therapy. However, for most people who injure themselves psychological treatment proves to be dissatisfying, as you yourself may have experienced.

Joan, a thirty-year-old educator, states, "I quit going to my therapist after a couple of months. During the first few sessions, when I was deciding if I wanted to keep seeing her, I was pretty up-front about hurting myself. But a few weeks later, when I actually started showing her my fresh wounds, she kind of backed off, like she was scared or something. She just wasn't giving me the kind of help I needed, so I quit."

There are several possible reasons for such dissatisfaction. First, in many cases, the topic of self-inflicted violence is not addressed. Rarely will a mental health professional inquire about this type of behavior. Clinicians often overlook the issue of SIV out of inexperience or ignorance or avoid it out of disgust. Either way, it is generally up to the client, to bring up the topic of self-injury. But, because of the shame and secrecy surrounding SIV, many clients never disclose this information. If this happened to you, it would hardly be surprising for you to feel dissatisfied with the treatment you received, given that such an important issue was not addressed.

Second, when clinicians do learn of self-inflicted violence, their reactions and strategies for treatment are not always in the client's best interest. Clinicians may demand that the client stop his or her self-injurious behaviors or risk being admitted to a psychiatric ward or hospital.

Either of these situations may have left you feeling as bad or worse than you did before entering psychotherapy. The topic of consulting a therapist is discussed in chapter 6. Chapter 10 discusses psychotherapy from the clinician's point of view, including the topics of reactions and therapeutic strategies.

Types of Self-Inflicted Violence

Self-inflicted violence is generally divided into three categories: Psychotic, Organic, and Typical. Forms of Psychotic SIV include removing or amputating body parts, including eyes, limbs, ears, and genitals. Historical and literary figures such as Vincent Van Gogh (who cut off part of his ear) and Sophocles's King Oedipus (who blinded himself) offer examples of Psychotic SIV. Often, these behaviors are a response to hallucinations or delusions the individual is experiencing. A hallucination is an experience of physically sensing something that is not real. For example, seeing an eight-legged beagle sitting in the middle of your living room would be a hallucination, unless you have a very strange pet. Similarly, hearing voices (through your ears, not just in your head) speaking to you when no one is around is another type of hallucination.

While hallucinations involve senses and perceptions, delusions are related to thoughts, when someone believes something which objectively cannot be true. For instance, thinking that you are Santa Claus or Cleopatra would be a delusion. Both hallucinations and delusions are sometimes responsible for people self-inflicting violence. While these types of SIV are severe, they are also easily identifiable, which is helpful in treating them.

Organic self-inflicted violence usually stems from autistic disorders, developmental disabilities, or other physiologically induced disorders. Organic types of SIV are always influenced by a physical or chemical problem in the body. Behaviors within this category include lip biting and head banging. These behaviors seem to serve a self-stimulating or self-soothing purpose.

In contrast, Typical SIV occurs for emotional or psychological reasons not stemming from psychotic (hallucinations or delusions) or organic (physical) factors. Most forms of SIV fall into this category. It is highly likely that if you are engaging in self-inflicted violence, you are performing one of the following acts:

- Cutting yourself

- Burning yourself

- Interfering with the healing of wounds by reopening them

- Biting your fingernails excessively

- Pulling out or plucking your hair to an excessive degree (trichotillomania)

- Hitting or bruising yourself

- Intentionally breaking your own bones

Typical forms of SIV generally are used as to make yourself feel better and cope with your life (as will be discussed in chapter 2). During an act of Typical self-injury, you do not lose touch with reality or enter a psychotic state.

As you can see, there are many forms of Typical self-inflicted violence. The following sections discuss some of the most common types of self-inflicted violence. Inevitably, some means of self-injury will have been omitted. Given the wide variety of ways people can hurt themselves, it is not possible to present an exhaustive list. The methods of self-injury presented here represent the most widely used and recognized types of SIV.

Cutting

Cutting is probably the most common of all the ways that people intentionally injure themselves. Most often the cutting is done with a razor blade, knife, piece of glass, or similarly sharp object. The majority of cuts are made on the arms, wrists, legs, and chest, but some people cut themselves on other parts of the body, including stomach, face, neck, breasts, and genitals. However, because of the accessibility of the arms and wrists, these continue to be the most frequently used areas for cutting. Cuts or scars on these areas of the body can also be explained more easily, making it less likely that others will suspect self-injury. Attributing a fresh wound to a slip of the knife while chopping vegetables is much easier when the wound is on your hand than when the wound is on your neck. Cutting is often known by other names, such as *slashing* or *slicing*.

Brett is a twenty-four-year-old waiter who frequently engages in episodes of cutting. "I use a scalpel that I bought at a swap meet. It's really sharp and makes it easy to slice up my arms. Watching the blood run down my arms calms me down. I don't really like hurting myself, but I like the way it makes me feel."

Burning

Burning yourself is also a relatively common form of self-inflicted violence, although it's not quite as prevalent as cutting. A wide number of methods are used to inflict the burns, including cigarettes, matches, lighters, kitchen-stove burners, heated objects (such as a hot skillet or a branding iron), and burning objects. Some people even use a flammable substance such as gasoline, propane, lighter fluid, or alcohol. The availability of such materials as cigarettes, matches, and lighters may promote these types of activities. Like cutting, burns are generally inflicted on the arms, wrists, legs, and chest.

Sally, a fourteen-year-old high-school freshman, describes her SIV. "Most of the time when I hurt myself, I do it with a lighter. I heat up the metal part on the end and press it real hard against my leg. Sometimes I'll do this five or six times in a row."

Interfering with the Healing of Wounds

Most of us at one time or another have interfered with the healing of a wound. It is common to see young children picking at their newly formed scabs. Many of us have unconsciously scratched or picked at a scab only to find it oozing fresh blood. Interfering with the healing of wounds is considered a self-injurious behavior when it is done with intention and purpose.

Much like other forms of SIV, interfering with wounds' healing process is a way of coping with overwhelming or disturbing emotional states. Some people remove stitches prematurely, insert objects such as pins, needles, or toothpicks into healing wounds, or do other things that reopen the wound. Disruption of the healing process is easily performed and can be done without particular tools. It also doesn't draw much, if any, attention, simply because it is a common—if not socially acceptable—practice. Therefore, although this type of self-inflicted violence is statistically less common than cutting or burning, it lends itself to situations in which there is little privacy or instruments for self-injury are not available.

David, an eighteen-year-old high-school senior, relates, "When I was younger I used to stick pins in my scabs. I liked feeling the sting and watching the fresh blood cover the old scab. My mom would always wonder why my cuts took so long to heal."

Hitting or Bruising

It's a common thing to see characters in television and films, upon making some sort of mistake, hit themselves on the head with their hands. This may be a case of art imitating life. Hitting or bruising yourself is a relatively common SIV activity. Hitting yourself with your fist is one such method of inflicting self-injury, and it often leaves serious bruises on the body. Both head and thighs are common sites for such battering, because of both their accessibility and the ease with which bruises there can be covered by clothing or hair.

Hitting or bruising yourself may not even seem like a form of self-inflicted violence, because of the relatively minor damage it causes. However, because it serves the purpose of alleviating disturbing emotional states, functioning in the same way as other forms of self-injury, hitting or bruising yourself can clearly be named as a method of SIV.

"Hitting myself on my thighs is my favorite way to self-injure," says Shaunna. "I like feeling the power of my fist and seeing the bruises start to form and turn my skin different colors. Hitting myself makes me feel strong and in control and helps me to get rid of some anger."

Excessive Nail Biting

Most of us at one time or another have bitten our fingernails during times of stress or anxiety or just to trim a ragged fingernail. What differentiates this nail biting from nail biting as a form of self-inflicted violence is the severity and frequency of the behavior. Excessive nail biting results in injury to the fingernails or cuticles. Poeple who do this often find themselves biting their nails to the point of drawing blood.

Like other forms of SIV, nail biting is a response to a state of psychological discomfort. The nail biting helps to alleviate this disturbing emotional state. During an episode of nail biting you may be unaware of your behavior and the extent of damage done. Thus, you will probably end a nail-biting episode only when you realize that physical injury has occurred, which is often evidenced by the blood from your injuries.

"Look at my nails, they're a mess!" exclaims Lisa, a thirty-year-old homemaker. "I've had this problem for years and years. I don't even realize that my fingers are in my mouth until I taste the blood. I once tried putting really bad tasting stuff on my fingers to make me stop, but even that didn't work."

Excessive Scratching

Excessive scratching follows a similar pattern to that of nail biting. Scratching, a perfectly normal behavior, becomes a form of self-inflicted violence when it becomes more extreme in frequency, intensity, or duration. This behavior usually results in an area of skin becoming raw and even bloody, producing serious damage. Areas of the body most frequently affected are the arms and legs and other easily accessed areas.

Typically, the scratching is done with just the fingernails, but in some cases a sharp or semisharp object such as a knife, comb, or pencil is used. Like other forms of SIV, excessive scratching serves as a method of coping, allowing for the release of tension. And like nail biting, excessive scratching can occur without conscious thought; awareness of the extent of damage may come only after the injury is serious enough to produce bleeding or similar consequences.

Mary, a forty-year-old attorney relates this about her SIV behaviors: "The first few times I noticed blood on my hairline, I didn't understand what had happened. Around the forth or fifth time of finding blood on my fingers and in my hair, I figured it out. I had been scratching my head so hard that I was making myself bleed."

Pulling Out Your Hair

Trichotillomania, the excessive and recurrent removal of your own hair resulting in a noticeable loss of hair, is the only form of self-inflicted violence to be recognized as a distinct psychological disorder in the *Diagnostic and Statistical Manual of Mental Disorders* (known as DSM-IV). The DSM-IV is used by professionals in the mental health field to determine psychological and psychiatric diagnoses.

Generally, hair is removed from the scalp, eyebrows, or beard. However, recurrent removal of hair from any part of the body would fall into this category of SIV.

Pulling out hair stems from a state of tension or unease, similar to the other types of self-inflicted violence. When you remove your own hair you may feel an incredible sensation of pleasure or relief. This sense of relief is one of the primary goals of any self-inflicted violent activity. One common result of trichotillomania is a noticeable bald spot, which the person often attempts to cover with a hat, bandage, or sunglasses (to hide the eyebrows).

A twenty-nine-year-old prison inmate describes his hair-pulling activities this way: "I wish I could just get a haircut so I wouldn't be able to pull out my hair . . . It's just something I do and I just can't stop. Look at me, I'm missing these big clumps of hair. I must look pretty scary. I know the other guys think I'm nuts. I feel like I've got no control over this."

Intentional Breaking of Bones

Although not as frequently observed as other types of self-inflicted violence, breaking your own bones is a serious form of self-injury. Breaking your own bones is often done with the aid of an instrument, such as a hammer, brick, or other heavy object. Sometimes people will throw themselves into walls or doors in an attempt to break a bone.

Broken bones are rarely suspected as stemming from SIV activities. Therefore, people who break their own bones generally receive some secondary gains or benefits (attention, help, communication), which may reinforce further such activities. If you have ever broken a bone (purposefully or otherwise), and had to endure the confinement of a cast, you can attest to the increase in attention and offered assistance derived from this plaster accessory. However, as a method of inflicting self-injury, this one has a "downside"—that bones take quite a long time to heal. Thus, engaging in this type of behavior with any frequency is virtually impossible.

"I was twelve the first time I tried to break my arm," states Randy, a twenty-year-old salesman. "I don't know what I was thinking or what the hell was going on. But, I remember taking a hammer and wailing down on my left arm. My aim wasn't so good and I ended up breaking my little finger. It hurt like crazy, but it felt good, too. Since then I've broken at least a dozen bones."

Activity 1.5: How I Hurt Myself

This activity is designed to help you identify and understand the ways in which you practice SIV. The information that you provide in this activity will be useful to you now and in the future. Later on, when addressing ways to stop injuring yourself, you will be referring back to this activity.

Some parts of this exercise may seem similar to questions you answered in previous activities. Nonetheless, it is important that you follow these instructions precisely. Take the time to write complete, detailed responses in your journal.

1. In activity 1.4, you wrote down the ways you have hurt yourself in the past and how you currently hurt yourself. On a fresh page in your journal, make a list of those behaviors. If as a result of reading the preceding sections on types of SIV you can add to that list, do so now.

2. Now, for each of type of SIV you practiced in the past, describe what you do or did in detail. For example, if you have cut yourself, on how many occasions have you done so? How old were you at the time? What did you use to cut yourself: a knife, a razor? How many cuts did you make each time? Be sure to describe each of the methods you have used in the same manner.

3. What method(s) of SIV do you typically use in the present? Use whatever words you use to describe the action to yourself.

4. How often do you hurt yourself?

5. Is anyone around when you hurt yourself? If so, who?

6. What do you typically feel before you hurt yourself: pain, anger, numbness?

7. What do you do when you hurt yourself? Where on your body do you injure yourself and to what degree? What are the consequences: Do you bleed, bruise, burn? How do you feel emotionally when you hurt yourself?

8. Do you have a routine or pattern that you follow each time, in terms of place, time, instruments used, and so forth? If so, describe it.

9. What do you do after you engage in self-inflicted violence? Do you contact anyone (friend, therapist, doctor)? Do you go to sleep?

10. Have you ever had to seek medical attention for your injuries? What happened? How were you treated by the medical professionals? Did you reveal how you really obtained your injuries?

The answers to these questions will be very helpful to you in understanding some of the ways by which you hurt yourself. Understanding how you inflict your injuries is a necessary step in beginning to change these behaviors.

The next chapter will give you a deeper understand of some of the reasons people engage in SIV.

CHAPTER 2

Why Do People Engage in Self-Inflicted Violence?

Why would someone purposefully and willfully hurt him- or herself? You may have asked yourself this question many times. If you are open about your self-injuries, you have probably even had to respond to this question frequently in answering inquisitive friends and family members. Whether or not you have tried to answer this question, you may not have a clear understanding of why you hurt yourself. This chapter presents some of the possible reasons why you engage in acts of self-inflicted violence.

Molly is a thirty-four-year-old lawyer who lives in Southern California. She has been cutting her arms for the past eighteen years, approximately twice a year. On these infrequent occasions, she generally makes only one or two small cuts on her upper arms. Molly hasn't told any of her friends or family that she hurts herself. The one time a coworker noticed and ask about Molly's wounds, Molly told him that she had been injured while trying to clip her cat's claws.

Molly isn't sure why she cuts herself. She describes her desire to cut as being like the desire to sleep—cutting feels like a need rather than simply a want. Molly feels a sense of relief and release after injuring herself. She feels more complete, whole, and at peace.

Like many people who hurt themselves, Molly is not readily able to recognize the motivations for her behaviors. She is, however, better able to identify her internal states and the results of her actions.

The reasons presented in this chapter are those *most commonly* cited when people explain why they hurt themselves. If you don't see your explanation listed, it doesn't mean your reason isn't valid. This chapter covers many, but by no means all, of the reasons you might hurt yourself.

Before reading further, take some time to complete activity 2.1, which will help you identify the reasons you engage in SIV.

Activity 2.1: Why Do I Hurt Myself?

This activity is the first step in gaining a better understanding of why you injure yourself, and it will lay the groundwork for changing this behavior (assuming you want to). In trying to change any habit or behavior, it's important to go back to the reasons why it occurs and try to alter the cause of the act. For instance, if you smoke cigarettes when you're stressed, changing the amount of stress you feel should change your desire to smoke. The same principle applies to SIV. So the first step in changing your SIV behaviors is to find out why they occur in the first place.

Write your responses to the following questions in your journal. In answering these questions, try to be as specific as you can. There are no right or wrong answers. The idea is simply to brainstorm as many possible things that are related to your SIV as you can. Even if you're not sure your answers are accurate, write them down anyway. Begin by thinking back to a time when you hurt yourself—a recent episode of SIV or an episode from a while ago.

1. What did you do? Describe this particular episode of SIV.

2. What were you feeling emotionally and physically right before you hurt yourself? Were you angry? Depressed? Sad? Numb?

3. What thoughts were going through your mind before this incident? Were you thinking that your life was a mess? That you were a failure? That no one cared about you?

4. What was happening prior to your hurting yourself? Had you had an argument with a friend? Had you been fired from your job? Had you been standing in a long line at the bank? What, if any, was the particular event that led up to this act of SIV?

5. What did you hope the SIV would do for you? Give you a way to release your pent up feelings? Get you some special attention? Make you feel more whole or more real? How did you think it would help?

6. Did the SIV help you in the way that you expected?

Relief from Feelings

As mentioned in chapter 1, one of the more common goals of SIV is to feel better at a time when you are emotionally overwhelmed. Most often, when people hurt themselves they are trying to relieve intense emotions and get some relief from tremendous internal psychic pressure. At times, such overwhelming emotions can seem uncontrollable, frightening, and dangerous. You may feel disorganized, disoriented, and as if your head might explode at any second. During these times it may appear as though there is no way to escape these feelings except to hurt yourself.

People who injure themselves often aren't able to regulate or control their emotions well. You may find it difficult to identify, express, or release your emotions. If you're like most adolescents and adults who hurt themselves, you never developed the ability to feel and experience emotions as others do: by crying, yelling, or screaming. Or you may not have been allowed to show or release your true emotions. Yet your feelings still exist, whether you show them or not. You may have adopted SIV as a strategy for getting relief from these intense feelings.

There are numerous reasons why you may not have developed a more typical way of releasing your emotions. It may have been unsafe—physically or psychologically—for you to express you feelings within your environment. For example, a common saying has it that "big boys don't cry." Perhaps in your family you were punished every time you shed a tear, and so you learned that you shouldn't show anyone your real feelings. Or maybe the expression of your feelings was ignored, denied, or disputed, any of which could certainly have a psychological impact. For instance, let's say that your mother was two hours late picking you up from school and you had to stand outside in the rain while you waited. When your mother finally arrived at the school, you got in the car, slammed the door, and told your mother that you were really angry that she had been so late. If your mother ignored you (by not responding to what you had said), disregarded your feelings (made a joke or said, "Well, you'll live," which you interpreted as, "So what if you're mad; I don't care"), or disputed your emotions (by saying, for example, "You're not really mad, you're just tired"), you probably would have been left with the impression that your feelings didn't matter. Once you believe that your feelings are not important to others, you are more likely to refrain from expressing them in a typical or direct way, by talking, crying, yelling, and so on.

A second reason you may not have developed a more common way of releasing your feelings has to do with the people around you. If your parents or other people you grew up around were not able to express their own emotions safely and directly, by talking, for example, you may not have been able to learn that method because you didn't see it demonstrated. Or if your parents physically fought each other when they were angry, you may have assumed that violence is a good way of expressing these feelings. Alternatively, you may have seen someone else you know using alcohol or drugs relieve feelings of depression or anxiety. In the same way that learning to read, write, or tie your shoes requires an instructor, learning how to appropriately express or relieve your emotions must be taught, either explicitly or by example (preferably both). If the people around you did not show you or teach you how to release your feelings in a typical or healthy manner, you wouldn't have been able to learn that skill.

A third reason you might have chosen SIV as a method to relieve your feelings also has to do with the behaviors of those close to you. As mentioned in chapter 1, if you saw others using SIV to release their feelings, you may have simply mimicked their behaviors. If you watch someone hurt him- or herself, and the results seem beneficial you might just try it yourself. This modeling of behavior is fairly common in such settings as jails, prisons, and inpatient psychiatric hospitals.

Whatever your reason for using self-inflicted violence to release overwhelming emotions, the effect is the same: Imagine that you are a can of soda. You're sitting there in your refrigerator, having a perfectly fine day, when suddenly something occurs that shakes you up—an earthquake, a passing truck, a mischievous kid; you don't know what. All you do know at this point is that you're very uncomfortable, feeling as if you're about to explode. If you think about it, you know that if you just wait, the feelings will pass and the tension will lessen. But because the tension at the moment is so extreme, you feel the need to pop your top. So you do this. This physical change gives you relief, but the price of this relief is extreme. You have behaved in a manner that changes you permanently.

People typically report that before engaging in an act of self-inflicted violence, they feel isolated, alienated, depressed, and frustrated. Whatever the source of the feelings—an event, a memory, or some unknown cause— they combine to create an uncomfortable level of tension and distress, which you must somehow escape or lessen. SIV helps you to reduce these negative feelings and offers a temporary escape from the seemingly unbearable tension.

Marge describes the way that SIV helps her to ease her feelings like this: "Have you ever seen that magic trick where the magician takes a dollar from someone in the audience and rips it into a hundred pieces? Then he does some kind of hocus-pocus thing, and presto, the dollar is whole again. Before I cut, I feel like that dollar that that's ripped in a hundred pieces. By the time I finish, it's like, presto, I'm whole again. That's why I cut: I get to feel whole again."

Marge is clearly using SIV to reduce her feelings of disorganization and tension—to get rid of her negative feelings and feel more whole and complete. If you're like most people, you have experienced a time when you felt really bad. During these times you just don't feel like yourself; instead you feel fragmented, tense, or empty. SIV helps decrease these negative feelings by providing an outlet for these emotions. It also creates a physical wound—as opposed to an emotional wound—which can later be nurtured and healed. The bottom line is that SIV makes you feel better, at least in the short term. Part of the reason self-inflicted violence is so difficult to stop is that at the moment you are distressed it is very effective at relieving your feelings.

Take some time now to look at how you typically handle your feelings by completing activity 2.2.

Activity 2.2: Dealing with Emotions

This exercise will help you understand how you handle your emotions. There are no right or wrong answers to any of these questions. However, your answers should give you an idea of the ways that you regulate and express your feelings and how they might contribute to your SIV behaviors. After each question a brief explanation is given that relates your answer to possible reasons you hurt yourself.

1. Are you direct in how you express your emotions? For example, when you are angry with someone do you tell them? Or do you keep your feelings to yourself? Or do you snap or lash out at other people because you're feeling so mad?

   Expressing your feelings in ways that are direct—such as talking about what you're feeling or confronting the situation that is making you emotional—will help you release your feelings in a more positive manner. Keeping your feelings to yourself or releasing them in inappropriate ways—such as yelling at your spouse when you're really angry at your daughter—will not help you get rid of the underlying emotions. These emotions will eat at you until you have to use an extreme measure like SIV to feel some relief.

2. When you are feeling intense emotions, do you prefer to be alone or with others? Does this differ with different emotions?

   Although it may be difficult for you to be with others when you are feeling intense emotions, doing so gives you a way to release your emotions and feel connected to others. Without this release and connection, you are likely to feel overwhelmed, alone, and helpless—all feelings which can lead to SIV.

3. When your emotions are intense, do you cry, scream, or release your feelings in some similar way?

   Crying, screaming, yelling, or similar methods of releasing emotions can prevent you from feeling overwhelmed. When you are able to release your emotions, you are less likely to want to hurt yourself.

4. Do you try to find ways to escape rather than deal with feelings or problems directly? For instance, if you are really stressed at work, do you quit your job rather than trying to work things out?

   Sometimes it's necessary to avoid feelings or problems. However, if you do this on a consistent basis, you are setting a pattern of instability and allowing fear to run your life. Generally, you don't try to avoid those things that don't scare you. Learning how to confront whatever it is that scares you will help you deal with your feelings effectively. When you are able to do this, you won't feel the desire to hurt yourself as strongly.

A Method of Coping

No one likes to feel bad or enjoys being in pain. In fact, we will go to great lengths to avoid pain and negative emotions. However, sometimes all our efforts at averting these disturbing sensations just don't work. At times, each of us feels bad. When we do, we generally try to use a coping mechanism to help get through these moments. We all have ways to contend with the pressures of the world. And the more difficult the situation, the more extreme the coping mechanism needs to be. For many of us, learning effective ways of coping is a long and difficult process. So when we find one that works, we're likely to use it a great deal. It is essential that we have and use these methods of coping so that we can function in the world and remain psychologically healthy.

All creatures have methods of coping. Coping is simply a behavior that is used to get through a difficult situation as well and as easily as possible—a survival tactic. Dogs bark when they feel scared, overwhelmed, or threatened (and sometimes if they're hungry). Opossum play dead when they fear danger. Humans too have established specific ways of coping, some of which are innate. When stressors get too great, our bodies are programmed to fight back. We sleep when we're physically or psychologically exhausted. Our heart rate and blood flow increase when we feel frightened, in case we need to react quickly.

Humans have a physiological reaction to stress, regardless of whether the stress which we experience stems from a physical, emotional, or psychological source. Some of these stressors may be ordinary, daily events (such as a traffic jam on the way to work); some will be extraordinary (such as an unexpected death or loss). Regardless of the source of the stress, we are programmed to try to defend ourselves—physically and psychologically— against these feelings. Sometimes the ways we defend ourselves are extreme, seemingly more severe than the original stressor. Self-inflicted violence is one example of such an extreme method. Nonetheless, its purpose is to help us through difficult times.

The way that SIV functions as a coping mechanism is complex. At first glance it seems odd or contradictory that SIV would be useful as a method of coping. As a coping mechanism self-inflicted violence is unique in that it is one of the few methods that also causes physical injury. It makes little sense logically that physical injury can provide a sense of relief. Yet, as you know, hurting yourself does just that—it provides a relief or lessening of uncomfortable physical or psychological sensations, and in that way it becomes a method you use to cope. The physical injuries force your body to employ its own coping strategies to deal with the pain and physical damage created by the SIV, as discussed in chapter 1. In this sense, although SIV is an effective strategy of temporarily dealing with psychological factors, it also creates additional situations—both physical and psychological—with which you must contend, such as physical trauma, shame, and guilt.

For each of us, various areas of our lives cause enough tension, stress, anxiety, and frustration that we can begin to feel overwhelmed. Traffic, long lines, finances, work, school, relationships, family problems, and many other areas in each of our lives present the opportunity for great stress or tension. And each of us has his or her own specific way of getting through the day. You may use SIV to help you cope, while your best friend goes to the gym and exercises. You may have another friend who uses drugs or alcohol when she gets overwhelmed. Maybe you even know someone who gets in fights as a way to feel better. There are many ways to cope with the pressures of life.

While all methods of coping help you to feel better (at least temporarily), some methods work better in the long run or have fewer negative "side effects." Generally, positive or healthy forms of coping (in moderation) will help you to feel better without producing results that could be harmful. Talking, exercising, writing, crying, breathing, doing artwork, and solving the underlying problem are all forms of positive, or healthy coping.

Behaviors that cause you further harm (immediately or in the long run) or that put you in a dangerous or uncomfortable position are considered negative or unhealthy coping strategies. Some examples of negative coping techniques include using drugs or alcohol, violent behavior toward others, overeating, gambling, smoking, and self-inflicted violence. Self-inflicted violence is a negative, or unhealthy coping strategy because it causes definite physical damage and possible psychological difficulties. So, while SIV is an effective method of coping and its use may even prevent you from behaving in a more drastic or destructive way (such as trying to kill yourself), learning to use other, positive coping strategies in your time of need will serve you well. These methods of coping and how to practice and use them will be discussed in greater detail in chapter 7. For now, activity 2.3 will help you explore the various coping methods you currently use.

Activity 2.3: How Do I Cope?

This activity will help you identify some of the ways you cope. Identifying as many of your coping strategies as you can now will help you later when you may need to use one of those strategies.

In the following list, circle each of the coping mechanisms that you use. Write any others that you use in the space provided.

Sleeping	Crying
Screaming	Walking
Talking	Exercising

Drawing	Painting
Drinking	Eating
Using drugs	Sex
Smoking	Meditating
Shopping	SIV
Gambling	Working
_____	_____
_____	_____
_____	_____

Now spend a few minutes thinking about why you use these methods of coping. Do particular coping techniques work for particular emotions or stressors? For example, does smoking help you feel better when you're really stressed and shopping work better when you're sad?

Using the coping techniques that you identified above, create a two-column table in your journal: In the left column of this table list each of the coping techniques you use; in the right column, list which specific emotion that technique helps with the most. The table should look something like this:

Coping Technique	**Emotion Helped Most**
running	*anxiety (from my job)*
talking (with my therapist)	*sadness*

When you are finished you will probably find that certain ways you cope correspond with certain feelings you experience. This information will be helpful when you are learning how to stop hurting yourself.

Now let's look at SIV specifically. You may have already listed SIV above. For most people who engage in SIV, it helps them feel better and cope with life more effectively—on a short-term basis. In your journal record all of the ways SIV helps you to cope. In other words, how does it make you feel better?

For example, a young man named Jason describes his experience like this:

> I feel like there's something rotting inside of me that's eating at me from the inside. I cut myself to get this rotten thing out of me, like it seeps out with the blood. Afterwards I feel clean and calm. I feel better.

For Jason, SIV helps to create a sense of calmness and inner peace, helping him cope with these terrible feelings.

Stopping, Inducing, or Preventing Dissociation

The word *dissociation* is used to describe a psychological state in which the individual experiences an alteration in consciousness, memory, and sometimes identity. During a dissociative episode, some people feel detached from their bodies. They may feel a floating sensation or a sensation similar to a hypnotic state. Many people also report a sense that they are actually separated from their bodies, and are watching themselves much as if they were watching a movie. Some people are able to dissociate to such an extent that they actually create separate identities, with separate lives, different abilities, and even differing physical characteristics.

Everyone dissociates to some extent; however, for most, dissociation is fairly mild. Some examples of typical dissociation include driving past your freeway exit, tuning out when someone is talking to you, or forgetting the page of a book you just read. As you can see, dissociation exists on a continuum, from mild to extreme. Each of us experiences this spaced-out state to some degree.

Although everyone dissociates to some degree, some people use dissociation as a defense mechanism, to protect them from overwhelming emotional or physical pain. However, sometimes these dissociative states themselves become overwhelming, due either to intensity or duration. Self-inflicted violence is one method used to reduce, prevent, or end a disturbing dissociative state.

It works like this: The state of high tension that precedes SIV tends to alter consciousness, often sending the person into a dissociated state in which physical pain and sensation is reduced. You have probably experienced the sensation of feeling numb or zoned out prior to hurting yourself. You may lose track of time or be unaware of your environment. And you may desire these zoned-out, dissociative feelings because they give you relief from emotional pain. You might even experience this dissociative state as quite calm or peaceful.

However, other people have precisely the opposite perception of dissociation. For some dissociation is very uncomfortable. The loss of connection with others (or sometimes with reality) and control over your own level of consciousness can be particularly frightening and alienating.

When you're in that spaced-out, dissociated state, your awareness of even yourself is extremely limited. Dissociation conflicts with self-awareness. But by doing things to increase your self-awareness you correspondingly decrease dissociation. SIV, which draws attention back to your physical being, is quite effective in increasing self-awareness, and in doing so helps to reduce or end a dissociative state.

Margaret is a twenty-three-year-old graduate student. She describes her self-injurious behavior as follows:

I have a hard time remembering many of the times I cut myself. All my memories become confused and melded together. Backgrounds switch, but the actions remain the same. I'm in the bathroom, looking into the mirror, staring into my own eyes. I don't know what I see. After minutes, hours, days (I lose track of the time), I pick up the razor blade and cut myself. I watch myself bleed with the same detachment as looking into my own reflection. I feel no pain, only the warmth of the blood trickling down my arm. The water makes the blood thin and spread. I use toilet paper to wrap my wounds and stop the bleeding. The pressure on my cuts stings, but also feels good. I can feel. I have survived.

By engaging in SIV, Margaret is able to end a dissociative episode and begin to feel again. Her experience is not rare. Many people report high levels of dissociation before and during an act of SIV. Changing your physical sensations through SIV serves to reduce the amount of dissociation you experience. Conversely, dissociation can also serve to reduce the experience of physical pain caused by the self-inflicted injury. In addition, for some people high levels of tension are so unbearable that they turn to SIV as a way to induce dissociation, and thus escape the emotional pain.

In its most severe form, dissociation can lead to alterations of identity, as in cases of dissociative identity disorder (formerly called multiple personality disorder). If you have multiple personalities, you may be particularly disturbed by these dissociated states, as they reduce the amount of control you have over which personalities surface. Inflicting self-injury is one method used to avoid, gain control over, or end this alteration of consciousness. Self-inflicted violence changes the physical sensations associated with dissociation, averting or disrupting this state.

As you can see, the role of dissociation before an act of SIV is complex. Some people hurt themselves in order to dissociate and thus relieve discomfort. Others use SIV as a way to eliminate or reduce a state of dissociation. In either case what is exceedingly clear is that dissociation does have a strong relationship with self-inflicted violence.

During the actual act of self-injury, dissociation takes on a simpler role. At this stage, dissociation mainly serves to block or reduce the perception of physical pain. In this altered state of consciousness it is much more difficult to experience physical sensations. You may have heard of people who successfully use hypnosis as an anesthetic during surgery. Hypnosis, like dissociation, alters typical conscious states, changing perceptions and sensations. Dissociation is particularly adept at altering the level of physical pain experienced during SIV.

However, high levels of dissociation can increase the physical risk associated with self-inflicted violence. In a highly dissociated state, some people lose awareness of the extent of injury they are inflicting. You may have had the experience of injuring yourself more severely than you had planned, later realizing that your wounds are more numerous or serious than you had perceived while dissociated. So the masking of physical pain experienced during SIV can have detrimental results.

After an episode of self-injury, the level of dissociation decreases. You experience a return to typical levels of consciousness relatively soon after injuring yourself. Sometimes this return to normal alertness is necessary so that your injuries can be treated. The decrease in dissociation also reflects the effectiveness of the SIV. Given that one of the main functions of SIV is to make you feel better, once this has occurred, the necessity to remain in a state of altered consciousness no longer exists. In short, when self-inflicted violence has served its purpose, dissociation is no longer necessary. Self-inflicted violence allows you to temporarily cope, tolerate, or reduce your overwhelming negative emotions and simultaneously control your level of dissociation.

Activity 2.4: How Much Do I Dissociate?

This exercise will help you assess the role dissociation plays in your life. As was mentioned before, all people dissociate to some degree, and dissociation is a very useful mechanism to deal with overwhelming situations.

Rate yourself on the following questions by circling the appropriate number in the scale following each question.

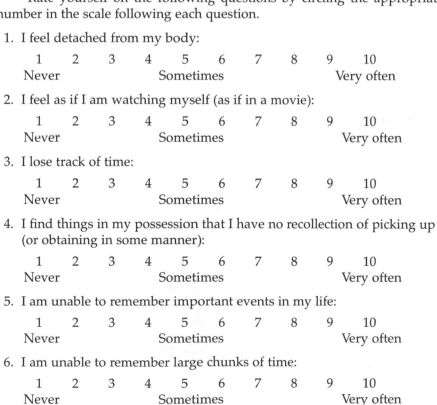

1. I feel detached from my body:

    1   2   3   4   5   6   7   8   9   10
    Never   Sometimes   Very often

2. I feel as if I am watching myself (as if in a movie):

    1   2   3   4   5   6   7   8   9   10
    Never   Sometimes   Very often

3. I lose track of time:

    1   2   3   4   5   6   7   8   9   10
    Never   Sometimes   Very often

4. I find things in my possession that I have no recollection of picking up (or obtaining in some manner):

    1   2   3   4   5   6   7   8   9   10
    Never   Sometimes   Very often

5. I am unable to remember important events in my life:

    1   2   3   4   5   6   7   8   9   10
    Never   Sometimes   Very often

6. I am unable to remember large chunks of time:

    1   2   3   4   5   6   7   8   9   10
    Never   Sometimes   Very often

7. I feel as if people, things, and the world in general are not real:

   1   2   3   4   5   6   7   8   9   10
  Never   Sometimes   Very often

8. I can't remember whether I actually said or did something or just thought about it:

   1   2   3   4   5   6   7   8   9   10
  Never   Sometimes   Very often

9. I become so absorbed in reading, watching television, or daydreaming that I don't notice when someone is talking to me or trying to get my attention:

   1   2   3   4   5   6   7   8   9   10
  Never   Sometimes   Very often

10. I do not feel pain (or much pain) when I injure myself:

   1   2   3   4   5   6   7   8   9   10
  Never   Sometimes   Very often

Add together all of the numbers you have circled. Your score will be between 10 and 100. Higher scores indicate more extreme levels of dissociation. So, the closer your score is to 100, the higher your level of dissociation. Scores of 80 and above indicate extreme levels of dissociation. Scores below 30 indicate low levels of dissociation. Scores between 30 and 80 could be considered average.

Again, there are no right or wrong answers or scores here. This activity is simply designed to help you see the role dissociation plays in your life.

Euphoric Feelings

During an episode of self-inflicted violence, you are physically traumatizing your body. Your body reacts to this trauma by working to minimize the pain you experience and heal as quickly as possible.

Dissociation is part of this process. Another part is the way that your body reacts physically to alter your perception of pain. This process is accomplished with the help of naturally occurring chemicals found in your brain. When you experience physical trauma, your brain releases substances called endorphins, which have effects similar to those of morphine. (Morphine works as a painkiller because it mimics these naturally occurring chemicals.) During an episode of SIV, endorphins are released so that you don't feel the pain associated with hurting yourself.

Like morphine, endorphins can also cause a very pleasant physical sensation—and they can become addictive. Thus you may engage in self-inflicted violence in order to produce feelings of euphoria, and may begin to rely on this act in order to stimulate these pleasant sensations.

You may have noticed that you feel a tingling sensation before hurting yourself. Or you may notice a general feeling of peacefulness or glee while engaging in a self-injurious act. You may even feel sexually aroused during an act of SIV. It is likely that each of these experiences is the result of the increased level of endorphins in your body.

One of the problems of using self-inflicted violence to produce euphoric feelings is that, like morphine and other means used to elicit such feelings, this method loses its effectiveness rather quickly—a tolerance can be built up. Therefore, the euphoric feelings produced by these chemicals will not be as strong in subsequent acts as they were during the first episode of self-inflicted violence. You may even find yourself injuring yourself more severely in order to experience the same type of sensations you felt when you were first engaging in SIV.

Physically Expressing Pain

As mentioned earlier, many individuals who engage in self-inflicted violence have difficulty expressing emotional pain. Emotions are often hard to identify, and can be even more difficult to release. Perhaps you can remember a time in your life when you really felt like crying, but couldn't produce the tears. Or maybe you felt really angry and wanted to scream, but you didn't due to your environment. At times like these, you might use SIV as a method of expressing and releasing emotional tension and pain.

Robert, a twenty-year-old artist who burns himself with cigarettes, describes, "I have a hard time talking about what's going on inside me. When I start talking, all of the crap I'm saying sounds so lame. I like looking at the scars on my arms because I know that they're real. It's like I'm trying to say, I've suffered, man, just look."

The results of self-inflicted violence—often cuts, bruises, burns, or broken bones—serve as an expression of internal conflict. By being able to actually view and feel something tangible, you are able to give your internal experience external representation. In other words, you can see how much you hurt by making what's real inside your mind and body become real outside. Physically expressing your emotional pain allows you to have concrete evidence of intangible, amorphous, or indefinable emotions.

Several goals are associated with physical expression of emotional pain. The first of these is to provide confirmation or evidence that you are suffering psychologically. Often, individuals who engage in SIV tend to minimize or doubt their own internal experiences. There are many possible reasons why a person would not trust his or her own experiences, but most often it has to do with a lack of verification from others that those experiences are real.

This concept may seem a bit confusing, so here's an example. Imagine that it is six o'clock in the morning and you are just getting up to go to school or work or wherever. You take a shower, comb your hair, brush your teeth, get dressed, and do all your morning rituals. A typical morning, right? OK, now imagine trying to do all of this while wearing specially made blinders, like racehorses sometimes wear, so that you are unable to see what you look like. You may think you put your clothes on correctly and combed your hair in the right direction, but you can't actually tell.

Now you step out of your house and face others. Their responses will tell you how good a job you did getting ready that morning. If you get strange stares, smirks, or all-out laughter, you know that your preparations didn't go quite as you hoped. If people stop and compliment you, you'll feel quite successful.

The point of this somewhat silly example is that others' responses are extremely important to our perceptions of our own experiences. We want those responses to match our experiences. When others respond in ways that are opposed to what we think or feel, we will begin to doubt ourselves.

If you doubt your own perceptions, it is likely that you did not get the kind of feedback you needed at critical times in your life, particularly in childhood. Receiving feedback from others that matches your experiences is sometimes referred to as *mirroring*. Through a lack of mirroring in your life, you may have developed a pattern of doubting your own internal experiences. By providing concrete evidence of your emotional pain, you can acknowledge, represent, and, in a way, mirror your own emotions. No one can question the gash on your arm. No one will doubt the cast on your leg. More importantly, through this physical expression, *you* will not doubt that your feelings are real and strong and painful.

Communication

Chris left her therapist's office feeling angry and abandoned. At the end of the session the therapist had mentioned that in the next month she would be taking off several weeks for vacation. Although her therapist had assured Chris that she would be able to contact another therapist in case of emergency, Chris didn't want her therapist to go. Chris felt as though she would fall apart without having her therapist to talk with and support her. Later that evening, Chris sliced her arms severely enough that she had to go to the hospital for stitches. From the hospital she called her therapist and left a message telling her about the SIV.

Sometimes SIV is used as a form of communication. Just as a picture is worth a thousand words, scars, wounds, and other visible signs of injury can also communicate a great deal. Your scars and wounds can express to others what you are thinking, feeling, or experiencing. In Chris's case, she was angry with her therapist and used SIV as a way of expressing her emotions. You may have difficulty expressing your feelings to others verbally, and, like Chris, you may use SIV to let those around you know what you are experiencing. Your friends may not realize the true level of your emotional or psychic pain until they see how you have chosen to represent this pain physically. (In fact, *you* may not realize the extent of your pain until you can see it physically.)

Although using SIV to communicate has serious drawbacks (such as shame, embarrassment, and the injury itself) it can be an effective way to express your needs, desires, and experiences to others. By exposing your pain and discomfort to others through SIV, you are more likely to receive what you need from them your friends and others. Without demonstrating a need for support or help, you probably will not receive them. In the example above, it is not likely that Chris's therapist canceled her vacation because Chris cut herself. However, it probably paved the way for a necessary conversation about Chris's fears, anger, and other feelings. Thus, by making your injuries visible, you may be trying to open lines of communication and precipitate a conversation about your experiences. You are indirectly showing others your inner world.

Chris used SIV as a way of expressing a fairly direct message: "I'm scared and angry that you're leaving me." But at times, self-inflicted violence is used to carry a symbolic message. For instance, you might injure yourself to create scars or wounds that mark a certain occasion; they become symbolic representations of that event. You may also self-injure to symbolically communicate to yourself the extent of your pain and your ability to survive. Although you may have no intention of showing others your wounds or scars, you create and witness evidence of your experience. Whether through symbols or more direct messages, SIV helps to create visible external representations of your feelings, and may allow you to communicate with others.

Self-inflicted violence undoubtedly sends many messages to others. But while SIV may be a potent form of communication, it may not always be effective. The meanings and messages behind an act of SIV may be misinterpreted. Fresh blood dripping from a newly opened wound makes a very powerful statement. However, like all forms of communication, the interpretation may not match the intended message.

When SIV is used as a method of communication, the intended messages generally reflect the great amount of psychic pain which the individual is experiencing: "I hurt." "I need help." "I'm in great pain." "I'm scared." All these statements reflect interpretations associated with self-injuries. However, interpretations such as "That person is crazy" or "She must be really nuts" or "He must have been trying to kill himself" may be made by others. Although it may be incredibly difficult, it might be wise to talk with friends about their understandings of what your self-injuries communicate. You may find that your intentions have been misinterpreted.

Often you will hear people talking about self-inflicted violence as an act of manipulation. Generally, manipulation is thought of in a negative sense. However, the fundamental meaning of the word is simply handling or controlling something. So SIV can be seen as an attempt to manipulate or control your environment—including the information you communicate to others—although the effectiveness of this method is limited by probable miscommunications.

We will return to the concept of control at the end of this chapter. For now, complete the following exercise, which will help you understand what you are intending to communicate through SIV.

Activity 2.5: What Does My SIV Communicate to Others?

In your journal, answer the following questions. You might want to think back to the last time you hurt yourself, because remembering a specific instance of SIV is easier than thinking of all your SIV episodes collectively.

1. If your injuries or scars could talk, what would they say?

2. To whom would they say these things?

3. How might these messages be misinterpreted?

If you are open with others about your SIV, ask them about their understanding of the messages your SIV behaviors communicate. Find out whether they are perceiving the message you are trying to send correctly, or whether they think your SIV means something different from what you intended. Write about this experience and what you have learned in your journal.

Self-Nurturing

Physically expressing pain through acts of SIV provides a way for you to nurture yourself physically, which becomes important when you are unable to do so emotionally. SIV is often used as an attempt to heal yourself, to make your internal wounds external and to nurture and heal these wounds. In other words, once the experienced pain or trauma is made external, as in a cut or burn, it is much easier to nurture and heal than when it existed only on a psychic or emotional level. The gratifying part of injuring yourself is the self-care which you get to provide afterwards.

Many people who engage in self-inflicted violence feel as if they are uncared for or as if they are alone in the world. This lack of connection with others is one of the primary influences of SIV. One of the results of self-injury is that it provides a situation in which nurturing must occur: When you are hurt, you have to take care of yourself.

You may have specific rituals around nurturing yourselves. Margaret, the woman described in the section on dissociation, would always wrap her wounds in toilet paper, using it to form a bandage which would help stop the bleeding. She would then cover the tissue bandage with an elastic bandage, enjoying the feeling of pressure on her arm. Caring for her own wounds was a way for Margaret to take care of herself and to receive the nurturing she greatly desired.

Often it is much easier to take care of a visible, tangible wound than to care for internal or emotional damage. Even if your wounds are not visible, such as when you hit yourself and no bruise is produced, you may still find ways to nurture yourself. In these instances, you may treat yourself as if you have physical wounds, such as wrapping your beaten thigh with an elastic bandage or taking a hot bath to ease the soreness from repeatedly pinching yourself. You may even find ways to nurture yourself for your emotional wounds, like eating a pint of chocolate ice cream because it helps to alleviate your feelings of self-pity or helplessness.

As mentioned previously, physical wounds can act as representations of psychological wounds. Therefore, by nurturing and taking care of your physical wounds, you are actually caring for your internal scars. As odd as it may sound, SIV may actually be a way for you to physically and psychologically take care of yourself. With work and the help of this book, however, you will be able to get to the point when you don't need to use SIV before you can take care of yourself. Take a minute now to write about the ways SIV allows you to care for yourself in the following exercise.

Activity 2.6: How Does SIV Let Me Take Care of Myself?

Nurturing provides a major role in SIV. This exercise will help you see how you take care of yourself after injuring yourself. Through this activity, you will likely discover that SIV allows you to nurture yourself in many ways. You might not take care of yourself to the same extent without SIV.

1. In your journal, describe how you care for your injuries. Do you wash them? Wrap them? Massage them? Do you seek treatment for your wounds?

2. If you have no visible wounds, do you find ways to care for them anyway? If so, how? Do you treat yourself better because you hurt yourself?

3. In what other ways does self-inflicted violence provide you with the opportunity to nurture yourself? Would you (or do you) care for yourself in these ways when you aren't injuring yourself?

4. How might you nurture yourself if you didn't injure yourself first?

Self-Punishment

It has been reported that more than half of all individuals who engage in self-inflicted violence were abused—physically, sexually, and/or emotionally—as children (this topic will be addressed in more detail in chapter 5). Often people who have been abused incorrectly blame themselves for the abuse or believe they "deserve" it because of their behaviors, thoughts, or feelings. As a child, you may have been taught that certain behaviors, thoughts, or feelings, deserved punishment. This lesson from your childhood may have remained and may influence the ways in which you treat yourself.

Jasmine is an eighteen-year-old woman who lives with her twenty-five-year-old sister and works as a waitress in order to support her infant daughter. The father of Jasmine's baby is no longer involved in their lives. When Jasmine gets upset, she makes a fist and hits herself as hard as possible, often leaving large bruises on her legs, arms, and stomach.

As a child, Jasmine was physically abused. Both her father and her mother would hit, slap, and throw things at her. Jasmine blamed herself for this abuse, feeling as though she deserved to be punished for "thinking bad thoughts." Now, Jasmine engages in a similar pattern, hitting herself to the point of bruising. Although Jasmine loves her baby, she sometimes feels overwhelmed and questions her decision to keep the child. When Jasmine catches herself having such thoughts, she punishes herself by engaging in SIV.

People who engage in self-inflicted violence are often overly critical of themselves. This internal criticism facilitates their acts of self-injury. Criticism—internal or external—leads to feelings of shame and blame, which lead in turn to self-punishment.

While it is important for people to continually assess their actions, thoughts, and emotions in order to act responsibly and ethically, it is not particularly helpful to physically harm yourself as a method of punishment. Punishing yourself does not change the past, nor does it change the present. When you feel bad about an act you have committed, a more proactive method of handling the situation would be to try to make amends, or change the situation. Although hurting yourself may make you feel better at that moment, SIV cannot alter the past. And many of the thoughts, feelings, or behaviors for which you punish yourself may not in fact be blameworthy. Activity 2.7 will help you explore some of the ways you may be blaming yourself for the things that were not your fault.

Activity 2.7: What Are My Self-Punishing Thoughts?

This exercise will help you understand the ways you may blame yourself for events that have occurred in your life. Although at times self-blame is appropriate, you will probably find that you've been blaming yourself for events that you did not cause.

Part 1. Think of an episode in your life that left you with some intense emotion—anger, sadness, guilt, remorse, disappointment, anxiety, or fear. If you have been abused, you might want to think about a time that you were abused as you complete this activity. Now describe the following in your journal (you can do this for more than one event if you wish):

1. The event itself—what happened.
2. The feelings you have about this event.

3. All the ways you blame yourself for this event. (Usually these statements begin *If only I . . .* or contain the words *should* or *ought*.)

For example, Sally, who is twenty years old, feels great sadness about the divorce of her parents, which happened when she was nine. Sally blames herself for the divorce. She thinks that if only she had been a better daughter, her father would have stayed. She also thinks that she shouldn't have fought with her sister so much and that her fighting helped to cause the divorce.

It is likely that once you write down some of the ways you blame yourself for these incidents, you will see that you really could not have influenced the event very much at all. You will probably find that you've been blaming yourself for things that really were not your fault.

Part 2. Another way you may be punishing yourself is by being overly critical of yourself. This section will help you to assess the ways you criticize yourself. (You will probably find that you are being overly harsh with yourself.)

In your journal, list your self-criticisms—all the ways you view yourself negatively. For example, your list may include statements like "I'm lazy" or "I'm stupid" or "I'm crazy."

Once you have done this, think about how you came to believe these statements. Did someone say these things to you? Do any of these statements remind you of a particular time in your life or a specific event? Write down any associations you have for each of these statements. Understanding the source of these ideas will be important later, when you are learning to be less critical of yourself.

Reenacting Previous Abuse

As mentioned in the preceding section, a large number of individuals who injure themselves have suffered some type of previous abuse. Often this abuse is of a physical nature. Self-inflicted violence is one method of reenacting abuse that took place at an earlier time.

The reasons people reenact previous abuse are varied. Some may replicate the abuse so that they can feel a sense of control—control that wasn't present during the original abuse. When someone is hurting you, particularly when you are a child, you have few ways of controlling the situation and making the abuse stop. However, as an adult inflicting injury upon yourself, you are in total control, able to determine when and where to hurt yourself and stop at any point you wish. (This idea is discussed further in the following section.)

Some people may act out the abuse as part of post-traumatic stress, during a flashback. A flashback is an episode in which you feel as if you are actually reexperiencing the traumatic incident. For example, you might be sitting at your desk at work and something happens to trigger a flashback.

Suddenly, although in reality you are still at your desk, you believe that you are six years old and being beaten by your father. You might even behave as if this is really happening at that moment—cowering in your chair, shaking, and crying. During a flashback, some people act in ways that replicate the original abuse, inflicting physical injuries as they do so.

Some individuals with dissociative identity disorder (formerly known as multiple personality disorder), may find that one alter injures another alter in order to reenact the abuse. *Alter* means each distinct personality that exists. Most people with dissociative identity disorder have ten or fewer distinct personalities. These alters present themselves as different people; they may have different ages, genders, sexual orientations, temperaments, and skills. Sometimes one personality will act violently toward another personality in order to inflict punishment or replicate previous acts of abuse. Since the violent acts actually hurt the same physical body, this is considered SIV.

Susan is a thirty-three-year-old nurse who has approximately eight main and distinct alters. Her alters range in age from three to thirty-two. One of her alters is a young boy; several are lesbian. Susan became aware that she had multiple personalities about five years ago. Prior to that time, she had experienced many strange and unexplainable occurrences. She would be unable to recall long periods of time and would find objects in her house that she had no recollection of purchasing; once she found a new stereo system in her living room. And she would find gashes and scars on her chest for which she had no explanation. Susan later came to learn that one of her alters (a particularly angry adolescent) habitually engaged in acts of SIV.

As discussed in the preceding section, replication of the original abuse may also be a method of self-punishment or a way to alleviate guilt. And some people do not know why they reenact the abuse, but simply feel the need to do so.

Replicating former abuse may take many forms. You might injure yourself in exactly the same way you were injured as a child. Or because of physical or psychological limitations, you may injure yourself in a slightly different manner. For example, if as a child you sustained injuries on your back, you might hurt your arms or legs instead. (While it is not impossible to inflict violence on your own back, it is rather difficult.) Your arms or legs, though not identical to the location of the primary abuse, are similar enough to serve the purpose of replicating the abuse.

It is not uncommon for the type of abuse to differ from the original abuse. For example, if you were sexually abused, you may now cut or burn yourself. Although the forms of the injury may differ, the way in which you perceive these injuries may be similar enough to serve the purpose of replication and allow you to feel control or relief of tension. Activity 2.8 will help you explore the ways your SIV might be connected to abuse you have suffered at the hands of others.

Activity 2.8: How Does Trauma Relate to SIV in My Life?

Not everyone has been traumatized or abused. If you are fortunate enough to have never been abused or traumatized, you will probably want to skip this activity. If you have the feeling that you may have been abused but aren't able to remember specifics, you might want to hold off on completing this activity until you remember a bit more. However, if you have had a traumatic experience that you can recall with some degree of detail, it is very important that you complete this activity.

Because SIV is so connected to trauma, it is important for you to confront the abuse you endured. Although this may be very difficult for you, remembering and processing trauma in your past will help you to take more control of your SIV. This exercise is designed to help you reflect on the trauma.

Part 1. In your journal, describe the abuse (physical, sexual, psychological) that took place in your past. You can either use a single episode of abuse or reflect on the abuse more generally. Provide as much detailed information as you can, using the following questions as a guideline.

1. When did the abuse occur?

2. How old were you?

3. Where did the abuse occur?

4. Who did this to you?

5. What were you wearing?

6. What did you look like?

7. What time of year was it?

8. What time of day was it?

9. Were you alone or were others around?

10. What were you doing right before the abuse happened?

11. What exactly happened?

12. What did you do afterwards?

13. Did you tell anyone?

14. How did you feel before, during, and after the abuse?

Try to recall as much as you can. This may be a very difficult process, particularly if you have not addressed these issues before. If this gets too uncomfortable or overwhelming, put this book away and call someone you can talk with (a friend, family member, therapist). It's really important that you be gentle with yourself during this activity.

Part 2. Now describe all the ways that your past abuse is similar to the ways you hurt yourself now. For example, if you were slapped in the face as a child, do you slap your own face now?

The goal of this activity is to gain understanding of how the trauma in your life has affected your SIV. After completing the activity, you should be able to start to see some parallels between what happened to you in the past and what you do to yourself now.

Establishing Control

Control is an essential component in each of our lives, and perceiving that we have this control is indisputably important to our mental health. When we feel in control of our environment, we feel better. We are more confident, happier, and even physically healthier when we have a sense of control. How real or absolute this control is really doesn't matter—it is the perception of control that counts.

One of the first things that we as humans learn to control is our body: our movements, our language, our bowels. And, as very small children, we feel great pride and accomplishment in this control. Not so long ago my mother received a telephone call from my niece. In this conversation my niece proudly exclaimed, "Nana, I went pee-pee in the potty!" This was clearly a significant moment in her life. As adults, we tend to take for granted the things that we have actual mastery over. Most of us can walk, talk, and, to use my niece's expression, go pee-pee in the potty. But our view of the power and control we do have becomes masked by events like waiting in long lines at the grocery store, being chewed out by a boss, having a lover tell you that the relationship is over. When your feelings of control are lessened, your emotional and physical discomfort is increased. During these times, self-inflicted violence is often used to decrease tension and ease psychological or physical discomfort by allowing you to feel a sense of control.

On a very primitive level, SIV replicates the sense of control we had when we were children; it is a way to control our physical being, one of the few things we truly can control. Many episodes of SIV are triggered by feelings of lack of control. Isolation, loneliness, frustration, sadness, and alienation are common emotions prior to episodes of self-injury. Each of these emotions may be perceived as outside the realm of our control. By planning and carrying out acts of self-harm, you are, in a sense, structuring your life by controlling your emotional states.

You may also use SIV as a way to control your physical experiences. When you hurt yourself, you may be trying to establish control over a dissociative state. As mentioned previously, SIV is closely connected to dissociation, and is one method used to end or avoid this alteration of consciousness. Self-inflicted violence alters the physical sensations associated with dissociation, thus averting or disrupting this state. In other cases, SIV serves to induce an episode of dissociation. The highly tense state that precedes an episode of self-injury tends to alter consciousness, often causing a dissociated state in which physical pain and sensation is reduced. The dissociated state may be either desired or undesired, depending on the person, the cause, and the likely result.

Thoughts can also be controlled through self-injury. By changing your behaviors, emotions, or physical sensations, you also affect your thoughts. Engaging in an act of SIV will cause changes in each of these areas. Therefore, you may hurt yourself in order to control intrusive, obsessive, or otherwish unwanted thoughts.

Control allows us to feel healthier, happier, more stable, more secure, and less anxious. We all need to believe that we can control certain aspects of our lives. Without this perceived control, we would feel as if we had little influence on our own lives, which could lead to feelings of hopelessness, helplessness, and depression. Through the use of SIV, you are able to clearly define and demonstrate a situation in which you do have complete control, allowing you to feel more control over your body, your thoughts, your behaviors, and even your emotions. Because of this, self-inflicted violence is an effective mechanism for temporarily increasing your perception of control in your life. It can help you feel more controlled, comfortable, and peaceful.

Activity 2.9 will help you explore the ways SIV may be helping you feel more in control of your life.

Activity 2.9: How Does SIV Help Me Feel in Control?

Because control is so essential in each of our lives, it is important to understand how it affects us. This exercise will help you determine how you perceive the control you have over your life as well as the way that SIV helps you feel more in control.

In your journal describe all the things in your life that you feel you have little or no control over. You may feel as if your entire life is out of control; however, in completing this activity, be as specific as you can. For instance, you may feel out of control in terms of your use of alcohol or drugs. You may feel unable to control your emotions. You may feel like you can't control your performance at work.

Once you've completed the first section, try to describe the ways that SIV allows you to feel more in control. Again, be as specific as you can. Understanding how SIV helps you feel in control will be important when you begin to look at alternative ways of getting this sense of control.

CHAPTER 3

The Nature of
Self-Inflicted Violence

Primarily because of the lack of information available on SIV, this behavior remains somewhat mysterious. For a long time, self-inflicted violence, or as it used to be called self-mutilation, was largely ignored by psychologists and other mental health professionals. Only now is SIV beginning to be considered a fairly common behavior and receive the attention it deserves. To date, very few articles, books, or studies have been published about typical forms of SIV. At this point, self-inflicted violence is simply not well understood by the professional community, and for this reason it is only possible to describe SIV in a general way. However, it appears that SIV tends to have some common characteristics from person to person. The general nature of SIV is discussed in terms of these characteristics in this chapter.

Shame and Self-Inflicted Violence

One of the most common factors associated with self-inflicted violence is that of shame. Shame is a powerful emotion, able to alter thoughts, feelings, and even behaviors. Embarrassment or shame related to SIV has a profound effect on all areas of life including relationships and school and job performance.

Often a sense of shame precedes SIV—stemming from events earlier in the person's life. As discussed in chapter 2, there is a strong relationship between self-inflicted violence and child abuse. For many people, engaging in SIV is associated with a traumatic history. And such trauma often causes feelings of shame and embarrassment. Many individuals who have been abused feel a sense of guilt, as if they in some way initiated, encouraged, or deserved the abuse. These thoughts and feelings become attached to memories of the abusive events, which are then transferred to the self-injurious activity. This is to say, if you feel guilty or shameful or think that you deserved abuse you received as a child, you might now want to act in ways that correspond with those beliefs. So if you feel as if you deserve to be punished, you may choose to punish yourself through an act of SIV.

The punishment in turn implies misbehavior or fault, and helps to foster feelings of shame and guilt. That is, because in theory punishment is administered when you have done something wrong—if you are punished you must have done something wrong. So an act of self-inflicted violence may induce feelings of shame that exacerbate those that preceded the SIV.

The shame resulting from SIV often breeds secrecy. It is likely that you keep your SIV activities a secret because of both your shame and your fears of being judged or labeled by others. The stigma attached to self-inflicted violence makes many people afraid to tell others about their experiences. The secretive nature of SIV serves to increase feelings of shame and isolation, which further perpetuate the cycle of self-injury.

Shame and embarrassment can result from many different components of self-injury. Scars, wounds, bruises, the type of SIV you use, emotions, alienation, loss of control, and feelings from related events may all affect the amount of shame associated with self-inflicted violence.

Wounds, Bruises, and Scars

Scars and visible wounds produce feelings of shame in most individuals who hurt themselves. Self-inflicted scars may be a lifelong reminder of the injurious episode and may produce shame from internal thoughts or feelings as well as from external sources. Scars or noticeable wounds resulting from self-inflicted violence can also be embarrassing when they become visible to others. Bald spots, bruises, and other visible, yet temporary markings caused by SIV can be equally as embarrassing as more permanent signs.

Some people find nothing more intriguing than other people's scars or wounds. "How did you do that?" "What happened?" "That looks like it must have hurt. What did you do?" Comments like these frequently result from exposing scars or other noticeable results of SIV, and can trigger feelings of shame or embarrassment. But scars or wounds that do not stem from an episode of self-injury do not carry the same type of shame. A scar from an old athletic injury, for example, might carry some embarrassment in that it may not be particularly attractive, but it could just as easily be worn as a "badge of honor." However, even a scar that evokes some shame because it was received in a moment of carelessness or ineptitude does not carry the same deep shame that a scar created intentionally does. The reaction of others to the cause of the scar or the wound varies considerably depending on its source, and those reactions will affect your feelings about the wound and its cause.

Veronica, an eighteen year old who works at a coffeehouse, relates the following story:

> I can remember being in junior high and some of my friends were showing each other their scars. There was a sort of pride in scars back then. I remember my friend Angie showing me this scar above her knee where she had to have stitches. She had fallen out of a tree or something. She seemed so proud of it, like it reminded her of something good. She asked about the scars on my thigh. At that time, I only had a few. I remember feeling embarrassed and I knew I couldn't tell her the truth. I made up some story. I was always making up stories about my scars. I think I blamed half of them on this old cat I used to have. When my friends would come over to my house and see the cat, they would look all scared and stuff. It was kind of funny. They didn't know he was declawed.

As this story illustrates, the way an injury is presented, reacted to, and valued depends largely on its cause. Imagine the following situation: It is a beautiful, sunny June day. Wearing a tank top and shorts, you are walking your beagle (Snoopy) on the beach. A tourist from Amsterdam stops to ask directions to the closest restroom. Before you can point in the right direction, she notices the raised, pink scars on your arms. She looks at you inquisitively and wonders aloud what happened. Let's consider two possible responses.

> **Response one:** "I used to work at the zoo, and I was attacked by a baby lion cub." At this response, the tourist may nod empathically and perhaps even engage you in a conversation about your former job (depending on how badly she needs to use the restroom).

> **Response two:** "I used to cut myself with razor blades when I was younger."

The probable reply to this response is a hasty nod and a sprint down the beach in the direction of the restroom.

Most people don't understand self-inflicted violence and will react awkwardly when it is mentioned. Others' responses often help to perpetuate and exacerbate your shame and embarrassment. By exposing your scars, you risk people noticing, wondering about, and reacting to your self-injurious activities. So when others notice your scars, in anticipation of their negative reactions, you may feel compelled to lie about the source of your injuries. For this reason scars are often kept hidden or covered.

Natalie is fifteen years old. She describes her attempts to hide her injuries as follows:

> I try to hide my scars. I wear long sleeves even when it's really warm outside. I'd rather have people think I'm a little weird than have them see my arms and know that I'm totally nuts. I can't stand it when someone does see my arms. I watch their face turn from a normal expression to this weird mixture of sympathy and disgust. They never know what to say. I never know what to say to them either. I just end up feeling bad, like I've done something to make them feel bad.

Many individuals who engage in self-inflicted violence try to hide their scars and fresh injuries. You might find yourself wearing long sleeves, long pants, or hats in the most sweltering heat, just to cover your injuries. You also probably consider the location of the injury and the difficulty of keeping it concealed when you are engaging in an act of SIV.

Recently I had the opportunity to meet with a prisoner, Gary, whose SIV consisted of pulling out his own hair. Gary had noticeable bald spots on his head, which formed a polka dot–like pattern. He stated several times during our discussion that he was really embarrassed by his appearance and was being harassed because of it by other inmates. Since the prison system has strict rules about clothing and accessories, Gary was unable to wear a hat to cover his bald spots, which would have allowed him to feel less self-conscious. As an alternative, Gary decided that it would be best for him to simply shave his head so that he would feel less ashamed. He was not planning to stop pulling out his hair, however. Rather, he had already decided that he would pull hair from other places on his body, such as his arms and legs, which would be less conspicuous.

As you can see, the shame and secrecy resulting from SIV can be very extreme regardless of your environment. Being judged or misunderstood by others can be very difficult to handle. Sometimes, the responses of others will cause you to alter your typical behaviors, causing you to shave your head, wear concealing clothing, or lie about your SIV.

By hiding your scars or distorting the truth about the source of these scars, you are continuing the cycle of shame. Try this instead: Remember that scars represent survival. Your body carries indelible reminders of how strong you can be. It is important to view these marks with pride and respect. Only when you respect yourself can you begin to demand the same respect from others. Activity 3.1 will help you begin to gain this persperctive about your "war wounds."

Activity 3.1: Wounds, Scars, and Shame

The goals of this exercise are to help you understand the way in which SIV causes you shame and embarrassment and to assist you in identifying your reactions to these feelings. Knowing more about how shame functions in your life will be important when you try to stop hurting yourself and begin reaching out to others.

The first part of this activity will help you realize the number of times you have hurt yourself and how you have positioned these injuries on your body. You may find that you have purposely chosen to injure yourself in places that you can conceal.

Part 1. For the first part of this activity, you will need a piece of paper at least as large as you are. (You could lay out newspaper or flattened paper bags on the floor and tape them together.) Alternatively, you can complete this exercise in your journal.

1. On the large paper draw the outline of your body, or have someone trace around you while you lie on the paper. If you are doing this on a smaller scale, simply draw the outline of a human figure on a page of your journal. Don't worry about your artistic ability.

2. On this figure, use a red marker to draw the location of each of your scars, wounds, or areas of injury—remember, not all wounds produce permanent scars.

The point of this activity is for you to be able to see how many of these injuries could have been hidden from others. You are likely to find that most of your SIV activities were done in places on your body that could be concealed.

Part 2. The second part of this activity focuses on the ways you hide your SIV and your scars. Again, the idea of this exercise is to understand the role that secrecy and shame play in your life in terms of SIV. This activity is not meant to induce feelings of guilt or shame. It is simply meant to help you understand yourself more fully.

1. Place a check mark next to each of the ways you keep your scars or injuries a secret.

_____ Not talking to friends, family, or professionals, about your scars

_____ Omitting the truth about the cause of scars

_____ Lying about the cause of scars

_____ Injuring yourself on places on your body that are usually covered

_____ Wearing clothes that cover scars or fresh injuries

_____ Wearing jewelry that covers your scars

_____ Getting a tattoo to hide your scars

_____ Injuring yourself on top of old scars

2. Are there other ways you keep your scars or injuries secret? List them here or in your journal.

_____

_____

_____

Part 3. The final part of this activity will help you look at how you explain the source of your injuries to others. Certainly other people have noticed or asked you about your scars, wounds, or injuries. You may explain these injuries in many different ways, depending on who is asking. Examining the ways you have explained your wounds and the reactions you received will enable you to plan future responses to these inquiries as well as better understand how shame influences your behaviors.

Think back to the times when others have asked you about your injuries or scars. In your journal, describe these situations, answering the following questions and including as much detail as you can.

1. Where were you?

2. Who asked you about your scars?

3. What did he or she say?

4. Were you surprised?

5. How did you respond? What did you say? (Remember that omission of information can be an explanation; for example, "Oh this gash on my arm? I can't recall.")

6. How did you feel about what you said?

7. How did the other person react?

Isolation and Alienation

People who engage in SIV are likely to feel shame simply because of the clandestine nature of this behavior. You probably feel alone or isolated in your SIV activities. This book may even be the first time you have known with certainty that others also engage in these behaviors. Because SIV is seldom discussed and has not yet been much exposed in the media, you have probably felt as if you are alone in these actions. You may feel different or abnormal. You may feel great shame about your self-injurious activities because you have not yet realized that there are others in the world who do similar things.

Self-inflicted violence, in this respect, is quite different from many other seemingly similar behaviors. Alcohol and drug use, eating disorders, gambling, even excessive sex and shopping each have received a great deal of media attention. This recognition and visibility allow people engaging in these behaviors to feel less alienated, less abnormal, less different. Similarly, most midsized to large cities in this country have easily accessible support groups for these various behaviors. But although a considerable number of individuals engage in SIV, it is rare to find similar amounts of attention and support for these activities.

Along with feeling different from others, some people feel embarrassed by the actual procedure of self-inflicted violence. The violence of self-injury may cause you to feel ashamed. You may feel guilt for purposefully wounding your own body, often drawing blood or creating permanent damage.

Vulnerability and Loss of Control

The sight of your own blood or wounded flesh may also produce feelings of shame. Exposing pieces of your physical being that used to be concealed—such as blood, flesh, or your scalp—may raise feelings of shame or embarrassment similar to those feelings evoked by the naked body.

Another internal source of shame is the feeling of failure to control your SIV behaviors. You may feel that engaging in a self-injurious act means that you are weak. You may have been trying to eliminate self-injurious behaviors, only to find yourself engaging in them again, resulting a feeling of failure and regret.

If you have discussed SIV with those close to you, you may find yourself reluctant to mention your recent self-injury. You may be embarrassed to admit that you felt the urge to hurt yourself. Thoughts like, *Why did I do this to myself again?*, *I thought I was over this*, or *What is my problem?* are common. You probably scold yourself for engaging in a behavior that, in many ways, helps you cope. However, the thoughts are not necessarily useful. Rather, they serve to amplify and perpetuate your feelings of shame and embarrassment It is the perceived loss of control or perceived failure that creates this shame.

For some people, rather than the action of self-injury evoking shameful feelings, it is the inability to recall engaging in these activities that causes embarrassment. As discussed in chapter 2, most people enter into a dissociated state before or during an episode of self-injury. Dissociation distorts consciousness as well as decreases the experience of physical pain. Some individuals dissociate more than others. You may dissociate so much that you are not able to recall what occurs during that time. This may leave you feeling confused, surprised, and ashamed when you realize what you have done. This lapse of memory may be as much or more of an embarrassment than the actual damage you have done to your body. While this level of dissociation is not particularly common, it can have severe emotional consequences, including high levels of shame.

Activity 3.2 will help you explore the connection alienation and loss of control have to shame in your life.

Activity 3.2: Isolation, Loss of Control, and Shame

Shame and embarrassment are common products of SIV. This activity will help you explore the relationship between these feelings and the behaviors you perform when you hurt yourself. You will probably find that when you engage in SIV you are also evoking shame or embarrassment.

Place a check mark next to each of the ways that injuring yourself creates feelings of shame or embarrassment.

_____ Injuring myself makes me feel different from others.

_____ I feel out of control when I hurt myself.

_____ I feel ashamed that I cannot remember injuring myself.

_____ I feel like I'm doing something I should not be doing.

_____ When I hurt myself I feel vulnerable and that makes me ashamed.

_____ The sight of my own injured body (or blood) makes me feel exposed and embarrassed.

_____ I feel like I'm being really violent and aggressive.

_____ I want to keep the fact that I hurt myself a secret.

_____ Hurting myself seems so weird that I'm afraid others will think I'm crazy.

Either here or in your journal list any other ways in which SIV creates shame or embarrassment in your life.

_____

_____

_____

What effect do you now think SIV has on the amount of shame you feel on a regular basis? Is it greater than you imagined? This topic will be discussed further in chapter 7.

Overcoming Shame

While shame is a useful emotion at times—telling us when we've violated our own moral or ethical codes—it can also be very damaging.

Secrecy, isolation, alienation, depression, and self-hatred are all consequences of shame. Many of these consequences will increase your desire to hurt yourself, thus playing a major role in the cycle of self-injury (which is discussed in chapter 4).

There are two main ways of reducing shame. The most obvious is to discontinue the activities that produce these feelings. However, it is likely that SIV still serves an important function in your life, that you use SIV as a method of coping. So, while ending the activity has a high rate of success in terms of reducing shame, it may not yet be a practical approach.

A second way to eliminate or decrease feelings of shame or embarrassment is to change the way you view the activity—how you think about it. Self-inflicted violence is a coping mechanism that you use as a way to control dangerous feelings or even to stay alive. Hurting yourself may actually have saved your own life, functioning as an alternative to suicide for example. The scars that you wear and the memories you have offer testimony to your ability to survive. If you begin to view self-inflicted violence as a method of coping, surviving, and caring for yourself, you are likely to decrease (and hopefully eliminate) shame and increase feelings of pride. Activity 3.3 will help you begin to do this.

Activity 3.3: Overcoming Shame

Begin by spending some time reading your journal and reviewing the activities you completed in chapter 2. As you recall, that chapter dealt with reasons you use SIV.

1. Once you have looked over these activities and given some thought to why you hurt yourself, turn to a new page in your journal. On this page, list all of the reasons you injure yourself. You may have reasons which were not discussed in the previous chapter so make sure to include those.

2. When your list is complete, rank your reasons in order of importance. Make the most important reason number 1; the second most important, number 2; and so forth.

3. Now think about the reasons you have just listed. What you have written probably doesn't contain anything that would make you ashamed. You have probably found a way to help you cope, to communicate, and to release your emotions. By learning to view SIV as a means to improve your life in some way (even if it's only temporary), you can reduce your feelings of shame regarding this action.

Ritual and Self-Inflicted Violence

Generally, self-inflicted violence follows some sort of ritualistic procedure. A ritualistic procedure is way of doing something, in this case SIV, that follows a certain pattern or that might be considered ceremonial. As mentioned in chapter 1, self-injury may be ritualistic in terms of environment, instrument, and/or procedure. Many people will not engage in SIV unless they are able to follow their ritual, and may arrange their life so that they can do so. For example, you might find yourself desperately wanting to harm yourself but unable to find the object you typically use. Without this object you are less likely to harm yourself.

Laura is a twenty-year-old waitress who lives by herself. She has lived on her own since the age of sixteen, when her mother threw her out of the house after catching her smoking marijuana in her bedroom. Over the past three years, Laura has regularly burned herself with cigarettes, usually several times per month. Her forearms and legs are severely scarred. In public, Laura always wears long-sleeved shirts and long pants.

Laura's SIV follows a highly ritualized process. First, when she feels the urge to injure herself, she goes home. Laura will only injure herself in her own home. Next, she turns off all the lights and shuts her windows and blinds. She then removes three small white candles from under the bathroom sink where she keeps them, and places them on the coffee table in the living room along with her pack of cigarettes. She uses a silver-plated cigarette lighter to light the candles. She then spends five to ten minutes simply staring into a candle flame, which helps her dissociate to a greater degree. Finally, she lights a cigarette, takes exactly one drag, and buries the burning embers in her flesh.

Some types of SIV are less likely to follow a ritualized procedure, including hair pulling, nail biting, and hitting oneself. These forms of self-injury are possible without the aid of objects (knives, matches, etc.) and can occur without much planning or forethought.

Environment

Like Laura, many people choose to engage in self-inflicted violent activities only in a specific location. For most people, this location is home, because it offers the desired seclusion and privacy. Also, feelings of alienation and isolation are more likely to occur in solitude. Since these emotions often precipitate episodes of self-inflicted violence, it makes sense that self-injury is typically performed at home.

You probably have a specific place in the house where you generally hurt yourself. A bathroom, bedroom, even a closet may be your favorite place for self-injury. Also, like Laura, you may tailor your environment in specific ways, such as closing the blinds and lighting candles.

You are also likely to have a particular time of day when you engage in SIV. Many people hurt themselves in the evening, when they are more likely to be alone and alternate methods of coping are no longer available or have lost their effectiveness.

Because SIV sometimes reenacts previous abuse, if you have been abused in the past—particularly if you suffered abuse on a regular basis—you may find yourself engaging in self-injurious activities at the same time of day, day of the week, or same time of year as the original abuse. For example, as a child, Jenny was repeatedly sexually abused by her uncle. Her uncle lived in another part of the state and would usually only come to visit on holidays and birthdays, so it was on these occasions that Jenny would be forced into performing sexual acts with her uncle. As an adult, Jenny has engaged in SIV on a regular basis. She associates certain holidays with memories of being abused, and each Christmas day, she takes a razor blade and cuts the inside of her thighs as a way of reenacting this abuse. Depending on your history or your schedule, you may find your episodes of self-injury gravitating to a particular date or time.

Instruments

The use of specific instruments to self-inflict violence may also follow a ritualistic pattern. Many people use one particular type of object or even one specific instrument when they injure themselves. It is common for someone to reject alternate objects that could produce similar injurious effects. For example, you might only cut yourself with single-edged razor blades. If only an ordinary knife or a double-edged razor blade is available, you might postpone your SIV activities until you can find a single-edged blade. Or perhaps you are planning to burn yourself, but you're out of matches. Even though you have a cigarette lighter at home, the ritual may necessitate that you ask a neighbor to loan you some matches. This selective use of instruments illustrates some of the ritualistic qualities of self-injury.

Procedure

The ritualistic characteristics of self-inflicted violence are perhaps most evident in the actual procedure. Laura, as described earlier, carefully prepared for her SIV activities. She set the stage by lighting candles and closing windows. She readied her instruments, placing her cigarettes and lighter on the table. Only then would she begin the actual process of SIV. She stared into the flame of a candle, inducing or strengthening a dissociated state. After doing this for several minutes, she would then light her cigarette, take one puff, and burn herself.

Many people follow similar types of rituals when engaging in self-injurious behaviors. Preparing the environment, readying the instruments, and engaging in some preinjury activity are all common components of this process. You may even find the actual ritual of SIV as gratifying as the injury itself. Or perhaps you need the ritualized procedure in order to complete your self-injury. As you may well know, the exact nature of the ritualistic procedure is highly personalized.

It is common to find ritualistic behaviors following the self-injury as well. You probably bandage or otherwise nurture your wounds the same way each time. Perhaps you apply a certain type of ointment after the injury, or maybe you always take a hot bath after you have hurt yourself. You may even document that you have injured yourself, taking a photograph or writing about the episode in a journal.

Take some time now to do the following exercise, to examine and record the routine surrounding your SIV activities.

Activity 3.4: What Are My SIV Rituals?

This exercise will help you explore the ritualistic qualities of your self-injurious behaviors. Identifying and understanding your rituals will be of great help to you when you begin working on reducing or stopping your SIV activities. Chapter 7 will ask you to refer back to this exercise.

Part 1. Spend a few minutes thinking about your most recent episodes of SIV. Then in your journal, answer the following questions:

1. Where were you when you hurt yourself? If you were in more than one location, list each place. What percentage of the time do you injure yourself in each of these locations? Have you hurt yourself in other locations?

2. What time of day did you hurt yourself? How often do you injure yourself at that time of day? Are there other times during the day when you injure yourself? What time are you most likely to injure yourself?

3. Is there a particular day of the week or time of the year when you are likely to hurt yourself? Do any holidays cause you to hurt yourself more often?

4. What instruments have you have used to injure yourself (knife, razor, matches, own hands)? Is there a particular object or type of instrument you use to hurt yourself? How likely are you to injure yourself if this instrument or type of instrument is not available?

5. What rituals or routine does your SIV follow? What do you usually do before, during, and after injuring yourself? Describe these ritualistic procedures in as much detail as you can.

Part 2. Now that you are more aware of your own rituals around SIV, try to answer two final questions. They will probably require more thought than the previous questions, and they may be difficult to answer. Don't worry if you are unable to respond to them.

1. How did these rituals develop? Were they something you were taught? How do you think you learned to use these rituals?

2. Why do you think you developed these rituals? Do they serve some function in your life, like making you feel more in control or letting your SIV seem more predictable? In what ways do they help you?

Is Self-Inflicted Violence Impulsive?

At this moment in courtrooms across the nation, jurors are busy pondering the idea of premeditation. Did Susan Smith plan to drown her two young children? Did Betty Broderick plan to kill her ex-husband and his new wife? The answers to these questions not only have profound implications regarding the character of the defendants but they determine the severity of verdicts and sentences.

In the legal world, impulsive actions are treated with more leniency than actions that have been planned. In the realm of mental health, however, this phenomenon is typically reversed. The mental health field views impulsivity in a more negative light. When an individual engages in an action that is not planned, not only is the action itself judged but so is the lack of control.

While the views of mental health professionals may have little or no bearing on your life, the question of the impulsivity of your self-injurious activities is of some importance. Acts that are impulsive are difficult to control. Conversely, behaviors that require more planning and forethought are easier to manage and control. Thus, you will be better able to reduce or eliminate those SIV behaviors that are not impulsive. (This topic will be addressed further in chapter 7)

For example, Philip is a seventeen-year-old junior in high school who picks the skin on his arms to the point where he draws blood and creates open sores. Philip has been doing this since he was fifteen, and has numerous scars on his arms as a result. Philip never plans to hurt himself. Rather, he begins picking his skin when he is nervous, and he is often unaware of his actions until he begins to bleed. Because he is not aware of what he is doing until he is well into his SIV behaviors, Philip's SIV will be more difficult to control. The events leading to the self-injurious act are not easily recognized or altered.

In contrast to this impulsive type of SIV, Jean's self-injury is much more planned. Jean is a nineteen-year-old college student who frequently cuts her legs with a Swiss army knife. Jean hurts herself mostly when she is feeling really tense or angry. Each time she hurts herself, she follows a ritualized procedure that includes returning to her dorm room (if she is not there already), locking the door, closing the blinds, laying out bandages, and heating the blade of the knife over the flame of a candle. Jean's actions clearly take quite a bit of planning and forethought. Because there are so many steps in Jean's SIV process, disrupting this process could occur at many points, which would decrease the chance that Jean would hurt herself.

The degree of impulsivity associated with self-inflicted violence in general is difficult to determine. Researchers studying this phenomenon have presented contradictory results, sometimes finding that SIV relates to impulsivity and sometimes finding that it does not. It appears that SIV and impulsivity have a complex, variable, unpredictable relationship.

Perhaps the mysterious role of impulsivity in self-injurious behaviors is related in part to the complex nature of SIV itself. Because SIV is often used as a coping mechanism, its course is unpredictable. For example, when I get overwhelmed with life and work and everything else, I often use exercise (swimming) as a way to cope. However, when these feelings occur I am often not in a place where it is possible to exercise—most of the time I'm either at work or driving on the freeway. Because I am unable to use this method of coping, I will plan to exercise later, therefore creating a planned activity. The same logic could apply to self-inflicted violence. If you are in a situation in which injuring yourself is not possible or not "safe," you may plan to engage in SIV later. In this case, SIV is not impulsive but planned.

However, sometimes SIV is impulsive. Continuing the previous example, if I were able to swim laps in the carpool lane or around the conference table while at work, I would be able to use my method of coping more impulsively. Likewise, if you are able to engage in self-inflicted violence at the moment when you need a coping mechanism, the activity might be considered impulsive.

To some degree, the role of impulsivity in SIV is dependent on the type of SIV being practiced. Some forms of self-injury are much more easily performed than others. Hair pulling, nail biting, skin picking, and hitting need no preparation and can be done fairly inconspicuously. These types of SIV are so accessible, in fact, that you might not even be aware that you're engaging in them. For instance, you could very easily be sitting at your desk at work pulling hairs from your beard without being conscious of your actions. Because these behaviors can be performed anywhere and need no specific preparation, they will generally be more impulsive way than other forms of SIV, which require more forethought and planning. Thus, the feasibility of injuring yourself using your chosen method in a given environment helps determine the premeditation of an act of self-injury.

In addition, the ritualistic qualities associated with self-inflicted violence suggest that these activities require more planning than researchers originally believed. As mentioned earlier, ritual may preclude impulsivity, since a given act of SIV often requires a great deal of preparation. You can't do something on the spur of the moment if you have to plan and prepare for it. Also, you may decide to not injure yourself if you're in the wrong location or don't have your usual instrument. Thus, you may plan to carry out your SIV activity later in the day instead of acting impulsively.

However, like any behavior and particularly like any coping mechanism, self-inflicted violence occurs when it is needed, and for this reason it may occur without planning. If you want to hurt yourself and have no reason not to do so, you probably will hurt yourself. And sometimes you may be in a situation in which SIV is contraindicated (such as at work), yet find yourself unable to control your self-injurious impulses. Perhaps your need for coping is greater than your need for privacy.

As you can see, many factors interact to determine the role of impulsivity in self-inflicted violence. So it is not surprising that research has found contradictory results in this area. What is evident, however, is that the relationship between impulsivity and self-injury is complex and is likely to vary depending on individual and situational factors.

Understanding the degree of impulsivity of your SIV will be an important step in determining the ways that will best help you control and eliminate this behavior. Techniques and strategies for stopping SIV are presented in chapter 7. For now, activity 3.5 will help you determine how impulsive your practice of SIV is.

Activity 3.5: Is My SIV Impulsive or Planned?

This exercise will help you to determine the degree of impulsivity and planning associated with your SIV. This will be important when you are finding techniques to help you eliminate SIV in chapter 7.

Spend a few minutes remembering a specific instance of SIV, either your most recent episode of SIV or an episode from further in the past. Try to remember as many details as you can.

Now, in your journal, describe the episode as a series of steps, for example:

1. *My boss yelled at me in front of my coworkers.*

2. *I felt embarrassed and angry.*

3. *I ran into the bathroom at work and locked the door.*

4. *I pulled out clumps of hair from my head.*

The more steps you have listed, the more planned your SIV activities probably are. If you have only one or two steps, it is likely that the ways you hurt yourself tend to be impulsive.

By completing this activity you are beginning to make progress in identifying ways of reducing your SIV activities. Later, you will see that the cycle of SIV can be disrupted at any of the steps you listed. It's just a matter of finding which step is easiest to alter.

CHAPTER 4

The Cycle of
Self-Inflicted Violence

Self-inflicted violence generally follows a fairly predictable cycle. Why and how you hurt yourself, the process of SIV, doesn't change much from one episode of self-injury to the next. Even if you alter the method of self-injury—for instance, cutting yourself one time and bruising yourself the next—the thoughts and emotions that occur during the process of SIV tend to follow a definite pattern. The first section of this chapter will help you better understand the cycle of your thoughts and emotions.

Although your thoughts and emotions are quite important, they are only two components of the entire process of SIV. The second part of this chapter presents different models that explain other parts of the cycle of self-inflicted violence. These models break down the process of SIV to make it more understandable and to help you to explore some of the reasons you engage in SIV, the possible functions self-injury may serve in your life, and what you experience physically and psychologically during the course of SIV.

Thoughts and SIV

Although you are probably not aware of it, it is likely that your thoughts follow a predictable cycle throughout the course of SIV. This section will help you identify and understand the thoughts during the cycle of self-injury. This will be helpful when you begin to work on stopping SIV in your life, which is discussed in chapter 7.

Thoughts Before SIV

Before you hurt yourself, many things are going through your mind. Some of these thoughts you are likely to be aware of, such as thinking of the method you will use to hurt yourself or even debating whether you will really injure yourself at all. However, you are probably also having many other thoughts of which you aren't so aware. Typically, these thoughts are one of the primary sources of the motivation to hurt yourself. Therefore, to create permanent change in your SIV behaviors, it is essential that the thoughts preceding these activities be identified and understood so that later they can be changed.

Bridget is a nineteen-year-old college student who is enrolled in honors-level courses and has many friends. She started burning herself when she was fourteen, stopped injuring herself for several years, and has now returned to the behavior. She typically burns herself using a cigarette lighter, which she always carries in her backpack. Bridget lives in the college dormitory and has a roommate, but finds the privacy to hurt herself when everyone else is asleep. She has many scars on her arms and legs and usually wears clothes that keep them covered. When people do notice her scars, Bridget usually implies that the scars are the result of a childhood accident.

Bridget has become able to identify some of the thoughts that typically appear prior to hurting herself. See if any of your thoughts sound similar to Bridget's:

No one likes me.

I hate my body.

Nothing ever works out right.

No one would ever want to be with me.

I'm so stupid.

Life sucks.

I hate everyone.

I can't stand my life.

I want someone to care about me.

Sometimes your thoughts will stem directly from identifiable events. For instance, if you received a poor evaluation at work, you might think to yourself that you are a bad employee. At other times, the origins of your thoughts will be more complicated and less clearly defined. For example, you may think that you are unattractive or lazy or stupid, and you may not be able to determine when and where this idea first originated.

Regardless of their origins, probably many of the thoughts you have before you injure yourself are negative. During the period preceding SIV, you are almost certainly thinking of yourself and your world in a pessimistic, despairing way. It is these negative thoughts that lead to the desire to self-injure.

Some people use SIV as a way to help control the negative thoughts (and emotions) they have. When you are experiencing thoughts that are extremely negative and destructive, you are likely to want to find a way to make them stop. SIV gives you an activity you can focus on—in a sense you deflect your negative thinking by substituting thoughts about the self-injurious act itself, such as planning a method or finding a place to hurt yourself. This is to say that your original thoughts of *I'm no good,* are replaced with thoughts of *I'm going to hurt myself.* Once you begin to concentrate on injuring yourself and all the details involved in that act, you push aside the original thoughts that led you to want to hurt yourself.

Although SIV is one method that allows you to control your thoughts and escape the discomfort caused by your negative thoughts, there are other options. Before you can exercise them, however, you must learn to identify your precipitating thoughts. Activity 4.1, at the end of this section, will give you some practice in doing this.

Thoughts During SIV

As mentioned in previous chapters, many people enter a dissociated state immediately before injuring themselves. In such a state you may feel as if you are not totally present in your body—as if you're floating or detached, or even like you're watching yourself in a movie. One of the functions of this state is to prevent the body from feeling pain, and it keeps you from feeling much pain when you hurt yourself. While dissociation is helpful in this sense, it is less helpful in other ways. Specifically, dissociation makes it very difficult to become aware of exactly what you are thinking at the time. However, it is precisely during this dissociated state that your thinking is likely to become the most irrational and often the most destructive. Here are some examples of thoughts that occur immediately preceding or during an act of self-inflicted violence:

I need to hurt myself.

This is the only way I can feel better. Just a few more (cuts, burns, bruises . . .) and I'll be OK.

Each of these thoughts is clearly illogical. At the time, however, each of them seems to make perfect sense.

Thoughts Following SIV

Immediately following an incident of self-inflicted violence, most people report an inability to access their thoughts. For many people, the physiological process associated with SIV causes their thoughts to become disorganized or scattered. However, shortly thereafter they regain the ability to identify specific thoughts. Thoughts during this time tend to focus on three major themes: shame, guilt, and relief. Bridget's thoughts after burning herself closely follow these themes:

I can't believe I just hurt myself again.

I can't tell anyone about this.

I'm so stupid for burning myself.

When am I going to stop doing this?

As dumb as it sounds, hurting myself makes me feel better.

Although thoughts filled with shame and guilt may be almost irresistible, generally they are not helpful. In all likelihood, negative feelings such as shame and guilt are part of the reason you want to hurt yourself in the first place. Allowing yourself to continue to think such thoughts will only make you want to inflict more injury on yourself. Instead of continuing negative and potentially dangerous styles of thought, it would be better for you to stop or change them. Specific methods of altering your thoughts will be presented in chapter 7, which focuses on stopping SIV. For now, the following activity will help you begin to identify the thoughts you have that make up a part of the cycle of your SIV.

Activity 4.1: The Cycle of My Thoughts

It is very important that you learn to identify and recognize the thoughts that you have during the process of SIV. Knowing what you are thinking will enable you to understand why you want to hurt yourself and to begin controlling your desire to hurt yourself.

This exercise will assist you in identifying and recognizing your thoughts throughout the process of SIV. This is an important initial step in changing your SIV behaviors. Exercises in chapter 7 will use the information you uncover here to help you learn some ways to control and change your thoughts. So you will need to complete this activity before doing the related activities in that chapter.

In your journal, begin keeping a log of all the thoughts that accompany episodes of hurting yourself. Since it may be difficult to remember the thoughts that you had from previous episodes of SIV, try to record your thoughts each time from now on when you want to hurt yourself.

1. Whenever you feel the desire to hurt yourself, simply take a few minutes and write down what you are thinking. Do your thoughts

have any common themes? Are they similar to Bridget's thoughts—filled with criticism and despair? (This step may have the side effect of lessening your desire to injure yourself.)

2. After you have hurt yourself, try to record any thoughts that you had during the actual process of SIV. What do you remember thinking?

3. List the thoughts you had after you injured yourself. Were your thoughts like Bridget's, in that they were self-critical or focused on shame? Or were your thoughts more filled with relief or plans for future self-injury?

4. How do you think your thoughts affect your desire to hurt yourself? Do you have specific thoughts that encourage SIV?

Emotions and SIV

Much like thoughts, the emotions experienced throughout an episode of self-inflicted violence tend to follow a predictable pattern. Although not everyone experiences these feelings, the majority of people engaging in SIV will encounter at least some of them. You may not even be aware of what you're feeling during various points in the self-injury process. By learning to identify your feelings, you will probably find similarities between your own experience and what is presented in this section.

Emotions Before SIV

Preceding an episode of self-injury, most individuals experience strong negative feelings that are overwhelming and intolerable. While the source of the feelings may vary, the emotions generally fall into several distinct, yet similar categories: anger and frustration, alienation, and depression.

People may feel frustrated or angered in response to any number of events, but in general these feelings usually stem from an inability to fulfill a desire. Thus, frustration may be caused by an inability to meet a variety of wishes or demands. For instance, you might feel frustrated because your partner is unresponsive to your needs, or because you are not able to control your own feelings, or because a television show you enjoy has been preempted by an infomercial. The possible sources of frustration are too numerous to imagine, and each episode of SIV may be related to a distinct source of this emotion.

Anger, while similar to frustration, generally stems from feelings of hostility. More often than frustration, anger often results from interactions with others that do not go as planned, and it is frequently directed at a specific person. Often anger is a response to treatment by others that you perceive as unfair. For example, say that after I have been standing in line at the grocery store for nearly ten minutes the checkstand next to me opens.

But instead of the new cashier helping the person who had been waiting longest (me), she helps the last person in the original line (who had just arrived). I perceive the situation as unfair, and I get angry. I feel hostile toward both the new cashier and the guy who simply sauntered up to the checkstand.

While frustration, anger, and hostility can be useful emotions, they can also be damaging if they aren't handled correctly. Emotions that are not released or transformed (particularly frustration and anger) tend to have negative side effects. In fact, it has been shown that hostility is significantly related to the occurrence of heart disease. As mentioned in chapter 2, many people who purposefully injure themselves do not know how to effectively manipulate these emotions.

Alienation is a second emotion that commonly precedes an act of self-inflicted violence. Like frustration and anger, feelings of loneliness, isolation, or alienation can stem from any number of events, including rejection by another, separation from an important figure in your life, abandonment, or mistreatment. General feelings of disconnection—perhaps caused by an inability to receive support from others—are common prior to SIV. And the fact that SIV tends to be practiced privately, in a clandestine manner, serves to increase these feelings of isolation and disconnection. It is difficult to be connected with others if you are in seclusion.

You may have also noticed that once you have hurt yourself, you tend to isolate yourself from others even more. You may do this physically, by staying away from other people, or emotionally, by hiding your SIV or omitting information about how you're really feeling. (This topic will be covered in greater detail in chapter 6.) Thus, alienation, isolation, and disconnection may be both an influence of SIV and a result of SIV.

The third type of emotion associated with self-inflicted violence is that of depression. Feelings of sadness, melancholy, or unhappiness frequently precede acts of SIV. Some people experience depression as boredom or emptiness or a feeling of dissatisfaction with their life. However you phrase it, this emotion is likely to produce feelings of pointlessness and hopelessness.

These feelings—anger, alienation, and depression—combine to form the ideal emotional environment for an act of self-inflicted violence. If you feel frustrated, alone, and hopeless, you are likely to use any means available to alter this overwhelming mood. The high level of tension produced by this emotional interaction also contributes to the urge to engage in SIV. While it is certainly possible to lessen this emotional state without the use of self-injury, many people who engage in SIV may not know how to use alternative means or may find themselves unable to do so at the time. Locating alternatives to self-injury will also be addressed in chapter 7.

Emotional States During SIV

During the self-injurious act itself, emotional states are difficult to ascertain. As mentioned previously, one of the primary goals of SIV is to alter or mask the experience of overwhelming emotions. Because SIV is so effective at this task, most people are unable to identify emotional states during this stage.

Many individuals dissociate while hurting themselves. Dissociation can be both an emotional as well as a physical state. That is, during a dissociative episode your level of consciousness is altered, which serves to obscure or distort your memories and make your emotions more difficult to identify. Finally, the release of endorphins (neurotransmitters that help block the feeling of physical pain) in response to the injury also masks feelings.

Emotions Following SIV

After an episode of self-inflicted violence, most people progress through two distinct stages of emotion. First, a great sense of relief is experienced. The enormous amount of tension that preceded the act has dissipated. In addition, the sense of calmness and happiness produced by the release of endorphins may continue for some length of time. For these reasons, immediately following an episode of self-injury, you probably feel pretty good. These good feelings are one reason why SIV is so self-reinforcing. Most people would probably like to feel that way more often, though not everyone goes to the same lengths.

The second emotional state you probably experience occurs after the positive feelings have worn off. This second stage includes feelings of guilt, regret, shame, and the return of the emotions that were evident before the act. By the time you reach this stage, you probably feel even worse than you did before injuring yourself. You may even feel so bad that you want to hurt yourself again. It is precisely this emotional experience that creates the cyclic pattern of SIV.

Frank is a twenty-two-year-old office worker who for the past ten years has engaged in SIV. When Frank hurts himself, he drops bricks or other heavy objects on his feet. He has broken bones in his feet many times. He explains the events like this:

> I hurt myself when I'm feeling frustrated and can't figure out a way to make things better. It's weird, but throwing bricks on my feet really helps, at least for a while. I get rid of that frustration and feel something real instead. It works for a while, but then the feelings come back anyway.

Activity 4.2 will help you begin to understand the cycle of your own emotions in relation to SIV, which is a first step toward breaking the cycle of SIV.

Activity 4.2: The Cycle of My Emotions

Understanding the specific emotions that are associated with SIV is necessary before you can change these behaviors. This activity will allow you to determine what you are feeling during the cycle of SIV. You will be referring back to this activity in chapter 7, when you are learning how to end your SIV behaviors.

For this activity you probably want to focus on a single incident. Try to think of a specific time when you hurt yourself that was fairly typical of most of the times you hurt yourself.

1. Focus on how you were feeling before the actual act of SIV. Sometimes it's hard to remember what you were feeling in the past. It might help you to try and remember some of the details of your surroundings at that time: Where were you? What were you wearing? What time of day was it? Try to get a clear picture in your mind of what was going on right before your injured yourself. Now try to remember what you were feeling.

2. Now, in the list below, write a *B* next to each of the emotions that you felt *before* you hurt yourself. Next, circle the emotions that are usually the most intense during this period. (Use the provided spaces to list any other emotions that you experience.)

_____	anger	_____	disconnection
_____	frustration	_____	depression
_____	hopelessness	_____	hostility
_____	sadness	_____	tension
_____	isolation	_____	fear
_____	alienation	_____	guilt
_____	shame	_____	loneliness
_____	anxiety	_____	emptiness
_____	relief	_____	euphoria
_____	numbness	_____	depression
_____	wholeness	_____	elation
_____	happiness	_____	pride
_____	_____	_____	_____
_____	_____	_____	_____
_____	_____	_____	_____

3. Then, place a *D* beside any emotion you experienced *during* SIV. As mentioned earlier, you may have great difficulty identifying any emotions during SIV. If you are unable to identify any particular feelings from this stage, don't worry. Simply go on to the next part of the activity.

4. Finally, place an *A* next to each of the emotions that you feel *after* you hurt yourself. Underline the emotions that are usually most intense during this period. It is likely that many of these will be the same emotions you felt before you hurt yourself.

Are you beginning to see how your emotions change throughout the cycle of SIV? Were you able to identify the emotions you feel most intensely? How do you think these emotions influence your desire to hurt yourself? Understanding the cycle of your emotions will be helpful to you when you begin to create strategies to reduce or eliminate your self-injurious activities.

Models of SIV

When I was a kid, I spent a great deal of my allowance and my time buying and assembling toy models. I loved the way the pieces fit together and made something whole out of what seemed like thousands of tiny parts. I also enjoyed learning how something that was really complicated could be broken down into smaller pieces that were easier to handle and understand.

As an adult, I have learned to deal with models of a different kind. In the field of psychology another kind of model is often used to explain complex ideas. Just like my childhood models, psychological models offer an easier way to understand ideas that may be very involved or complicated. They help to break down large, complex ideas into smaller pieces that can be more easily understood. Although toy models involve actual tangible parts, psychological models consist of concepts, concepts that represent the inner workings of a behavior, thought, idea, or feeling—things that can't really be seen. Yet, like physical models, psychological models help us to understand their subject as a whole.

Several models are used by psychologists to better understand the nature and cycle of self-inflicted violence. While each of these models appears to have some validity, I urge you to use your own experiences to judge the accuracy of each model as it applies to you.

The Addiction Model

The first model of self-inflicted violence is very similar to models used to explain various addictions, including substance use, eating disorders, gambling behaviors, sexual addictions, and compulsive shopping.

Figure A represents the process and essential components of this model. As you can see, this model is cyclic: Self-inflicted violent behavior continues in part due to the direct effect of the behavior and its consequences. In other words, while SIV may help you to feel better, it may also lead to further acts of self-injury. The following sections describe the particular components of this model and the ways in which they create the cycle of self-inflicted violence.

Figure A: The Addiction Model of SIV

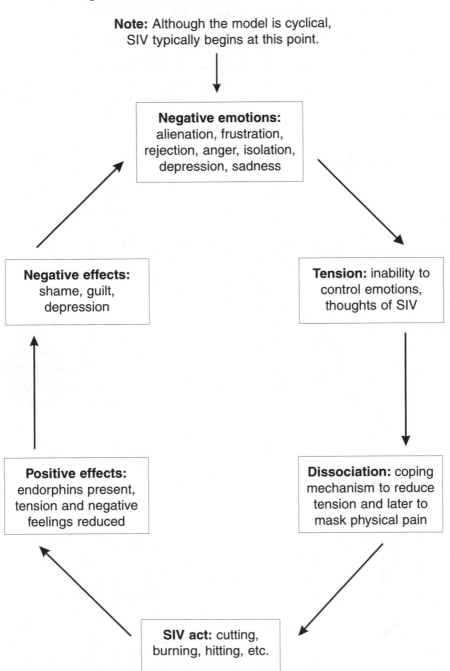

Negative emotions. Negative emotions generally mark the beginning of the SIV cycle. As previously discussed, negative emotions may stem from any number of sources and tend to fall into three main categories:

- Anger, hostility, and frustration

- Alienation, isolation, disconnection, rejection, and loneliness

- Sadness, depression, and simply feeling bad

Usually these negative emotions are experienced as overwhelming, uncontrollable, or fragmenting (a feeling of being scattered or not whole). This highly uncomfortable state makes you want to find ways to feel better quickly. Although the effects are sometimes extremely detrimental in the long term, SIV does provide an effective, short-term way of overcoming these emotions.

Tension. Once SIV has been considered as an option for reducing these negative feelings, the emotional experience shifts to a state of anxiety or high tension. So, while you may have started out feeling frustrated, depressed, or sad, you are now dealing with very intense feelings of tension or anxiety. This tension is partially a product of the anticipation of inflicting self-injury; once you begin to think about hurting yourself, you begin to anticipate the actual act of self-injury.

Because SIV may be either desired or undesired, or both, your anticipation may contain elements of excitement and/or anxiety, either of which will make you feel tension. The sense of excitement that may precede an episode of SIV stems from the fact that self-injury can produce feelings of euphoria and relief, as discussed earlier. Thus, when you are anticipating this event, you may feel a different kind of stress called *eustress*, which is stress or tension stemming from a positively viewed source. However, you may also feel fear or anxiety when anticipating an episode of SIV. You may view SIV as a necessary, but undesired event. You may feel anxious because of the actual danger involved or because you feel unable to your control emotions in a more traditional manner. You might even see self-inflicted violence as a last resort, an extreme attempt to retain a sense of sanity.

Dissociation. Dissociation is the next stage in the SIV cycle. Dissociation stems directly from the high-tension level produced by overwhelming or uncontrollable emotions. Dissociation (discussed in chapter 2) serves a very useful dual purpose in that it both acts as a coping mechanism and allows you to withstand intense emotional and physical pain, reducing your experience of tension and later masks the physical pain produced by the injury.

The SIV Act. During this stage you are actively engaging in self-harm. Cutting, burning, hitting, bruising, pulling hair, picking scabs, nail biting, and excessive scratching are all common SIV behaviors. During these actions dissociation tends to be at its highest, minimizing the experience of physical pain. At this time endorphins are also released, aiding dissociation in limiting the amount of pain you perceive. It is the combination of endorphins and dissociation that causes many people to report a surprising lack of physical discomfort as they engage in self-injurious activities.

Positive effects. Immediately after the self-injurious act comes a sense of relief. At this point the endorphins stimulated by the SIV continue to be present, allowing you to experience a sense of euphoria (joy and calmness) and well-being. In addition, the SIV act has enabled you to successfully transform your uncontrollable negative emotions into something more tangible and controllable—the self-injury. By performing and then nurturing the self-injury, you have turned a negative psychological state into something manageable, regaining control over your emotional and physical states. It is the effectiveness of this coping mechanism that allows SIV to provide such a strong and necessary sense of temporary relief and freedom from psychological distress.

Negative Effects. One of the problems with self-inflicted violence as a method of coping is that its effects are only temporary. As the endorphins dissipate and the consequences of the self-injurious behavior become more clear, you are likely to experience negative emotions such as shame, guilt and remorse. In addition, negative emotions such as you felt before you hurt yourself will often reappear at this point or shortly thereafter. As a result of having engaged in self-inflicted violence, you may be left feeling worse than you did before hurting yourself. And it is these negative emotions that will plant the seeds for your next episode of self-inflicted violence.

Liz is a seventeen-year-old high-school junior. She described her process of SIV as follows:

> It all starts cause I'm not feeling much of anything. I mean, I know I'm depressed and stuff, but I just can't feel it. So I decide to cut myself, and I know I'll feel better after. When I'm getting my stuff together, you know, the razor blade and the paper towels and the bandages, I feel like I've got lots of energy. I get into this state where it seems like I'm not really real but I can feel every piece of my body tingling. It sounds weird, but it feels really good. And when I cut myself, this feeling actually gets stronger. I feel alive. I love how the blood feels running down my arm. It's all warm and stuff. Usually by the time I finish putting the bandages on my arm, the tingling feeling is gone and I just feel kind of drained. Sometimes I'll even go sleep afterwards. Later, when I think about what I've done and I see the slashes on my arm I start feeling bad again. I don't like having to hurt myself.

Activity 4.3 will help you examine how applicable the addiction model is to the pattern of SIV in your life.

Activity 4.3: My SIV and the Addiction Model

Understanding how your own cycle of SIV operates will help you later when you begin to change this pattern and decrease your self-injurious activities.

1. Think back to a specific time when you hurt yourself. You may want to use your most recent episode of SIV since it is probably freshest in your memory. In your journal, list the three emotions you felt most intensely before you hurt yourself. (If you're unable to recall, you might want to review Activity 4.2.) For example:

   1. *Sadness*

   2. *Anger*

   3. *Disappointment*

2. Now, try to describe in your journal how you felt when you began to think about hurting yourself. You were feeling bad and you got the idea to hurt yourself. Then how did you feel? Did you experience a change in your negative emotions? Did you become tense or excited or nervous? Or did you become numb or dissociated? Did your feelings change even more as you got closer to injuring yourself? What happened?

   For example:

   Once I decided to hurt myself, I felt really excited and full of energy. I didn't feel sad anymore because I knew I was going to do something that would make me feel better. Right before I hurt myself I felt really zoned out, but even that was a calm and good feeling.

3. Describe as best you can what you went through when you injured yourself. Write about what you did, what instruments (if any) you used, how long the process took, your experience of pain and/or dissociation, how you felt, and anything else you think is important. How did your feelings change throughout the process? When were you more tense, less tense, more dissociated? Do you have difficulty remembering the specifics of this stage of SIV? Describe whatever you felt or can remember.

4. Take a few minutes now to think about what happened after you hurt yourself. In your journal describe what you went through afterward. How did you feel? Were you calm, peaceful, tired, anxious? (Again, you might want to refer to the preceding activity to help you remember some of these feelings.)

5. Because relief is one of the primary feelings resulting from SIV, it is important to explore exactly how SIV causes this experience

and how you define relief. In your journal list all the ways that self-inflicted violence gave you relief.

6. Finally, you need to examine the ultimate stage of the SIV cycle—the negative results and return of your negative feelings. Knowing when you might experience the return of negative feelings will be very important when you try to stop hurting yourself. Using the same episode of SIV you've been following throughout this activity, think about how long it took after hurting yourself before you began to feel bad again. Was it minutes? Hours? Days? Weeks? Were the feelings the same as before you hurt yourself? If they weren't, how did they change? Was it the intensity or the actual emotions that changed? How long do you usually go between episodes of SIV?

Hopefully, this activity has helped you to see how your SIV activities follow the basic addiction model. By understanding your behaviors in terms of a model, you will be better able to control your self-injuries and prevent yourself from engaging in these activities.

You have probably noticed by now that many of these activities ask you to describe what you go through when you injure yourself. Although this process of describing your experience may seem redundant and unnecessary, it is actually designed to be helpful. Going over what you feel, think, and do when you hurt yourself not only enables you to remember more and more important details, but improves your ability to deal with self-inflicted violence. By repeatedly bringing SIV to your consciousness, you lessen the impact of remembering these events. You probably already have a much easier time thinking about specific times when you hurt yourself now than you did in earlier exercises. The shame, embarrassment, and other emotions you feel lose some of their power as you confront them more often, which will be helpful when you begin to work on stopping SIV.

The Operant Conditioning Model

A second model used to explain the cycle of SIV is that of operant conditioning. Operant conditioning states that what happens following a behavior (the consequences) influences the likelihood of that behavior reoccurring. According to this theory behaviors followed by positive outcomes (reinforcers) will be strengthened, whereas behaviors followed by negative outcomes (punishments) will be weakened. This theory of learning and behavior is called Thorndike's Law of Effect.

In simpler terms, this model means that the consequences of your SIV activities will affect the probability that you will use SIV in the future. For instance, if a result of an act of self-inflicted violence was that it made you feel better, you would probably hurt yourself again. But if you injured yourself and it hurt much more than you expected, you would be less likely to try SIV in the future. The concepts of reinforcement and punishment are explained more fully in the following sections.

Reinforcement. *Reinforcement* is a psychological term that basically means the same thing as reward. When you experience reinforcement, you receive a reward or a pleasurable consequence for some behavior. Reinforcement always makes it more likely that you will repeat whatever behavior produced the reward. For example, although I really enjoy working, there are some days I would rather stay in bed or go to a movie or do anything but go to work. But because I drag myself out of bed and go to work anyway, at the end of each month I receive a pretty nice (and necessary) reward—a paycheck. The paycheck acts as a reinforcer and makes it likely that I'll continue to go to work.

Reinforcers can be both positive and negative, but they're always rewards. Unlike the way we typically think of *negative* and *positive*—as *good* and *bad*—when relating to reinforcement these terms take on slightly different definitions. *Positive reinforcement* means to provide a consequence that is desired. For example, there are few things in the world I enjoy more than going to the beach. So to give myself an incentive to finish a task, I promise myself that when I finish I can go to the beach. When I receive this incentive I am positively rewarding myself, giving myself something that I desire. This is an excellent way of strengthening any behavior, and it helps me to get my work done.

Self-inflicted violence provides several positive reinforcers, as discussed in chapter 2: the euphoric feeling produced by endorphins, self-nurturing of wounds, expression of feelings, connection or communication with others via your injuries, and so on. Because it offers so many rewards and positive consequences, your SIV behavior is likely to be strengthened.

Negative reinforcers are a second type of consequence that also strengthens behavior. *Negative*, in operant conditioning language, refers to the removal of something, as opposed to the receipt of something (a positive reward). Negative reinforcement occurs when something unwanted is removed or reduced, thus strengthening the behavior that removed or reduced the undesired thing.

Let me provide an example: Several years ago I had some neighbors who, when they saw that I was home (when either I was visible or my front door was open), would simply walk into my house and announce their presence. Although they viewed this as neighborly, I like my privacy and so their behavior bugged me. One day I discovered that I could lock my screen door, forcing my neighbors to use the doorbell to announce their arrival. My behavior of locking the screen door reduced undesired intrusions by my neighbors. And since this was a highly effective way of keeping them out of my house, I began to lock the screen door frequently. My screen-locking behavior was strengthened because the consequences were so rewarding.

Negative reinforcement works similarly in terms of SIV behaviors. Think of your negative emotions as troublesome neighbors. Once you find a behavior that reduces or eliminates their intrusion, you're likely to engage in that behavior quite often. Self-inflicted violence works well to reduce the presence of negative emotions. It is similarly effective at ending or preventing undesired dissociative episodes. Because SIV is so good at reducing or eliminating negative emotional states, it has exceptionally strong negative-reinforcement properties. The numerous reinforcements, both positive and negative, that self-injurious behavior can provide help strengthen the likelihood that SIV behaviors will continue.

Punishment. You may be wondering about the flip side to reinforcement: punishment. When your behavior creates a consequence that you don't like, that is undesired, that consequence is called a *punishment*. Unlike reinforcement, which strengthens the likelihood a behavior will reoccur, punishment weakens a behavior.

Like reinforcement, punishment can be either positive or negative. Positive punishment means the presentation of something undesired. For example, as a child I once used my mother's lipstick to paint my face like an Indian warrior—at least my imagined version of what one should look like. I did not know that Indian warriors needed permission to paint their faces, as well as appropriate paints. Needless to say, I got in trouble and was punished for my behavior. If I had been spanked for my actions, I would have received positive punishment. The presentation of something undesired, the spanking, would have decreased the likelihood that I would use my mother's lipstick as war paint in the future.

My parents chose a negative punishment instead: I had something I enjoyed taken away from me. When something that you enjoy or desire is removed from you as a consequence to your behavior, it is called *negative punishment*. I was not allowed to watch television for the rest of the weekend. Taking away my beloved television was a form of punishment that decreased the probability that I would ever use lipstick again (for war paint or otherwise).

Both positive punishment and negative punishment reduce the chance that you will again engage in the original behavior. Self-inflicted violence has properties of both positive and negative punishment. Among its several forms of positive punishment are undesired wounds or scars and feelings of shame, regret, and embarrassment.

Negative punishments, although less obvious than the positive punishments, also result from self-inflicted violence. The feelings of shame and embarrassment (positive punishers) typically produced by self-injury may cause you to avoid certain situations or activities you might desire. If, for example, you wear long-sleeved shirts or long pants in the summer so that others won't see your scars, SIV is preventing you from going swimming or wearing clothes that are more comfortable and appropriate to the season. SIV may also reduce the honesty, pride, and connection with others you experience. Because these desired things are reduced or removed by your self-injurious activities, those activities are exerting a negatively punishing consequence.

As you can see, self-inflicted violence produces both reinforcing and punishing consequences. So if SIV has consequences that increase the likelihood of this behavior and also has consequences that decrease its likelihood, what does this mean? The answer is in many ways quite simple: As the saying goes, "Timing is everything."

The timing of a consequence has a profound effect on the fate of the behavior. Consequences that occur immediately after, during, or even slightly before a behavior have the greatest effect on the perception and future of that behavior. Return for a moment to the addiction model of SIV. Before, during, and immediately after an act of self-injury the consequences consist primarily of reinforcements (you feel better or at least less bad; endorphins are released). It is not until later that the punishing consequences make their appearance (you feel physical pain; you have to cover your body; you feel shame). Thus, because reinforcement is more closely associated in time with self-inflicted violence, the likelihood that acts of self-injury will recur is great.

Take some time now for the following exercise, which will help you to look at the ways your SIV has been affected by the principles of operant conditioning.

Activity 4.4: How Operant Conditioning Affects My SIV

In this exercise, it is likely that you will discover that in many ways the consequences of your self-injuries have influenced your desire to continue to hurt yourself. In chapter 7, several operant conditioning techniques will be employed to help you stop hurting yourself.

1. First let's focus on the ways that SIV offers you positively reinforcing consequences. In trying to decrease your SIV behavior, you will want to consider these consequences. Place a check mark next to each of the ways that self-inflicted violence provides you with positive reinforcement. Use the blank lines to list additional positive reinforcers. Remember, positive reinforcers are those consequences that give you something rewarding.

_____ Produces good feelings	_____ Lets me nurture myself
_____ Allows for communication	_____ Provides control
_____ Produces tangible results	_____ Enhances dissociation
_____ _____	_____ _____
_____ _____	_____ _____

2. Because negative reinforcement is also involved in strengthening a behavior, it is important for you to understand how you decrease or eliminate unwanted situations, feelings, or things through your own SIV activities. Place a check mark next to each of the ways that self-inflicted violence provides you with negative reinforcement. Again, use the blanks for additional negative reinforcers. Remember, negative reinforcers are rewarding in that they reduce or eliminate something you don't like.

_____ Decreases dissociation   _____ Decreases tension

_____ Decreases anger or frustration _____ Reduces sadness

_____ Reduces depression   _____ Decreases need for others

_____ Decreases hopelessness   _____ _____

_____ _____   _____ _____

3. Now let's focus on the ways that SIV introduces punishments in your life. Place a check next to each of the ways that SIV acts as a form of punishment. Once again, blank lines have been provided for your use.

_____ Produces shame   _____ Reduces connection with others

_____ Increases secrecy   _____ Produces wounds or scars

_____ Increases isolation   _____ Enhances feelings of failure

_____ _____   _____ _____

_____ _____   _____ _____

Did you find that SIV is better at providing you with reinforcement than punishment? You probably wouldn't continue to hurt yourself otherwise.

Opponent Process Theory

Opponent process theory states that a reaction to an event will automatically produce the opposite reaction. For example, you are walking down a dark alley and from behind you comes a loud noise that startles you. Your heart begins to race and your breathing becomes shallow as you turn to find out the source of the noise. When you realize it was a car backfiring, your fear reaction gradually yields to feelings of relief and calmness—hence "opponent," or opposite, part of the theory's name. Self-inflicted violence works in a similar manner. Feelings of great tension and fear before SIV are later replaced by the opposite emotional state, relaxation and peace, the *opponent process* of relief.

Over time, as you engage in acts of self-harm, you begin to expect this sense of relief. Because you have learned to expect this desired emotion, you may begin to enjoy the act of self-inflicted violence, just as some people love to bungee jump because after the jump their hearts stop pounding and they feel much less tense than before the jump. Other people enjoy eating extremely spicy foods because it feels so good when their mouths stop burning. These people learn to anticipate the cessation of fear or pain and so look forward to the activity that causes it. The same is true for SIV. You may feel excitement, anticipation, and euphoria just before or while you hurt yourself because you know that this act will lead to relief of intolerable negative emotions and help you to feel better when you're through. So not only do you begin to expect this sense of relief, but you begin to seek it out by instigating negative sensations, as when you intentionally injure yourself.

Observational Learning

Observational learning works on a very simple premise: We do what we view. There is no question that we learn by watching others. We model our behaviors on the behaviors of others. And when we see others engage in a behavior that appears to be rewarding, we are likely to try that behavior ourselves. When we see others engage in a behavior that seems to have undesired consequences, we are less likely to try that behavior.

As a child, I once watched my older brother hold an oral thermometer up to a lightbulb in order to make it appear as if he had a fever. The result of his behavior was that he was permitted to stay home from school that day and that his family (except for me) treated him kindly. This seemed like a pretty good deal to me. So the following week, when I really didn't want to go to school, I tried his technique. It worked, and I remained out of school for several days. I had observed and modeled his behavior to gain something I wanted—a few days off.

We can also apply this model of learning to self-inflicted violence. Say you witness someone in great emotional pain. You watch as she intentionally injures herself, and you see her seem to gain great relief and pleasure from this action. You may even see her get extra attention from others or get treated in a different, desirable manner. The next time you are in great emotional pain, it is likely that you will remember this episode and you may try these self-injurious methods for yourself.

As mentioned in chapter 1, in the section on how SIV develops, if you were ever in a confined setting such as a psychiatric ward of a hospital or a prison you may have seen others use SIV. You may have even modeled the SIV behaviors you witnessed and started your own self-injurious activities.

Within environments such as these, modeling can and does occur, significantly spreading the occurrence of SIV.

If you have not been in such a setting, it is not likely that you would have had the opportunity to observe and model SIV behavior. As mentioned previously, SIV usually occurs in isolation and is a very secretive type of activity. Therefore, away from these confined environments, modeling of SIV behaviors does not seem to occur.

If you are like most people, you have probably never witnessed anyone else performing this behavior. However, even though you may not have actually seen someone else performing SIV, you may have had some exposure to self-injury in less direct or obvious ways. Your reaction to those instances would also influence the chance that you would hurt yourself.

Activity 4.5 will help you explore some of the ways you may have been exposed to SIV. Although you may not have observed and modeled these behaviors, their presence may still have affected you in some way.

Activity 4.5: How Have I Observed SIV?

1. Begin by circling each of the ways that you have had some exposure to self-inflicted violence: Add any other ways in the blanks.

_____ Television	_____ Movie
_____ Magazine	_____ Book
_____ Hospital	_____ Psychiatric ward
_____ Prison	_____ Detainment center
_____ Friend	_____ School
_____ Newspaper	_____ Newsletter
_____ Religious group	_____ Athletic group
_____ Family member	_____ Client
_____ Coworker	_____ Internet/computer
_____ _____	_____ _____
_____ _____	_____ _____

2. Now go through each of the items circled, and to the left of the item put a plus sign (+) to indicate that the result of the self-injury seemed rewarding, a minus sign (–) to indicate that the result seemed negative or punishing, or an equal sign (=) to indicate that the result was neither rewarding nor punishing.

3. Look back and count how many items you circled. Then count up the plus, minus, and equal signs. Chances are, your view of SIV

matches whichever type of sign you see most often. That is, if you have mostly plus signs, you probably saw SIV used in ways that were rewarded and are likely to have tried injuring yourself to achieve similar rewards. If you have mostly minus signs or equal signs, your decision to hurt yourself was probably not influenced by modeling because what you were exposed to did not seem rewarding.

Psychodynamic Explanations

The psychodynamic perspective of psychology basically states that behavior stems from hidden forces within our personalities. According to this theory, our actions are strongly influenced by those thoughts and feelings that remain beneath our conscious awareness.

There are numerous explanations for self-inflicted violence from a psychodynamic perspective. While some of these reasons seem to make sense on an individual basis, as a general model that explains how and why SIV occurs, this theory is not particularly helpful. However, because these ideas may be useful to some people, several of these theories are discussed briefly below. Although there are many other psychodynamically oriented explanations of SIV, those presented here seem to be the most relevant and logical. Because the overall applicability of these models seems limited, further exploration of these additional explanations is not merited.

Suicide. One psychodynamic theory proposes that self-inflicted violence is a form of partial suicide, that self-injury is a wish to die and the actual behavior is a thwarted attempt at suicide. While this may be true in a few cases, it is likely that death is neither a primary nor a secondary goal of your SIV activities. In fact, you probably use SIV as a method of coping, a method of staying alive and sane. Although it is possible to cause critical injuries during an episode of SIV, this would seem more of an accidental result rather than an actual goal.

Depression. Self-inflicted violence from a psychodynamic perspective can also be viewed as an action rooted in depression. Many psychodynamic theories posit that depression is anger directed toward oneself. So from this perspective, SIV is simply an expression of this anger. While there are many ways to turn rage inward, self-injurious acts would appear to be an especially direct and potent one. Maintaining the integrity and safety of our bodies is one of our most necessary and primary tasks. By hurting your own body you are punishing yourself and communicating on a very primitive level an intense sense of the anger you have turned against yourself.

The psychodynamic interpretation of depression also encompasses a sense of helplessness or hopelessness. You choose to take these rageful emotions out on yourself because you feel either unable to direct this anger toward others or as if a direct expression of your anger would be futile or useless. Consequently, you choose to injure yourself to express and release the anger that stems from your helplessness.

Reintegration. In addition, at a very basic level self-inflicted violence is useful as a method of reintegrating your sense of physical being. When you injure yourself you are probably experiencing some sort of disturbance in your sense of physical self, possibly stemming directly from the dissociative state that typically precedes the act of self-injury or from an earlier state of psychological distress. You may feel fragmented, zoned out, or as if you aren't all there. The act of self-injury allows you to physically reconnect with yourself and reexperience yourself as a whole, unique, living being. In psychodynamic theory, learning to differentiate yourself from others and experiencing yourself as a distinct entity are primary and essential goals of development. When you use SIV as a method of reconnecting with yourself physically, you are reinstating a sense of your boundaries and distinctness from others.

CHAPTER 5

Self-Inflicted Violence and Other Psychological Factors

Self-inflicted violence does not exist in a vacuum. As with most behaviors, many other factors influence, result from, and are related to SIV. Some of these factors may contribute to the desire to harm yourself, such as remembering traumatic events from your past or needing to feel more connected with your body. Other factors are produced by SIV, such as shame and embarrassment, as mentioned in chapter 3. And some factors, such as use of substances or certain patterns of eating, simply coexist with SIV.

Sometimes it's difficult to understand the different types of relationships other factors have with SIV. Perhaps the following analogy will help. Say you are at your physician's office complaining of a sore throat and headache. Your doctor examines you and gives you feedback about your problems. Your doctor might tell you that your sore throat and headache are two distinct problems, which just happen to occur at the same time, coexisting with each other but not influencing each other. It might also be that your doctor informs you that your sore throat has caused or exacerbated your headache, and that treating your throat will help reduce your headache. Or, your doctor could tell you that your sore throat and headache are related to each other, both being symptoms of some greater problem like the flu.

As you can see, the ways factors relate to each other can get a bit confusing. You may find that certain factors, such as trauma or substance abuse, have any or all of these types of relationships with SIV. That is, SIV can influence (or be influenced by), coexist with, and/or relate to other psychological factors. This chapter will help clarify some of the psychological factors that have some type of relationship with SIV.

Trauma

It is virtually impossible to discuss self-inflicted violence without discussing trauma. As discussed in earlier chapters, an overwhelming number of individuals engaging in self-injurious behaviors have suffered some form of childhood abuse. Significant correlations exist between both sexual and physical forms of childhood violence and SIV. Other violence within the home has also been determined to be related to self-injury, as has emotional abuse. In addition, SIV has also been linked to having been a participant in or witness to acts of ritual abuse. The short- and long-term effects of abuse are far reaching and severe, impacting emotions, memories, relationships, self-esteem, behaviors, and even identity.

In some ways self-inflicted violence can be viewed as a reaction to trauma. If you have endured and survived trauma or abuse, you can attest to the horror of these events. During episodes of abuse you have probably felt violated, helpless, and powerless—as if you had no or little control over your environment or even your body. It is likely that you were confused by the way in which you were being treated. You may have even felt guilty. Given the intensity and severity of the psychological effects of trauma it became necessary for you to find some way to cope. Self-inflicted violence and its related processes may have helped you to deal temporarily with the aftereffects of these traumatic experiences by giving you a way to escape your negative feelings and to feel in control.

Self-inflicted violence, as mentioned previously, can serve many functions. It may be a way of recreating some of the violence you endured or witnessed as a child, allowing you to reenact the trauma through self-injury. Replicating previous traumatic experiences allows you to symbolically alter the original course of the abuse because, when you perform these self-injurious acts, you have control. This control helps change your reaction to these events. By using SIV, you are able to go from a situation in which you felt helpless and powerless to a situation in which you have complete control, autonomy, and power.

Self-inflicted violence is also used to relieve psychological tension. This extreme tension may be the direct result of prior abuse (as in the case of memories or flashbacks) or may be an indirect result of the abuse (such as an extreme reaction to loss or isolation). You may have experienced times when you are unable to rid yourself of painful images or memories of the trauma. At these times you may have used SIV as a way of eliminating these overwhelming memories.

Jerry, a thirty-five-year-old restaurant owner, is a self-described head banger. When Jerry gets upset or overwhelmed, he bangs his head against a wall. He has been doing this for as long as he can remember. Jerry associates his current SIV practices to physical abuse he endured as a child. In Jerry's words,

> When I was a kid, my daddy would get real upset and slam me against the wall. He was usually drunk at the time. My daddy was a big drinker, you know. He would have me pinned against the wall and have his hand in my hair and he would just keep slamming my head into the wall and calling me stupid and stuff. He would do this for the longest time. If I cried he'd do it even longer, so I tried real hard not to cry. Now I do this to myself. When I've screwed up or done something stupid, it's like I hear my daddy's voice and I just start banging my head.

Because abuse and trauma have so many related consequences, it is likely that you have used SIV to cope with some of these results. For example, during the period of the abuse you may have found it dangerous to form good connections with others, and so subsequently you still have difficulty connecting with others. If, for example, those closest to you were the same people who were hurting you, you would have been unable to trust them. Or because of the abuse you might have kept secrets from other family members or friends, which would also interfere with your ability to connect with others. You may have also used self-injury to reduce the emotional pain related to the abuse. A lack of connection with others and difficulty trusting others fosters the same feelings that lead to hurting yourself. Because of patterns set up in your abusive past, you may use SIV to both replicate these patterns as well as control and relieve the accompanying intense emotional pain.

Activity 5.1 will help you examine the effects of abuse or other traumas on your life.

Activity 5.1: How I've Been Affected by Trauma

Part 1. In understanding the connection between SIV and trauma, you need to recall the trauma you experienced. If you are certain you have not experienced any trauma or abuse you may wish to skip this exercise. You may also wish to skip this exercise if you cannot recall the specific events of abuse that took place or if you find this activity too upsetting.

In your journal list each of the events you consider traumatic. This list may be very long and difficult for you to generate. Or perhaps you will have only a few items. If many events were similar (for instance, if you were sexually abused over a period of years), you may choose to list them as a group rather than separately. Try to describe each event or group of events in as much detail as you can.

If writing about these activities feels uncomfortable, you can also draw pictures or another type of artwork that symbolizes what happened to you.

Part 2. The next part of this activity will allow you to explore how trauma has affected your life. You may find that your life has not been severely changed by the trauma. On the other hand, you may discover that it has greatly influenced certain areas of your life.

Place a check mark next to each of the items that describes an area of your life which has been affected by abuse or trauma. Then circle the three areas in which you think you have been most affected. Blank spaces are provided so you can include any areas that are not listed.

_____ Trust	_____ Sexual activities
_____ Anxiety	_____ Fear
_____ Shame	_____ Guilt
_____ Responsibility	_____ Consistency
_____ Boundaries	_____ Fear of abandonment
_____ Independence	_____ Dependence
_____ Creativity	_____ Spontaneity
_____ Substance use	_____ Anger
_____ Work/school	_____ Parenting
_____ Relationships	_____ Sleep
_____ Eating	_____ Isolation
_____ Secrecy	_____ Risk taking
_____ Self-discipline	_____ Communication
_____ _____	_____ _____
_____ _____	_____ _____

By exploring trauma and the ways it has affected your life, you will begin to see some connections between what happened to you and why you hurt yourself. Knowing how trauma relates to your SIV behaviors will be of help to you when you begin to change your patterns of self-injury.

Boundaries

One of the areas that is damaged by abuse, particularly sexual abuse, is that of boundaries. Boundaries are limits we place on ourselves and others that help us to maintain our sense of separateness and independence. As children we learn to separate ourselves from others and experience ourselves as whole, independent beings. We take great pride in determining what is ours and what is not ours. For a brief period in each of our lives we are encouraged to be selfish. For example, as a toddler I can remember mastering the word *mine*. I would walk through my house pointing and identifying most objects as being "mine." Although I'm not exactly sure what a three-year-old would need with a vacuum cleaner, I had claimed possession.

One of the things that children lay claim to is their own body, believing that their body is their own and no one else is allowed to use, touch, or disturb it without permission. We tend to carry these same rules, or boundaries, into adulthood. However, children who are abused often are not allowed to learn about boundaries. Sexual or physical abuse leads to confusion over these very basic rules of ownership. Children who have been abused learn that their body is able to be hurt or manipulated by others. They learn that their bodies are not their own—that their boundaries are variable or nonexistent.

Self-inflicted violence allows people to experience their body as their own. In this way, self-injury helps illuminate or restore some basic boundaries lost due to childhood trauma. Injuring yourself may help you to feel more real, more separate, more whole. You are the one who is hurting yourself. You are making the changes in your body. You, and you alone, are in charge of your body. In this way, SIV helps you maintain your sense of separateness and your sense of self. Activity 5.2 will help you examine your boundaries.

Activity 5.2: Understanding My Boundaries

There are no right or wrong answers for this exercise; simply circle the number for each statement that best indicates how well the sentence describes you and your experiences. An explanation of the scoring is provided at the end of the activity.

1. I try to help people, even when they refuse my help out of politeness.

   1   2   3   4   5   6   7   8   9   10
   Never   Sometimes   Very often

2. I like to surprise my friends by dropping in unexpectedly.

   1   2   3   4   5   6   7   8   9   10
   Never   Sometimes   Very often

3. I have difficulty saying no to others.

   1   2   3   4   5   6   7   8   9   10
   Never   Sometimes   Very often

4. Others, even my friends, take advantage of me.

   1   2   3   4   5   6   7   8   9   10
   Never   Sometimes   Very often

5. I sometimes have to use subterfuge or clever tactics to get my way.

   1   2   3   4   5   6   7   8   9   10
   Never   Sometimes   Very often

6. My friends can talk me into doing just about anything.

1	2	3	4	5	6	7	8	9	10
Never				Sometimes				Very often	

7. Sometimes I borrow things from my friends and then forget to return them.

1	2	3	4	5	6	7	8	9	10
Never				Sometimes				Very often	

8. When I am talking with others, I sometimes get so involved in the conversation that I interrupt to make my point.

1	2	3	4	5	6	7	8	9	10
Never				Sometimes				Very often	

9. I feel as if most things I own are really not mine.

1	2	3	4	5	6	7	8	9	10
Never				Sometimes				Very often	

10. Most people don't really say what they mean, so I go ahead and do what I feel like doing anyway.

1	2	3	4	5	6	7	8	9	10
Never				Sometimes				Very often	

Add up all the numbers you have circled. Scores of 10 to 40 indicate that you have strong boundaries. You respect the boundaries set by others and have set your own as well. Scores of 41 to 69 demonstrate an average use of limits and boundaries in your life. You may occasionally have difficulty establishing or maintaining clear boundaries with others. Scores of 70 to 100 show that you have difficulties standing behind the boundaries you make in your own life and may also impinge on those set by others.

While this is by no means a scientific psychological test, it should provide you with a sense of the strength of your boundaries.

Dissociation

As discussed before, dissociation is an integral part of self-inflicted violence. Dissociation is also related to trauma. Often the mechanism of dissociation is a necessary tool for surviving abusive situations. Dissociating from the physical or emotional pain may have helped you to cope with the trauma. However, as an adult you may find it difficult to regulate your dissociative states. SIV provides an effective means of controlling dissociation, helping you to enter or end a dissociative state.

Lisa is a nineteen-year-old who was sexually abused by her stepfather from the ages of eight to twelve (at which time her stepfather was imprisoned for an unrelated offense). For the past six years, Lisa has been cutting herself on her legs using a razor blade. She describes how her SIV relates to her past traumatic experiences as follows: "I cut myself when I feel numb or empty. Cutting is an easy way to get in touch with myself and feel real again. It makes me feel alive and whole."

Eating Disorders

The relationship between self-inflicted violence and eating disorders is both interesting and complex. Research shows that most women who engage in self-injurious activities also have some type of eating disorder. (The relationship between SIV and eating disorders in men has not yet been formally explored.)

Although numerous types of eating disorders exist, only anorexia nervosa and bulimia nervosa are recognized by the American Psychiatric Association as distinct and diagnosable problems. Anorexia nervosa involves maintaining a body weight significantly lower than what would be considered normal for the person's age and height. Anorexic individuals often have a distorted view of their own body shape and size. While anorexics are severely underweight, people with bulimia nervosa generally weigh within the normal range for their age and height. They engage in episodes of binge eating (eating excessive amounts while experiencing a feeling of lack of control over food intake), and some also purge (eliminate the food eaten by inducing vomiting, using laxatives, exercising excessively, or using another method). Compulsive eating and frequent use of fad diets may also be considered forms of eating disorders.

As it is with self-inflicted violence, trauma is a common antecedent to eating disorders: Slightly more than one-third of individuals who have eating disorders also experienced some type of trauma, typically sexual abuse, as a child. Eating disorders, like SIV, may stem from a need for an adequate coping method or mechanism of gaining control. Many other factors can also influence the development of an eating disorder. However, in terms of its connection with SIV, these represent several of the most frequently noted roots of eating disorders.

A tendency toward dissociation is also common among individuals with eating disorders. If you have an eating disorder, you may find yourself experiencing dissociative states similar to those that occur when you injure yourself. In fact, the overall pattern of eating disorders is very similar to that of SIV. The course of bulimia, in particular, seems to mirror the addiction model presented in chapter 4: Negative feelings produce a state of tension, which leads to a state of dissociation, which is regulated by an act of binge eating (or purging), which then induces feelings of euphoria, which wear off and give way to feelings of guilt, shame, or remorse. And so the cycle goes.

If you have an eating disorder, you may alternate between actively engaging in SIV and the eating behavior. You may even engage both behaviors simultaneously. Each type of activity may be used as a way of coping with great internal pain. Both can provide a way to relieve or release tension, of communicating to others your own internal state, to regulate dissociative states, and to physically express your psychological state. As you can see, eating disorders and SIV have a great deal in common.

Although self-inflicted violence and eating disorders can directly influence one another, it seems that their true relationship is more indirect. In psychological terminology the relationship between these two behaviors would be labeled as spurious. A spurious relationship is one in which two things are connected by a common source, rather than cause and effect. The following diagram illustrates:

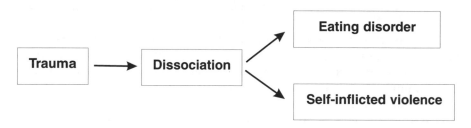

As you can see, trauma leads to an increased tendency to dissociate, an ability that may have been necessary to survive the traumatic event both mentally and physically. The dissociation can (but does not necessarily) lead to either eating disorder behavior or an episode of SIV or both. The trauma is the common source of each of these behaviors and is responsible for the apparent relationship between eating disorders and self-inflicted violence. This is not to say that trauma always leads to an eating disorder, nor to SIV. Likewise, both eating disorders and SIV can develop independently without the presence of trauma. However, using this model to look at the relationship between self-inflicted violence and eating disorders helps to explain their complex association. It seems that both of these behaviors, while often stemming from common sources, also provide similar functions as coping mechanisms.

Activity 5.3 is designed to help you assess your perceptions about food, weight, dieting, and your body.

Activity 5.3: My Eating Patterns

Part 1. Circle the number for each statement that best reflects what is most true of you at this time.

1. I dislike how I look (physically).

    1   2   3   4   5   6   7   8   9   10
   Never   Rarely   Sometimes   Often   Always

2. I am on a diet.

    1   2   3   4   5   6   7   8   9   10
   Never   Rarely   Sometimes   Often   Always

3. I obsess about food.

    1   2   3   4   5   6   7   8   9   10
  Never   Rarely   Sometimes   Often   Always

4. I binge (eat a great deal of food at one sitting).

    1   2   3   4   5   6   7   8   9   10
  Never   Rarely   Sometimes   Often   Always

5. I restrict my food intake so I can lose weight.

    1   2   3   4   5   6   7   8   9   10
  Never   Rarely   Sometimes   Often   Always

6. Others tell me I need to gain or lose weight.

    1   2   3   4   5   6   7   8   9   10
  Never   Rarely   Sometimes   Often   Always

7. I eat when I am upset or bored.

    1   2   3   4   5   6   7   8   9   10
  Never   Rarely   Sometimes   Often   Always

8. I feel out of control in terms of my eating habits.

    1   2   3   4   5   6   7   8   9   10
  Never   Rarely   Sometimes   Often   Always

9. I vomit or purge after eating.

    1   2   3   4   5   6   7   8   9   10
  Never   Rarely   Sometimes   Often   Always

10. I think I have, or have had, an eating disorder.

    1   2   3   4   5   6   7   8   9   10
  Never   Rarely   Sometimes   Often   Always

Now add up all the numbers you have circled. Scores of 10 to 40 suggest that you have few issues with food, weight, or eating patterns. Scores of 41 to 69 are fairly average, indicating that while you may have issues around food, weight, or eating disorders, they are not particularly troublesome or out of the ordinary. Scores of 70 to 100 suggest that you may have some of the views or behaviors that correspond to an eating disorder.

Part 2. Because SIV and eating disorders are related in many ways, it is important to understand the dynamics of these issues in your life. This second part of this activity will help you to explore the connection between these two phenomena.

In your journal, describe in your own words how you view the relationship between eating disorders and self-inflicted violence in your own life. How do you think that they relate to each other? Do you use food to regulate your emotions in the same ways you use SIV? Do your patterns of eating correspond to those times when you are engaging in SIV?

Substance Abuse

The word *substance* in the context of substance abuse or substance use can mean any drug (over-the-counter, prescription, or illegal), including alcohol, nicotine, and caffeine. These substances may be inhaled, ingested, or injected. The term also includes chemicals that are deliberately inhaled for the purpose of getting high, such as certain glues, paints, and solvents. Many other types of substances may also be included within the realm of substance-related disorders.

Substance-related disorders is a general term that includes a wide variety of specific uses of substances and patterns of involvement with these chemicals. *Substance use, substance abuse,* and *substance dependence* each refers to a different degree of impact that the chemicals have on your life. In addition, the many side effects produced by these drugs often lead to other problems ranging from insomnia to brain damage. Because substances are often used to alter our psychological or physical states, they have much in common with self-inflicted violence. Self-injury is typically used to change how you feel: to alter your level of dissociation, decrease tension, and increase euphoria. In this sense, SIV has similar effects as certain substances. However, although substance use often serves a similar function as self-inflicted violence, the two behaviors are not as related as you might expect.

Many people begin using and continue to use substances as a method of regulating their moods. When you feel depressed or sad, you may find yourself wishing you could change your mood. Drugs can effectively do this, although there are numerous possible detrimental side effects. Most of us use one chemical or another at times to regulate our moods and physical states. How many times have you reached for a cigarette or a glass of wine or a Valium when you've been upset or anxious? Most mornings I find myself downing a cup of coffee before I even attempt to greet the day.

As you know, the use of substances such as caffeine, alcohol, and nicotine is much more prevalent and widely accepted by society than that of others, such as heroin, amphetamines, and marijuana. Although you could probably easily imagine bringing a thermos of coffee with you to school or work, and maybe even sharing some with a coworker or classmate, you might have more difficulty picturing yourself snorting a line of cocaine while sitting at your desk (and you definitely would not want to share it with those around you). Most of us use some type of substance to help get us through the day. However, the overwhelming majority of these substances are both legal and culturally sanctioned, making them more difficult to identify, recognize, and understand as a problem.

The true relationship between substance use and self-inflicted violence is difficult to establish, in part simply because much substance use goes unrecognized as such. You probably would not consider yourself a drug addict or as abusing or dependent on substances. It is likely that you don't even realize when you are using chemicals to alter your state of being, such as drinking coffee to become more alert. Also, the use of legal substances like caffeine is rarely considered problematic or unacceptable. This lack of awareness of actual drug use makes it hard to grasp the true nature of substance use as it relates to SIV.

Most people who engage in self-injurious acts do not use or abuse illegal substances. In fact, fewer than one-third of those who injure themselves have ever used street drugs. Furthermore, the majority of SIV activities do not occur under the influence of any substance, legal or otherwise— although again, the role of substances such as nicotine and caffeine is difficult to assess.The reason for this is that both self-inflicted violence and substances are used as short-term methods of coping. Everyone has his or her own preferred way of dealing with the world. Some methods work better on certain occasions, some better on others. The use of these two behaviors in conjunction appears to be unnecessary in that either action produces a temporarily effective way to cope. Once you have found something that works, the immediate problem is solved—you don't need to use another coping method.

Consider this analogy: You have a bad headache, so you take an aspirin. Once your headache is gone, you wouldn't have any reason to take another form of pain reliever. Once you use either a drug or SIV to help you cope with your emotional pain, you will probably not try to use the other behavior at that particular moment. Thus, while SIV and substance use are related, they are not likely to occur simultaneously.

Activity 5.4 will help you explore your use of substances and the relationship (if any) that use has with your SIV.

Activity 5.4: Exploring Substance Use

Part 1. This first part of the exercise will help you explore the role of substances within your own life. You will probably be able to recognize at least some of these chemicals as ones you have had experience with.

For each of the following items listed, indicate whether you have used, are currently using, or have never used each substance. Use a *C* to indicate current use, a *P* to indicate past use, and an *N* to indicate that you never have used the substance.

_____ Marijuana/hashish		_____ Quaaludes
_____ LSD (acid)		_____ Caffeine
_____ Inhalants (solvents, glue)		_____ Cocaine/crack
_____ Nicotine		_____ Amphetamines/ crystal meth

____ Alcohol   ____ Valium

____ Heroin   ____ Rohypnol (roofies)

____ Painkillers (e.g., Vicodin)   ____ Xanax, Halcion

____ Hallucinogenic mushrooms   ____ PCP

____ Opium   ____ Ecstasy

____ _____   ____ _____

____ _____   ____ _____

____ _____   ____ _____

Part 2. The next part of this activity will help you to see the ways in which substances may be related to SIV in your life. You may find that you rarely or never use drugs when you are hurting yourself.

In your journal, answer the following questions.

1. How often have you been under the influence of a substance when you hurt yourself?

2. Did you feel any differently than you do when you hurt yourself when you're sober? If so, in what way?

3. Why do you think you hurt yourself when you were under the influence of a substance? Was the effect of the drug not enough to make you feel better? Was the drug so strong that you didn't realize you were injuring yourself?

Suicide

Angela walks into the emergency room at her local hospital. Her left arm is wrapped in a blood-soaked towel. She is sobbing. The nurse inspects Angela's injuries and finds several deep gashes on her wrists and forearms. She concludes that Angela's wounds are the result of a suicide attempt. After her injuries are treated, Angela is told she must be transferred to the psychiatric ward of the hospital for several days so that she can be observed, evaluated, and treated for suicidal ideation. Angela disagrees with the doctors, telling them that she wasn't trying to kill herself, that she only wanted to feel better and that she now wants to go home. The doctors disregard Angela's side of the story and place her in the psychiatric ward.

Angela's case is relatively common. It is often difficult for others to distinguish injuries resulting from self-inflicted violence and injuries caused by a suicide attempt. Cuts, scratches, gashes, and burns look the same regardless of intent. However, people who engage in self-injurious activities find the distinction between these two behaviors remarkably clear.

Suicide, as is commonly said, is a permanent solution to a temporary problem. The intent of suicide is cessation of life. Chronic feelings of distress and depression can lead to someone deciding to end his or her life. Suicide is often the result of immense psychological discomfort; hopelessness and helplessness are emotions that frequently precede a suicide attempt. On some occasions this great psychological pain is the result of overwhelming and inescapable physical pain, as in the case of the terminally ill. While suicide is used to end psychological pain, people who attempt (or succeed in) suicide are not trying to find a way to adapt to their psychological state. In contrast, self-inflicted violence is used to cope—to adapt to severe psychological discomfort.

Self-inflicted violence is not intended to produce any type of life-threatening injuries. You hurt yourself so you can feel better. This goal of feeling better is in direct contrast with suicide's goal of not feeling at all. The means, intent, and often the result of self-injurious acts are vastly different than those of suicide. Self-injury is not a mild form of suicide, nor is it a suicide attempt gone awry. Instead, SIV is a means of coping during a time of intense or overwhelming distress.

Activity 5.5 will help clarify the difference between any suicidal feelings you may have had and your SIV behaviors.

Activity 5.5: Exploring Suicidal Feelings

This exercise will help you to assess the suicidal feelings you may have had in the past as well as in the present. If you currently feel suicidal, I highly recommended that you discuss these feelings with someone—a friend, family member, therapist, doctor, or crisis worker. There are people out there who care and can help you. Remember, there are always other options.

Part 1. Answer the following questions related to suicide.

1. Have you ever thought about killing yourself?   Yes   No

2. Did you have a specific plan to kill yourself?   Yes   No

3. At this moment, do you feel like killing yourself?   Yes   No

4. Have you ever tried to kill yourself before?   Yes   No

5. If so, did you change your mind during or before the attempt?   Yes   No

6. Have you ever been hospitalized or under a doctor's care for wanting to or trying to kill yourself?   Yes   No

7. Was the method you used or planned on using considered highly lethal (e.g., shooting yourself versus swallowing five aspirin)?   Yes   No

8. Have you known someone who committed suicide?   Yes   No

9. Do you have a terminal illness?   Yes   No

10. Do you currently have the means to kill yourself?   Yes   No

Now take a minute or two and look over your answers. If you answered yes to many of these questions, you have probably had moments in your life when you were very serious about killing yourself. If you have never felt seriously suicidal in the past, you may skip the rest of this activity.

Part 2. The second part of this activity will help you understand the difference between wanting to kill yourself and wanting to hurt yourself to feel better.

1. Think back to the times when you felt suicidal. In your journal, describe what was going on in your life at that time. Had you just lost a job? A relationship? Were you imprisoned? Were you dealing with issues of abuse or trauma? Did you just have a few really bad days in a row? What was you life like during that time in your life?

2. Now describe why you didn't kill yourself. What kept you from attempting suicide or succeeding in killing yourself?

3. Finally, think about and describe the ways that SIV is both different from and similar to suicide. It may help if you focus on the purpose of each act or on what causes you to want to hurt yourself as opposed to what made you feel suicidal.

Understanding the difference between suicide and SIV will help you to further clarify the role of SIV in your own life. This will assist you when you look for alternatives to self-injury in the next chapter.

Borderline Personality Disorder

Out of the entire spectrum of psychological diagnoses, self-inflicted violence is most often associated with borderline personality disorder (BPD). With the exception of trichotillomania (the pulling out of one's own hair) and sexual masochism (which sometimes involves self-injurious activities), borderline personality disorder is the only psychological diagnosis that specifically identifies self-injurious activities as a criteria for diagnosis. For this reason clinicians are apt to diagnose individuals who purposefully injure themselves as having borderline personality disorder based primarily on that one behavior. Because of the lack of diagnostic options where self-injury is concerned, you may have been incorrectly diagnosed with BPD.

Borderline personality disorder has many distinguishing features other than self-injurious activities. Personality disorders—whether borderline or another type—are characterized by long-term patterns of behavior that lead the person to feel distressed or impaired in some manner. Usually these patterns of behavior will affect functioning in several areas of life, including employment or school, social relationships, and/or personal well-being. In general terms, BPD is characterized by chronic, intense instability and chaos. This instability can present itself in the realms of identity, relationships, moods, and impulsivity.

People with borderline personality disorder seem to fluctuate between extremes. While most of us view life as a spectrum of color and choices and experiences, individuals with borderline personality disorder see the world as a more black-and-white, all-or-nothing experience. If people were light switches, most of us would have dimmers. We could illuminate and perceive our surroundings in varying degrees. Individuals with borderline personality disorder seem to have an "on-off" switch. Life is either great or terrible, effortless or hopeless.

In addition, people with this disorder frequently do things that undermine their own success. Goals are often thrown aside just before being met. Promotions, graduations, and relationships may be thwarted before successful completion. Self-defeating behaviors such as substance use, overspending, and engaging in physical altercations are common.

There is no question the worlds of people with BPD are chaotic. Several years ago the Sega company produced a video game (and later a television show) called Sonic the Hedgehog. In the game, Sonic was safe from his enemies as long as he curled up in a tight ball and kept spinning. Once he stopped spinning and stood up, he was vulnerable to the attacks of various other creatures. People with borderline personality disorder are like Sonic: As long as they keep spinning—creating and repairing chaotic situations within their lives (and in consequence in the lives of those close to them)—they feel safe. When their lives get too calm or too stable, vulnerability, tension, and anxiety emerge, and instead of experiencing those intense and unpleasant feelings, they seek new chaos. Stability sends these folks spinning.

For people with borderline personality disorder self-inflicted violence serves several functions. First, self-injury is a direct response to overwhelming psychological pain. The emotions experienced during those moments of stillness are often incredibly intense, and SIV is a method of relieving and releasing some of those feelings.

Last summer I spent a great deal of my free time snorkeling in the waters of Southern California. On most days the water was reasonably clear and had decent visibility. I could see a wide variety of marine life, including fish, lobsters, and rays. I enjoyed this activity and felt comfortable in the water with these strange but harmless creatures. However, one calm, clear day I entered the water to find that the visibility was much better than usual. I could easily see depths of thirty to forty feet, as opposed to the typical fifteen to twenty feet. As I ventured out into deeper water, I was able to see things that previously had been hidden. Sharks, skates, and large fish glided along the ocean bottom. Although logically I knew that these creatures were generally harmless (yes, sharks typically present little danger), I was scared. As I swam (very quickly) back toward the shore, I found myself longing for the days when the ocean wasn't so calm and the visibility wasn't so good. As much as I enjoy snorkeling, there are some things in the ocean I would rather just not encounter.

In a similar way, people with borderline personality disorder feel frightened by the thoughts, memories, and emotions that emerge during their moments of calm. Inflicting self-injury is a way to release those feelings. It also serves to prevent those feelings from emerging further. The dissociation that accompanies self-injury pulls the plug on these overwhelming emotional states.

In addition, the injuries produced through SIV provide another type of chaos to focus on. The wounds allow a transfer of attention from the original, distressing emotions and experiences to the new emotions and experiences resulting from the self-injury. For instance, you might have been feeling empty or alone before hurting yourself, whereas afterward you feel ashamed or guilty. The shift may be not in the intensity of the emotions but in the direction. For whatever reason, you may feel safer experiencing emotions linked to the self-injury than those emotions linked to past events. In short, self-inflicted violence plays an interesting role within individuals with borderline personality disorder. Self-injury, for a variety of reasons, acts as an agent for producing internal states which are better able to be tolerated.

Activity 5.6 asks a series of questions related to symptoms of borderline personality disorder. These questions are intended to help you gain a fuller picture of yourself and your life, which will be useful when you progress to the next chapter.

Activity 5.6: Borderline Personality Symptoms

The following questions deal with some of the behaviors, thoughts, and feelings associated with borderline personality disorder. Note that these questions will not tell you if you have this disorder. They may simply help you understand yourself and the ways in which you relate to others and the world around you.

1. I will go to great means to avoid being abandoned
   by others.   Yes   No

2. I tend to have intense relationships with others.   Yes   No

3. My relationships with others are fairly unstable.   Yes   No

4. I find that I either really like or really dislike most
   individuals.   Yes   No

5. I don't really know who I am.   Yes   No

6. My life is always in chaos.   Yes   No

7. I am impulsive.   Yes   No

8. I find that I do things that I really hadn't planned on doing.	Yes	No
9. I have threatened to kill myself before.	Yes	No
10. I have purposefully hurt myself before.	Yes	No
11. I sometimes drive recklessly.	Yes	No
12. I have abused drugs or other substances before.	Yes	No
13. My moods are constantly changing.	Yes	No
14. I feel bored or empty frequently.	Yes	No
15. My friends would describe me as moody.	Yes	No
16. I have difficulty controlling my anger.	Yes	No
17. I dissociate frequently.	Yes	No
18. I have problems with self-control.	Yes	No
19. My boundaries with others are not very clear.	Yes	No
20. I tend to see things as black or white.	Yes	No

Answering yes to many or all of these questions does not necessarily mean that you have BPD; most of these statements are also related to other issues. The point here is simply to recognize feelings and behaviors that may be problematic for you.

Dissociative Identity Disorder

Dissociative identity disorder, previously known as multiple personality disorder, occurs when an individual has two or more discrete identities. Each of these identities, or alters, has its own way of being in the world and may have its own memories, own history, own style of thought, and own temperament. Some of the personalities may be unaware of the presence of some or all of the others, while some alters know and communicate with other distinct personalities. Roughly half of those people with dissociative identity disorder have between two and ten distinct personality states.

In many ways an individual with dissociative identity disorder is much like an extended family. Each of the "family members" has a distinct personality with particular strengths and weaknesses. One family member may be very artistic, one may excel at business, one may be depressed, one anxious, one angry. There may be children, adults, and adolescents. Some family members may be male, some female, some heterosexual, and some homosexual. Within the family, some of the members may communicate well with each other, some may communicate ineffectively, and some may not communicate with each other at all. With dissociative identity disorder, however, all these family dynamics occur within the same individual.

Dissociative identity disorder is generally related to intense trauma experienced as a child. Severe sexual or physical abuse as a child is a common antecedent of this disorder. Ritual abuse, which is often both intense and chronic, also has been related to dissociative identity disorder.

The psychological mechanism that allows someone to establish and maintain separate identities is dissociation. Since both abuse and dissociation very often appear in conjunction with self-inflicted violence, it makes sense that dissociative identity disorder would also coexist with SIV.

Self-inflicted violence serves many functions for people with dissociative identity disorder. In addition to the usual wide variety of purposes SIV serves (communication, release of emotions, and so on), it has some particular applications among individuals with dissociative identity disorder. First, the ability SIV has to control dissociation is of particular importance because of the high level of dissociation that occurs in those with dissociative identity disorder. The need for this control is paramount.

Sometimes SIV is used to prevent an alter from emerging. The physical sensations experienced during an act of self-injury may be enough of a reminder of reality to inhibit certain personalities.

SIV can also be used to induce the emergence of a specific identity. One alter may be in so much emotional or physical pain that it becomes necessary for a different identity to take over. This change in identity may be either purposeful or accidental.

In addition, just as violence sometimes exists in families, violence can occur between the identities contained in an individual. Self-inflicted violence is sometimes a violent act perpetrated by one alter on another. Many people with dissociative identity disorder have at least one alter who is angry, violent, and abusive. These alters may take their rage out on the other identities—and in reality, of course, their own physical selves.

Self-inflicted violence may also occur as a result of internal dialogue between different personalities. Occasionally, one identity will produce an internal voice that directs another alter to injure him- or herself. Depending on the strength of this identity, the result may be an episode of self-injury.

One woman with dissociative identity disorder describes her SIV activities as follows (in her description she uses *we, our,* and *us* to refer to the group of identities that make up who she is, just as you might describe your family):

> The last time it [SIV] happened was after talking to our therapist. We had been telling about what was done to us when we were little. That didn't go over so well. When we got home he [one of her alters] cut us up pretty bad. We weren't supposed to tell. The little ones [her personalities who are young children] got so scared that they went and hid. The rest of us couldn't hide, we had to stay there and take it. It was pretty bad that time.

Because of the nature and extent of the dissociation that occurs in dissociative identity disorder, it is not uncommon for an alter to find wounds and be unable to recall the source of these injuries. The inability to remember an act of self-injury may be as upsetting to the person as the actual injury. Being unable to recall important events or information is a common characteristic of this disorder. This inability to recall often produces feelings of frustration, anger, helplessness, and despair. As you know by now, these emotions are common antecedents for an episode of self-injury. Thus the severity of the dissociation involved with dissociative identity disorder, as well as both the causes and the results of this dissociation, will affect the likelihood of SIV activities and sometimes the extent of the injuries also.

Dissociative identity disorder is an extreme and complex type of psychological problem. If you know or suspect that you have multiple personalities, and you want help with that or with SIV, it is probably best for you to obtain professional assistance so that you can treat the causes underlying these issues.

Assessing for Other Factors

Now that you have read about the principal psychological factors that often result in, are caused by, and coexist with SIV, take some time to record information about factor that may be affecting your life. Activity 5.7 will help you do this.

Activity 5.7: Other Factors and My SIV

Because SIV coexists with so many other psychological factors—trauma, substance use, eating disorders, and so forth—it is important for you to identify and understand these factors and the roles they play in your SIV. Exploring how these factors affect SIV will assist you when you are trying to stop hurting yourself. This activity will help you identify other problems, behaviors, or psychological diagnoses you have in addition to SIV.

1. Spend a few minutes now to think about your life and some of the other problems you may be experiencing. If you have been to psychotherapy, you may be able to give these problems specific names or diagnoses, such as anorexia nervosa. If you do not know a specific term that is used to identify a problem, just describe it in your own words. In your journal, make a list of all the problems you have identified: psychological diagnoses, behaviors, moods, physical problems, or thoughts. For example, you may list items like depression, drug use, shame, physical abuse suffered as a child, overeating, and tension.

2. When you have finished making your list, look over the items and decide whether they caused or influenced SIV, are the result of SIV, or are unrelated to SIV. Place a C next to those items you think caused or contributed to your SIV; an R beside those items you think resulted from your SIV; and an X next to those items that simply coexist with your SIV behaviors. You may place more than one letter next to some items, showing that, for example, some-thing can be both the cause and result of SIV. Some factors or behaviors may have different causes at different times—some re-lated to SIV and some not. That's perfectly OK; record whatever leters make sense to you.

When you are finished your list should look similar to the following example:

1. Depression —C, R

2. Anxiety —C

3. Bulimia (diagnosis from therapist) —X

4. Alcohol use —X, R

5. Sexually abused by uncle —C

This list will be helpful to you as you learn about ways to prevent yourself from self-injury in the next chapter.

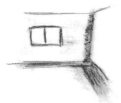

PART II

Ending Self-Inflicted Violence

CHAPTER 6

Talking to Others About
Self-Inflicted Violence

The first section of this chapter examines the ways your SIV behaviors can affect your relationships with others and how others may respond to your SIV. It also discusses some ways of overcoming those reactions.

The second section explores the process of finding and interviewing a therapist and what to expect if and when you begin therapy. Chapters 9 and 10 address specific ways that friends, family members, and therapists can offer assistance for SIV. Once you have opened lines of communication with others, it may be useful for them to read one of these chapters.

How SIV Affects Communication
With Friends and Family

Nearly everything we do has an effect on others, whether we intend it to or not. Even our "nonbehaviors" can affect others. For instance, responding to what someone says with silence makes a very strong statement, as does not showing up when you're expected. Our facial expressions, body language, silence, tone of voice, and actions all affect the reactions and behaviors of others. Similarly, the behaviors of others have an impact on us. When you tell others you care about that you are purposefully injuring yourself, they are likely to have many strong reactions. The following section discusses a few of the most prominent ones along with how to overcome their negative effects.

SIV Keeps Others at a Distance

Although SIV may serve many functions within your life, such as help-ing you to cope and survive, it can have some detrimental effects on your relationships with others, one of which is to keep others at a distance, both emotionally and physically.

Self-injury promotes emotional distance from others in several ways. First, the secrecy and shame attached to many SIV behaviors causes a lack of honesty and open communication between you and the important others in your life. You may not tell others about your self-injury. You may omit information about your behaviors and your emotional states. You may even go so far as to lie about your actions and feelings. Each of these impairs or severs communication and intimacy with others, thus creating distance. You cannot be close to others if you are not honest with them.

The dissociation that accompanies self-inflicted violence also creates emotional distance. Remember that dissociation can be both a precursor to SIV and a result of self-inflicted violence (see chapter 2 for a more complete discussion of dissociation). It is impossible to feel connected with another when you are in a dissociated, spaced-out state, since during dissociation you feel disconnected from yourself. You cannot feel emotionally close to someone else when you are distant from yourself. SIV, to the extent that it contributes to dissociation, will cause you to feel isolated and removed from those around you.

In addition, you may keep others physically distant because of your wounds or scars. You may sleep in a separate bed or room from your partner so that your injuries are not discovered, and you may refrain from sexual or intimate contact with others for the same reason. Even when oth-ers know of your injuries, you may not wish to have them exposed or touched in any way. You may feel very self-conscious or ashamed when others notice your scars.

Tanya is a twenty-nine-year-old lawyer who has been slashing her arms for about fifteen years. She mostly cuts herself when she is feeling angry or overstressed. She has numerous scars on her arms which she hides by wearing long-sleeved shirts. She has this to say about how her SIV affects others:

> I think the biggest way my slashing affects others is by keeping them away. I've only told three people about this problem. I al-ways keep everyone at a distance: I don't want them to find out that I hurt myself. I'm afraid of what they would say or think. I wouldn't want this to get out into the professional community. I'm afraid if it did, my career would be over. When people find out that you slash your own arms, they think you're a mental

case. So instead of taking that chance, I just stay away. I get lonely sometimes, but it's better than what could happen.

Activity 6.1 will help you to understand the ways in which self-inflicted violence causes you to remain separate physically and emotionally from others. Once you are able to see the effects of SIV on your relationships, you might be more motivated to change your SIV behaviors.

Activity 6.1: Keeping Others at a Distance

Before you complete this exercise, you might want to review your journal, particularly activity 3.1, "Wounds, Scars, and Shame." In rereading your responses you will probably see how it is primarily your shame about SIV that creates distance from others.

In your journal list each of the ways SIV contributes to your distance from others, for example:

Lying about SIV reduces open and honest communication.

I won't let others touch me because of my scars.

Closing the Gap

Having explored the ways that SIV helps keep you separate from others and hampers communication, you may now be better able to reduce this distance between yourself and others. Ending your SIV behaviors is one way to decrease this distance. By not engaging in SIV, you do not create the results (shame, wounds, etc.) that cause you to pull back from others. However, although this solution is easy to propose, as you know, it is far less easy to implement—and you may simply not be ready to end your SIV behaviors. Therefore, instead of stopping your self-injurious activities, you might choose to decrease distance and/or create intimacy between yourself and others by not allowing yourself to engage in those behaviors that serve to create distance.

For example, if you refuse to let others physically touch your scars because you are self-conscious or ashamed of them, by doing so you are distancing yourself. To promote more intimacy with others, don't allow yourself to act in this way. Let other people touch your scars. Stop omitting information about the cause of your injuries. Begin to talk to others openly and honestly about SIV.

Although this will be difficult and will require a great deal of risk-taking and courage on your part, you will feel more connected with others, which in turn will decrease your desire to hurt yourself. Stopping SIV, as well as creating intimacy and decreasing distance with others, is likely to be a difficult and long process. However, with some perseverance and courage you will be successful. Chapter 7 will go into the process of stopping in greater detail.

Coping with Others' Reactions to SIV

It is important for you to realize the extent to which your actions affect others around you. SIV creates many specific emotions and reactions in others. Although your intention may not be to provoke a reaction (you may not even want others to know of your self-injuries), it is likely that they will react.

Jessie's case may help to illustrate this point. Jessie is fourteen years old and in her freshman year of high school. She lives in an affluent suburb of a large city with her mother, ten-year-old brother, two dogs, and several goldfish. Jessie began to injure herself last year following the divorce of her parents. She typically sticks pins and nails into the flesh on her arms and legs.

Jessie recalls when she first told her mother about her SIV behaviors:

When I first told my mom about hurting myself, I was hoping that she would help me. Instead, she totally flipped out. I didn't even think about how she would react. I only thought of how tough it was for me to tell her.

Most of the reactions others have to your SIV will be negative. If you have noticeable scars or wounds you probably already know this. You may find people staring at your scars or wounds, or you may overhear derogatory comments about your psychological state or mental capabilities. You may also find that you are treated differently after exposing your self-injurious behaviors. Jessie lost several friends because they "just couldn't handle" her self-inflicted injuries. There is little doubt that many people see SIV as disgusting, sick, and crazy.

Like Jessie, you may suffer some type of negative reaction because of your self-injuries, if you have not already. And you may be unprepared for that reaction. You may be so focused on the great courage and effort it takes to tell others about your self-injuries that the possible ramifications for others don't occur to you. Eventually though, you will notice some of the negative effects of exposing your SIV. You may lose friends because they are unable or unwilling to deal with your self-injurious behaviors. You may notice more subtle changes in your relationships with others, such as friends or family members visually inspecting you for signs of fresh wounds. You may find that friends and family focus conversations and attention on your self-injuries rather than on the many other aspects of your life. Each of these reactions will change your relationship in some manner.

One of the more difficult and damaging forms of reaction to self-inflicted violence is nonreaction. Sometimes those around you simply will not respond to your behaviors, leaving you feeling invisible. As stated before, SIV is often tied to feelings of isolation and alienation. When you are ignored, the feeling of invisibility can lead right back to the feelings of isolation and alienation that are part of the cycle of SIV.

Consider the following situation: You are in a grocery store, standing in the checkout line. The woman in front of you has a four-year-old boy with her. She is chatting with the checker. Meanwhile, the boy is staring up at her saying, "Mom, mom, mom." He gets no reaction. Then he starts to pull on her leg, and says in a louder tone, "Mom, mom, mom!" Still nothing. Finally, the kid starts to scream "Mom! Mom! Mom!" at the top of his lungs. He is lunging at his mother's leg, trying desperately to get her attention. She places a hand on the boy's head and continues to speak with the checkout clerk. The boy stops screaming and begins to cry. His need for attention was met with an insufficient reaction—a nonreaction—causing him to feel alone and uncared for, which is why he is crying.

When self-inflicted violence is met with a negative response or a non-reaction, you will experience negative emotions of your own. Humans are social animals, and the interactions that take place between us can have profound effects on our relationships and our internal psychological experiences. When your SIV behaviors are met with a nonreaction, you might react very much like the little boy in the grocery store. You might begin to hurt yourself more visibly or more often. You might begin to make your injuries more and more severe until they can no longer be ignored. And eventually you might give up trying to provoke a reaction and end up feeling more rejected, more invisible, and more isolated than you had initially.

Although self-inflicted violence does create reactions in those around you, this is not a sufficient reason to try to stop or even decrease your self-injuries. You may indeed decide to change your SIV behaviors, it is essential that you do this for yourself, and not in an attempt to please or mollify others. You are not responsible for controlling or changing the emotions of others, nor is this possible. (Chapter 7 will discuss this more thoroughly.)

Although it would be nice for you to be unaffected by the reactions of others, this isn't likely to happen. Regardless of the actual response of others to your SIV activities, it will almost certainly have an impact on you. One method you can use to cope with the reactions of others is to try to understand why the other person is reacting in that way. For example, if after you tell your best friend about your SIV, she begins to call you every twenty minutes to make sure that you're OK, you might want to talk with her about her reaction. Understanding her motivation to act in this way may not change her behavior, but it may help you to feel better. Since you cannot control the reactions of others, you can only try to understand.

The main point of this section is simply to illustrate the ways that your self-injurious behaviors can affect others. Knowing that this will occur will allow you to understand some of the ramifications of your self-injurious behaviors as well as prepare you for the possible reactions of others. Activity 6.2 will help you to explore the reactions that your self-injurious activities have on others.

Activity 6.2: Reactions to My SIV

In your journal, list each of the people who knows about your SIV. Describe each person's reactions to your SIV behaviors. Also indicate how these reactions affected your emotions, thoughts, physical state, or relation-ship with that individual. Feel free to list the reactions of strangers as well, even if you don't know their names. Here's an example:

Name	Reaction	How It Affected Me
Mom	*Shock, later she cried*	*It made me feel guilty and like not telling her about hurting myself. (I don't like to see her cry.) I feel more alone.*

Learning to Communicate Directly

Communication is a key to any relationship—platonic, intimate, cas-ual, or romantic. Communication is most effective when it is direct and clear. As an example, say two friends, Dick and Jane, are talking on the telephone, trying to make plans for that evening. They have been consider-ing going out to dinner and to a movie. Here is their conversation with an interpretation of the meaning behind their words added.

Dick: So have you thought about what you want to do?
Meaning, I want you to make the decision.

Jane: No, not really.
Meaning, I have thought about it, but I want to hear what you think first.

Dick: Yeah, me neither.
Meaning, I'm really not sure I want to do anything with you tonight.

Jane: You know, you've been really busy this week. If you want some time alone, I'd understand.
Meaning, I really don't feel like doing anything with you tonight.

Dick: I don't really need time alone. But I don't want to go out just to go out. If we can't come up with some good ideas, I guess we'll both end up staying home.
Meaning, Don't make it seem like it's my fault we're not going out! Now I really don't want to go out with you tonight.

Jane: Yeah, I don't want to go out just to go out either. I can't think of anything fun to do, though.
Meaning, Let's just forget about going out tonight.

Dick: Me neither.
Meaning, Let's just forget about going out tonight.

Jane: My dog is whining up a storm. I'd better go feed him. Why don't you call me if you think of anything you want to do?
Meaning, I just want to get off the phone and relax.

Dick: OK, that sounds good. Call me if you think of anything.
Meaning, Cool! I get to stay home tonight!

Jane: Sure. I'll talk to you later.
Meaning, Cool! I get to stay home tonight!

Imagine how different this entire conversation would have been if Dick or Jane or both of them had simply been clear, direct, and honest about his or her desires. Each would have better understood what the other wanted. Without direct communication, implications and confusion abound.

Self-inflicted violence is a very indirect method of communication. The messages others receive when they learn of a self-injurious act are likely to be distorted and inaccurate. You may think that your SIV communicates one message, whereas in fact it communicates many messages, most of which are not what you intended.

Miscommunication has many results. First, because you are unlikely to get your point across, your needs will be left unmet. If, for example, you are using SIV as a way to communicate your inner pain, your wounds may be misinterpreted by others as an indication of a state of mental instability. Or you could be trying to ask for help and support, only to find yourself cast off by your friends because they view you as dangerously self-destructive.

Self-inflicted violence is also often misinterpreted as an act of manipulation. Because it is an indirect form of communication, others may view your self-injury as an attempt to provoke a response or reaction from them. In some cases this may be true, but most often, manipulation of others is not the goal of SIV. However, because you are not being direct about your intentions, your needs, and your internal processes, you leave yourself open to a wide variety of misinterpretations, many of which will not be favorable.

Instead of using self-inflicted violence as a form of communication, you would be better served to speak about SIV directly, communicating through words rather than through actions. The messages you are striving to transmit will be communicated much more clearly with words than by self-injury. This is not to say that you need to stop injuring yourself; you can only do that when you are ready and have alternate means of coping. However, communicating directly about the ways you use, view, and think of SIV will help clarify some of the possible areas of miscommunication. Activity 6.3 will help you begin learning and practicing more direct forms of communication.

Activity 6.3: Talking to Others About SIV

The goal of this exercise is to find out how your self-injurious actions have been interpreted by others.

1. In Activity 2.5, "What Does My SIV Communicate to Others?", you listed some of the messages your SIV actions relay to others. Take a few minutes now to review that activity.

2. Now for the hard part. Select at least one person you trust to talk with about your SIV activities. This person might be a friend, family member, or therapist. You may even have spoken with him or

her before about hurting yourself. Now ask this person to spend some time talking with you about SIV. What did your friend think your SIV behaviors were communicating? Does he or she think that SIV has changed your relationship? If so, in what ways? Has this person always known about your SIV?

3. In your journal, describe this conversation in as much detail as you can. The principal goal of this activity is to determine whether your SIV activities have been misinterpreted by those around you, so be sure to address this issue in your writing.

4. If you do find out that your self-injurious activities communicated something other than what you had intended, be sure to talk about this with your friend.

Although this activity will be very difficult to do, it is also very important in that it will help you to open the channels of communication and feel more connected with others.

Deciding to Begin Therapy

This section is designed to help you explore and evaluate the option to enter psychotherapy.

Why Do You Want to Be in Therapy?

The decision to enter psychotherapy is rarely easy. You may find that you need to put a great deal of thought into it. Before entering into a therapeutic relationship, it is important that you understand why you will be going to therapy. Most people who enter therapy do so because they want help with a particular problem. A few enter therapy out of curiosity or a desire for self-growth. Even fewer people enter therapy against their own will, such as in court-ordered cases. The more motivated you are to be in therapy, the better the results are likely to be.

If you are considering therapy for help in dealing with issues of self-inflicted violence, there are several questions it would be helpful to ask yourself before making your decision. First, what particular issues or problems would you want to address in psychotherapy? Are you trying to control your self-injurious behaviors? Are you seeking therapy to deal with factors related to SIV, such as past trauma or eating disorders? Are you considering therapy to learn how to deal with stress or to better manage your environment? Being clear about what you want to address is an important factor in your decision to enter therapy.

A second important question to ask yourself is what you hope to achieve through psychotherapy that you cannot achieve on your own. Your answers to this may be numerous and varied. Perhaps you hope to get an objective opinion about your problems. Maybe you just want someone to talk to who can give you support during difficult times. You might hope to gain some knowledge or insight about your behaviors or even some suggestions as to how to control them. Through this question you may determine that you are able to achieve your goals without the help of a psychotherapist. Your answer to this question will undoubtedly affect your decision to enter therapy.

Why now? This third question will also help you determine if you wish to enter therapy at this time. What is going on in your life right now that is causing you to consider therapy? How have things changed in the past week, month, or year that you feel you might benefit from seeing a psychotherapist? Perhaps you are feeling more out of control than usual, or maybe you are currently hurting yourself more than you care to. Or you might simply now have time or money to devote to therapy that you didn't have before. Or you may have utilized all your current coping mechanisms and support systems and need some outside assistance.

Whatever your answers to these questions, they should help you clarify whether you really want to enter psychotherapy at this time. If you do decide that you wish to begin psychotherapy, please understand that it is not a magic cure for your problems. You will not go to therapy and "get fixed." Psychotherapy often requires a great deal of effort, time, and expense. You are likely to feel worse before you feel better, and you may also experience times when you feel as if therapy is no help at all. At times therapy can be wonderful, fun, enriching, and motivating. However, like most things, psychotherapy has its ups and downs, its good and bad qualities, as well as many in between. Psychotherapy requires both motivation and a commitment to be helpful. Thus, your decision to enter psychotherapy should be given considerable thought. Activity 6.4 will help you through the decision process.

Activity 6.4: Why I Want to Be in Therapy

Spend some time answering the following questions about the option to enter psychotherapy in your journal. Your answers to these questions should help you clarify whether you want to be in therapy, if you need to be in therapy, and if therapy is likely to provide the help you desire.

1. What issues or problems do you want to work on in psychotherapy?

2. Are you able to address these issues on your own? What has happened before when you tried to work on these issues by yourself or with the help of friends or family?

3. How do you anticipate that your self-injurious behaviors will be dealt with in therapy?

4. How would you respond if your therapist determined that you should decrease or eliminate your SIV behaviors?

5. Why are you seeking therapy at this time? Did something occur recently that increased your desire for professional help?

6. What do you hope to achieve in psychotherapy? What do you expect to be like when you are "done"? Are these goals realistic?

7. How motivated are you to be in therapy? How long will you commit to being in therapy?

Finding a Good Therapist

Once you have decided to enter psychotherapy, you will need to find a therapist. Although it is generally easy to locate a therapist, it is more difficult to find a therapist who is well qualified and suited to your particular needs. You may be able to locate a therapist through a referral from a friend, physician, family member, or someone else who knows you well. You will generally have better luck finding an adequate therapist through a referral than you would using the yellow pages or other advertisement. Regardless of how you find a therapist's name and telephone number, you should ask some questions before entering therapy with that person.

Because psychotherapy involves such an intense and personal relationship between therapist and client, it is important to find a therapist with whom you feel comfortable. Your comfort level may be determined by many factors, including the therapist's academic degree, knowledge, psychotherapeutic approach, age, sex, experience, and personality. It is perfectly fine to ask a potential therapist questions to determine his or her "fit" for you before entering a therapeutic relationship. Typically therapists will not answer highly personal questions. They should, however, be willing to answer questions directly related to your treatment or your role as client.

While you are not likely to find a therapist who fits all your criteria, it is extremely important that you feel comfortable and confident with your therapist—at least once you get over the initial fear and doubt that accompanies entering psychotherapy. The following questions will help you in your search for a therapist.

What type of degree and/or license do you have? Most therapists have some graduate training in psychology, social work, human behavior, or medicine. The therapist's exact title will depend on the actual degree or license obtained—PhD, PsyD, MFCC, LCSW, MD, and so on. Psychiatrists, who are actually medical doctors, are the only type of therapist allowed to prescribe medication. Psychologists, psychiatrists, social workers, and marriage, family, and child counselors each have slightly different approaches to therapy based on their training. You may wish to inquire about these particular approaches or the specific types of training required for their degree.

In my opinion, it really doesn't matter what specific degree the therapist possesses. Most psychotherapists are able to perform a variety of functions. However, it is essential that the therapist be licensed through a state accrediting agency. Licenses to practice therapy are generally designed to protect you, the client, and to ensure some type of quality control. The therapist's possession of a valid license ensures that you as a client have some recourse if you are dissatisfied with the nature of the therapy. While there may be some wonderful practitioners who operate without a license (not all states or countries require a license to practice), I would generally recommend against seeking treatment from an unlicensed therapist.

How much experience do you have in treating self-inflicted violence? If you are entering therapy to work on issues of self-injury, it only makes sense that you ask about the therapist's experience in this area. As mentioned earlier, most therapist's will have little, if any, formal training in dealing with SIV behaviors. Yet some therapists may have more practical experience than others in this area. You should feel comfortable with the therapist's level of experience or knowledge, or at least with his or her willingness to obtain education in this area. (This book is one possible source of knowledge about SIV that professionals can use; chapter 10 is written especially for therapists. The last section of chapter 8, "Resources," lists some additional publications and sources of information.)

What is the normal course of treatment for self-inflicted violence? With this question you are really asking how the therapist generally responds to issues of self-harm. Is this therapist likely to suggest medication or hospitalization? Will he or she be able to discuss issues of SIV with some level of comfort? You need to determine what might happen if you were to enter therapy with this particular therapist. By asking this question up front, you will be less likely to be surprised by the way SIV is handled in the therapy.

How much do you know about areas related to SIV (such as eating disorders, dissociation and dissociative disorders, trauma, or abuse)? Because SIV is such a complex behavior with relationships to various factors, I recommend that you assess the therapist's knowledge and experience in these areas as well. You may want to specify those areas that are relevant to you in particular.

How long do you expect that I'll have to be in therapy? Most therapists will not be able to give you an exact length of time you are expected to be in therapy (although your insurance company might). Generally the course of therapy is better determined after you have spent some time in therapy, at which point the therapist can make a better-educated guess of the treatment, rather than simply picking a number without really knowing you or the dynamics of your case.

What is your general availability? You will want to assess the therapist's availability—not just for scheduled sessions but also for events like emergencies, after-hours calls, and additional sessions. Does the therapist carry a beeper? Is he or she available for an emergency appointment? How often does he or she go out of town or take vacations? How long does it normally take for the therapist to return phone calls? In dealing with SIV you probably need a therapist who is generally available for you and any emergencies that may arise. This is not to say that you should expect your therapist to return your 2:00 a.m. phone calls every night of the week, but the therapist should be responsive to your needs in a manner that is both fair and effective.

How much do you charge? The fees for psychotherapy should be within a range you can afford. While psychotherapy is seldom inexpensive, you will need to find a therapist who fits within your budget. Some therapists may offer fees based upon your income level or financial situation (sliding scale). Some agencies provide psychotherapy at rates considerably lower than therapists in private practice.

Bear in mind that the amount of money you pay a therapist does not necessarily correspond directly to his or her skill or competence. In other words, just because someone charges a great deal of money doesn't mean that he or she is an exceptional therapist, and vice versa. Be sure to discuss the cost of therapy before setting up the initial appointment.

Is there anything else that you think I should know about you or the way you do therapy? This question is simply intended to provide the therapist an opportunity to inform you of any relevant factors that may influence your decision to engage in therapy. The therapist may tell you of a particular psychotherapeutic orientation to which he or she subscribes. You may find that the therapist discloses information about cultural factors, sexual orientation, age, office location, or accessibility for the differently abled. With this question you may learn something about the therapist that may either increase or decrease your desire to enter therapy with that person.

These are just some of the questions you may wish to ask while you are interviewing therapists. When you enter therapy, you are entering into a relationship. It is important that you be as informed as possible before beginning this new relationship.

You may find that you have many other questions as well as those discussed above. Don't be afraid to address all these issues before or during the first session. Activity 6.5 is a worksheet you can use to interview potential therapists.

Activity 6.5: Interviewing a Therapist

You might want to make several photocopies of this page so that you can use this when interviewing each therapist.

List the questions below that you will ask potential therapists. The eight questions discussed above have already been entered for you. Feel free to add your own in the space provided and to deviate from the order shown here. Beneath each question indicate the therapist's response as well as any notes that might help you in your decision. Generally, you will be asking many of these questions over the telephone before setting up an actual appointment.

Most therapists won't mind answering questions relating to your decision to make an appointment or begin therapy. Remember though, they generally won't answer personal questions.

When you are interviewing prospective therapists, keep in mind that you are the consumer and you are essentially trying to determine whether you want to purchase a particular product.

Therapist's name: _____

Telephone number: _____

Address: _____

Date interviewed: _____ In person? _____ By telephone? _____

What type of degree and / or license do you have?

_____

How much experience do you have in treating self-inflicted violence?

_____

What is the normal course of treatment for self-inflicted violence?

_____

How much do you know about areas related to SIV?

_____

How long do you expect that I'll have to be in therapy?

_____

What is your general availability?

_____

How much do you charge?

_____

Is there anything else that you think I should know about you or the way you do therapy?

_____

_____

Overall Impressions:

_____

_____

_____

What Happens in Therapy?

Each person's experience in therapy will differ because much of what happens in therapy depends on you. How you choose to use each session, your therapist's approach and experience, and your own knowledge, experience, and motivation will all help shape your therapy.

In most cases, the first few sessions of psychotherapy will be spent relating historical or factual information and developing or defining therapeutic goals. During these first few sessions you are getting to know your therapist, and vice versa, and determining whether this therapeutic relationship will suit your needs.

After these initial sessions, the real work begins. You are likely to experience times when you feel overwhelmed, anxious, sad, angry, or dissatisfied. You may think that therapy is not helping you at all. Or you may think that therapy is helping you too much—that all your success and positive feelings are due to therapy or your therapist. You will probably go through fluctuations in your perceptions of therapy and your therapist, as well as of your commitment to therapy. All these experiences are normal and to be expected.

The nature of the therapy itself and the therapeutic relationship is impossible to describe because it is so personal. Everyone perceives therapy differently and will benefit from psychotherapy in different ways and to different degrees. I cannot tell you what will occur once you enter therapy. However, if at any time you are dissatisfied or confused with the way in which therapy is progressing, I strongly recommend that you discuss this with your therapist. Good luck in your new adventure!

CHAPTER 7

Deciding to Stop
Self-Inflicted Violence

At first glance, the decision of whether or not to end self-inflicted violence seems simple. You would probably agree that ending a self-damaging behavior would be wise. However, the decision to end SIV is not as simple as it seems. As you have learned in previous chapters, self-inflicted violence serves many functions, not all of which are damaging. In fact, in many ways SIV helps you cope better or serves some other useful purpose. Giving up any long-standing behavior can be incredibly difficult—habits are hard to break. For these reasons, the decision to end self-inflicted violence is very complex.

This chapter is designed both to help you decide if you want to stop hurting yourself and to give you some ways to do so. It contains a lot of material, some you may be ready for and some you may not. Take your time working through the chapter; there's no need to rush. You will probably find that progressing through this material is not as easy or as straightforward as it is first appears to be. You may want to skip over those sections that you feel you are not quite ready for and come back to them later, or you may decide to repeat particular activities or topics that need more attention. Make the most of this chapter by using it in whatever way works best for you.

Why Should I Stop?

Several questions need to be asked and answered before you can make a decision to stop hurting yourself. The first is, Why do you want to give up

SIV? Although this question seems as if it would have a simple answer, typically it does not. You may have several reasons for wanting to stop hurting yourself, or you may not be able to identify any clear rationale. Your answers to this question will affect whether you try to eliminate your SIV behaviors and how successful you will be if and when you do.

To Escape Pressure from Others

You may want to end self-inflicted violence because important others in your life are urging you to do so. A therapist, spouse, partner, or friend may pressure you about your SIV behaviors. It is not uncommon for therapists and other mental health professionals to demand that self-injurious behaviors stop during treatment. Similarly, it is likely that your spouse, partner, or friends will ask that you refrain from SIV. While these people may sincerely care about you, and they may truly believe that they are helping you by insisting that you control your self-injurious behavior, this pressure may not be especially helpful. Support is more helpful than demands, suggestions, or coaxing. You need to determine your actions on your own accord. You need to decide to end SIV because you want to, not because someone else wants you to. Ending self-inflicted violence, or changing any other behavior, at the insistence of another will most likely end in failure.

To Reduce Shame, Embarrassment, or Secrecy

The decision to end self-inflicted violence may not be influenced directly by others, but may instead result from your own shame or embarrassment about hurting yourself. As mentioned elsewhere, shame is an important component of SIV. To reduce your feelings of shame, you probably don't tell others of your self-injurious behavior and you attempt to keep this activity secret, covering your scars and fresh injuries. Reducing this embarrassment may be a primary motive for you to discontinue your self-injurious behavior.

Stopping your SIV behaviors may allow you to be more open and honest with your friends and family—not that you are dishonest when you omit information that could be linked to the self-inflicted violence. It's simply that hiding things from those you care for makes it difficult to feel close to them. Consider this fictitious conversation between friends:

Dick: So, what did you do last night?

Jane: Not much. How about you?

Dick: I didn't do much either.

Now let's see the same conversation without the omission:

Dick: So, what did you do last night?

Jane: I was going to go to the movies, but I decided to stay home and slash up my arms with a razor blade. Want to see?

Dick: (Silence)

Understandably, it can be very difficult for you to admit to another that you purposely injure yourself. Often the reaction of others is disbelief, disgust, or shock. Ending self-injurious behavior would alleviate much of the shame and embarrassment associated with this act.

Because SIV Doesn't Work Like It Used To

A third reason some individuals decide to conclude their SIV behavior is that it does not provide a permanent solution to deal with problems or overwhelming feelings and is no longer even an effective short-term coping mechanism. Rarely will people give up an activity, thought, or behavior that is pleasing and gratifying. However, the gratification received from SIV decreases with repetition. At first, SIV was probably effective at reducing your negative feelings and emotions; otherwise you wouldn't have done it. However, after many episodes of self-injury, it becomes increasingly difficult for SIV to produce the same effect. Compare self-inflicted violence to riding a roller coaster. The first ride is new and exciting, producing feelings of stimulation and glee. But, after the tenth ride, the feelings produced resemble nausea, or maybe boredom, more than excitement. Although this example is a bit extreme, repeated SIV activities can have similar results. The feelings that once produced changes in your emotional states no longer have the same effectiveness. Thus, the decision to stop hurting yourself can stem from SIV's reduced effectiveness.

When you decide to end SIV simply because it doesn't work like it used to, you run the risk of falling into another pattern of coping that could be even more harmful than SIV. It is not uncommon for self-inflicted violent behavior to be exchanged for something with equal or greater potential harm, such as drugs or alcohol. While using these substances may seem to meet your needs at that moment, these alternative coping mechanisms can be very dangerous—possibly more dangerous than SIV. Excessive eating, shopping, sexual activity, reckless driving, gambling, and many similar behaviors all have great potential for harm.

If SIV's ineffectiveness is one of your reasons for stopping, it is essential that you identify and try out as many possible positive alternative methods of coping as you can. You will probably be able to find a new method of coping that is nondetrimental and helpful to you. Alternate methods of coping are discussed later in the chapter.

To Improve Psychological and Physical Health

One of the most positive reasons for ending self-inflicted violence is a desire to be healthier, both physically and psychologically. While SIV at one time may have been a method of survival and coping for you, it may no longer be necessary. As an adult, you have a much greater capacity for enduring difficult situations and taking care of yourself than you did as a child or adolescent. Out of this added strength can emerge a desire to end self-inflicted violence in order to improve your well-being.

Although SIV temporarily helps reduce feelings of depression, isolation, alienation, and frustration, it can also increase these same negative feelings over time. Over time, the shame, embarrassment, guilt, and physical consequences of SIV take their toll. You may decide to end this vicious cycle and promote a healthier psychological and physical existence by stopping your SIV. Ending your self-injurious behavior is likely to increase your desire for the support of others, decrease your isolation, and make you feel better physically. (Repeated damage to the body—no matter how small the trauma—can have serious physical and emotional consequences.) Additionally, a feeling of pride can be gained from abstaining from a desired behavior. Ending self-inflicted violence can produce feelings of accomplishment and satisfaction and a give you a healthier outlook on life.

Activity 7.1 is designed to help you explore the reasons you want to stop hurting yourself.

Activity 7.1: Exploring Reasons to Stop SIV

Part 1. The first part of this activity will help you assess others' influence on your decision to end your self-injurious behavior. In your journal, complete the following exercises.

1. List all the people who know that you hurt yourself.

2. Now circle the names of those who have suggested (or demanded) that you stop hurting yourself.

3. Next describe the possible reactions they might have if you did stop. How would you feel if they reacted this way?

4. Now describe the possible reactions they might have if you did not stop. How would you feel if they reacted this way?

5. In what ways do you feel your decision to stop SIV relates to the possible responses of others?

Although the decision to end SIV may be influenced by others, it is unlikely that you will be successful unless you yourself also want to stop self-injuring.

Part 2. The second part of this exercise will help you understand the ways that your SIV has changed since you first began injuring yourself. You will probably find that SIV doesn't work as well as it used to, and this may affect your decision to stop your SIV behaviors.

1. Look through your journal, paying particular attention to activities 2.1 ("Why Do I Hurt Myself") and 4.3 ("My SIV and the Addiction Model"), which relate to your initial experiences with SIV.

2. Now describe what injuring yourself is like for you at present.

3. Write about your emotions, physical sensations, behaviors, and thoughts. How has SIV changed for you over time? Does it still help you cope with your life as it used to?

Part 3. List the reasons you want to stop injuring yourself. Your list may be very long or very short. The number of reasons really doesn't matter. What does matter is that the decision to end SIV is your own and that you have a strong desire to stop hurting yourself.

When Should I Stop?

One of the more difficult things to determine is when to stop hurting yourself. You may be ready to change this behavior at this very moment. You might be mentally scanning your living environment, thinking of each place where you have stored an instrument that could be used for SIV. You may have even gone so far as to gather these instruments and throw them in the back of a closet, or maybe even in the trash. However, since you are reading this book right now, it is more likely that you are still wondering if it is time to stop hurting yourself.

Change is always challenging and difficult—and often scary. Few of us face major changes with enthusiasm and without fear. For this reason, it is unlikely that you will feel secure in your decision to end SIV. You will be unsure. You will be scared. But—if you decide to and you're ready—you will be able to end this behavior.

You may not yet want to stop SIV; it may still serve an important function in your life. It is vitally important that *you* decide when you are ready to end this behavior. If you are not yet ready to give up SIV, don't. If you try to stop hurting yourself when you aren't really ready or don't really want to, you are only setting yourself up to fail. Instead, wait until the timing is right. If you think that you can only reduce the amount that you are injuring yourself, but not eliminate SIV altogether, then start with that. You are the best judge of your readiness. No one else can make this decision for you. Do remember that, no matter when you decide to end self-inflicted violence, it will be a difficult decision, and you will most likely feel scared, unsure, anxious, and uncomfortable. Although you may be looking forward to changing this behavior, you are also likely to question your ability to succeed. Each of these thoughts and feelings is normal and to be expected. Try not to let them influence your decision.

Activity 7.2 will help you determine whether you are ready to stop engaging in SIV.

Activity 7.2: Am I Ready to Stop?

You can use the following checklist to help determine how ready you are to end self-inflicted violence. While it is not necessary that you meet all these criteria before stopping SIV, the more of these statements that are true for you before you decide to stop this behavior, the better.

	Yes	No
I have a solid emotional support system of friends, family, and/or professionals that I can use if I feel like hurting myself.	____	____
There are at least two people in my life that I can call if I want to hurt myself.	____	____
I feel at least somewhat comfortable talking about SIV with three different people.	____	____
I have a list of at least ten things I can do instead of hurting myself.	____	____
I have a place to go if I need to leave my house so as not to hurt myself.	____	____
I feel confident that I could get rid of all the things that I might be likely to use to hurt myself (razor blades, cigarette lighters).	____	____
I have told at least two other people that I am going to stop hurting myself.	____	____
I am willing to feel uncomfortable, scared, and frustrated.	____	____
I feel confident that I can endure thinking about hurting myself without having to actually do so.	____	____
I want to stop hurting myself.	____	____

Even if you have decided that now is not the right time to stop engaging in SIV, keep reading this chapter. The information that follows will give you not only a good idea of what is involved in stopping but can help you build the support structure and alternative coping strategies you will need when you are ready to stop.

How Do I Stop?

Once you have decided that it is time to stop hurting yourself, the next question to be answered is how. Many methods can aid in stopping or reducing SIV behaviors in the short-term—when you feel the need or desire to harm yourself. Before we look at these techniques, however, it is necessary to examine some general long-term approaches.

Behaviors, thoughts, feelings, and physical sensations are all linked; each influences the others. Therefore, by changing what happens in one area, you also change what occurs in the others. The ultimate goal is to alter each of these areas enough so that you not only no longer hurt yourself but you also no longer feel the desire or need to hurt yourself.

Changing Your Behaviors

Many people feel that changing what you do, day to day, is the best way to make the alterations in thoughts, feelings, and physical sensations that are necessary for permanent change. To alter these daily behaviors, you must first determine the characteristics of your SIV actions.

Begin by reviewing in your journal the exercises you've done in previous chapters in which you have described your SIV. Activities 1.4 and 1.5 ("SIV's Course Through My Life" and "How I Hurt Myself") and Activity 3.4 ("What Are My SIV Rituals?") are probably most relevant. This information will provide a good starting place for devising a plan for change. As you review these activities, try to get a sense of the particular patterns of your SIV. To change your self-injurious activities, you first have to understand what they consist of. Examining these patterns makes it possible to create some ways to change them.

Let's look at Jackie's pattern, as an example. Jackie is a twenty-five-year-old college-educated woman who lives alone and works at a bank. She has cut herself using razor blades since she was about sixteen. Typically, she cuts herself on her upper arms and her legs so that no one can see her wounds. She generally cuts herself about once a month and makes two or three cuts during each episode. When she is going through difficult times, she hurts herself more often. Each time Jackie has hurt herself it has been in the early evening after returning home from work. She is always alone when she cuts herself. Jackie keeps her razor blades in the bathroom, under the sink and cuts herself in that room. Afterward, she carefully wraps her wounds with bandages, throws away her used razor blade, cleans the sink, and goes to bed.

Anytime you change your behaviors, you change the organization of your thoughts, feelings, and physical sensations. Changing behaviors is an effective way to produce change in these other areas. Therefore, altering the behaviors associated with SIV will alter not only the frequency of and the manner in which you engage in this activity but also some of the fundamental reasons for doing it.

Time and place. As mentioned in chapter 3, many people have a particular time of day when they are more likely to hurt themselves. For you, this may be a time of day when you tend to feel particularly vulnerable or isolated, such as morning or evening. Jackie generally engaged in SIV in the early evening. It is important to monitor and assess when you are most likely to hurt yourself. By changing the pattern of your activities during these times, you can decrease the likelihood of self-injury.

One really easy way to change your SIV behaviors is to change where you are or who you're with at the times when you are most likely to hurt yourself. For instance, placing herself in an environment incompatible with self-inflicted violence in the early evening when she typically cut herself, Jackie was able to greatly reduced the likelihood that she would harm herself. She made a plan to stop over at friends' houses after work most evenings. By doing this she was able to avoid the time and place that was most dangerous for her as well as get plenty of good dinners made for her by her friends.

Formulating a plan of how, when, and where to change your surroundings is important. By placing yourself in an environment or situation in which you are not likely to injure yourself, you can control your SIV activities. It is important to remember that this will be more effective if, whenever possible, you can put yourself in an environment incompatible with SIV before you have any thoughts or feelings about wanting to hurt yourself. Changing your surroundings when your self-injurious desires are already present makes avoiding the behavior much more difficult. However, as mentioned before, difficult does not mean impossible and you may still be able to find ways to alter your environment or situation.

Although changing your environment is one method of avoiding self-harm, it is not foolproof. Sometimes you may not be able to avoid the environment where you injure yourself, or you may find yourself in a situation in which the desire to hurt yourself is so great that you are unable or simply don't want to leave. Finding somewhere to go at six o'clock in the evening is a lot easier than finding a place to go at 4:00 a.m. when you really feel like hurting yourself. At these times, other short-term behavioral changes can decrease the likelihood of self-injury, as will be discussed at the end of this chapter.

Means. Another important change is to get rid of any instruments that you usually use to hurt yourself. Do this before you feel the desire to self-injure. If you use razor blades, throw them away. If you use a lighter, throw that away. If you can't bring yourself to actually discard these objects, then place them in a box and bury it in the backyard or hide it in the back of a closet under something really heavy or hard to move. Make whatever instruments you usually use as inaccessible as possible. This will make it more difficult for you to hurt yourself and thus decrease the chance that you will do so.

Jackie could not bring herself to throw her razor blades away. However, she was able to place them in a locked box, which she kept at the back of her closet. Because the key for the box wasn't psychologically associated with anything, she was able to throw it away. Thus, when Jackie really wanted to hurt herself, she was unable to get to her store of razor blades, and, to get more blades, she would have had to leave her house. This changed her environment, making her less likely to hurt herself.

Ritual. Changing the patterns or rituals associated with self-inflicted violence will also alter your behaviors. Jackie always cut herself in the bathroom, then bandaged her wounds, threw away the razor blade, cleaned the sink, and went to bed. This was her ritual. Changing any part of your ritual will make SIV more uncomfortable and less reinforcing for you. In other words, by altering the routine you have for hurting yourself, you change your level of comfort and awareness. The less comfortable you feel when you injure yourself, the less likely you are to engage in this behavior. Also, changing your routines makes you more aware of your surroundings and your behaviors. As mentioned earlier, awareness conflicts with dissociation and consequently decreases self-injury.

Besides changing her environment and the means by which she hurt herself, Jackie also changed her routine so that she was less likely to engage in SIV. For instance, Jackie added a step to her ritual of self-injury. Before going into the bathroom to cut herself, Jackie forced herself to go outside and walk twice around her house. In changing this one routine, Jackie not only delayed her self-injurious activities but she also increased her awareness of her behaviors and made it less probable that she would hurt herself. Jackie also removed a step from her ritual. She stopped cleaning the sink immediately after cutting herself. Instead, she waited until the next day to wash out the sink. Seeing the mess the next day made Jackie more aware of what she had done and also made the whole process a bit less gratifying for her because it took considerable effort to clean up the dried blood in the sink.

Anything you can do to change your routine, either by adding steps to or removing steps from your ritual will help to increase your awareness and prevent SIV. Activity 7.3 will help you to develop some ideas for how to change your behaviors when you think you might injure yourself.

Activity 7.3: Changing My Behaviors

In this exercise, you will focus on ways to change your situation, environment, and routine to make it less likely that you'll hurt yourself.

Part 1.

1. Spend a few minutes thinking about environments where you are least likely to hurt yourself, such as work, school, the mall, the movies, the gym, a friend's house, or your therapist's office.

2. In your journal, make a list of these places. Be sure to include every environment you can think of. Even though you may choose not to go to that place, it's always better to have options.

You can refer back to this list (and hopefully go to one of these safer places) the next time you feel like hurting yourself or feel as if the desire may be coming on—when you've had a bad day, for example.

Part 2. When you are unable to change where you are, it becomes that much more important that the environment around you is as safe as possible.

1. Think of all of the instruments in your environment that you might use to injure yourself.

2. Now formulate a plan to make these instruments as inaccessible as possible. For instance, if you use razor blades to cut yourself, plan to throw them away or put them in the garage or put them in a locked box and throw away the key. Write your plan in your journal.

3. Once you have written down your plan, carry it out.

4. When you are finished making your environment safer, spend a few minutes writing in your journal about what you did, how you did it, how it felt, what you feel like now, and any thoughts, questions, or concerns you may have about this step.

Although this step may seem pretty simple, the actual process of changing your environment and removing the instruments you use to injure yourself will probably be quite difficult for you. It's OK to feel scared and worried. It's even OK if you were only able to hide some of the things you use to hurt yourself. You're still making progress.

Part 3. As a final step in changing your behavior, you will need to change some of your rituals or patterns of behavior. In Activity 3.4, "What Are My SIV Rituals?," you identified the pattern you follow when you hurt yourself. You may want to reread this section of your journal.

1. Once you have your rituals in mind, think of all the ways you could change them. Could you change the time of day or what you do before you injure yourself? Could you nurture your wounds differently? Could you use an alternate instrument? How could you do things differently?

2. Write down all these ideas in your journal.

When you are thinking about hurting yourself, review this section and try some of these ideas. Your desire to self-injure will almost certainly change as a result.

Getting Support

Because the desire for self-inflicted violence often arises from feelings of isolation and alienation, it is essential to reduce these feelings. Most individuals engage in SIV when they are alone. By creating and using a solid support system and participating in activities with others, your feelings of isolation and alienation decrease. Also, by placing yourself in situations where others are present, you make it less likely that you will harm yourself.

Jackie chose to spend evenings with her friends. This not only got her out of a potentially dangerous environment at critical times of the day, but it also placed her with others—a situation incompatible with cutting herself.

When you feel like you want to hurt yourself, call a friend. Or call several friends. Have someone come and sit with you, or go sit with someone else. Use your support systems.

One of the most simple, yet effective methods of changing unwanted behavior is based on one simple rule: Never engage in any activity unless you are able to tell at least two people of your plans. Chances are, if you can't tell two people what you plan on doing, it's not a good thing for you to do. This rule can apply to taking a trip, buying a car, doing drugs, robbing a bank, anything at all, including self-inflicted violence. And by talking with at least two other people, not only are you receiving feedback on your planned activity but you are increasing the behavior that leads to a decrease in negative feelings—you are connecting with others.

Activity 7.4 will help you look at your existing support system and to prepare for those moments when you might need to use it.

Activity 7.4: My Support System

List all the individuals who you could safely contact when you feel the desire to hurt yourself. Include their phone numbers, addresses, and times when they are likely to be available. You may want to include friends, family members, your therapist, a crisis line—anyone who might be helpful when you are feeling like hurting yourself. The goal in creating this list is to identify as many sources of support as you can, so it's important that you list people you feel comfortable contacting and who you trust not to make matters worse. You might include people on this list who don't know that you hurt yourself but who would offer you enough of a distraction that your desire to engage in SIV decreases. Or you may list only people in whom you place a great deal of trust and would be able to be completely honest with about your desire to hurt yourself. The idea is to create a list that gives you as many options as possible.

Keep a copy of this list in a place where you have easy access to it—or make several copies, one to keep by the phone, one to carry with you, and so on. You never know when you'll need it.

Name	Phone Number	Address	Times Available

Changing Your Thoughts

Another component of ending or reducing SIV is to change the thoughts you have regarding these activities. In chapter 4 you explored your thoughts throughout the cycle of SIV. This is a good time for you to spend a few minutes reviewing your journal, particularly Activity 4.1, "The Cycle of My Thoughts." You need to become aware of your thoughts during the process of SIV in order to change them. By drawing attention to these thoughts and beliefs, you will be able to identify and alter the style of thinking that leads you to hurt yourself.

Joel is a sixteen-year-old, high-school sophomore who is active in school theater, a member of the varsity swim team, and a straight A student. He also has a part-time job at a movie theater and has a girlfriend who works there as well. Several years ago Joel's parents were divorced, and his family went through great turmoil. Joel's younger sister went to live with her father while Joel remained with his mother. It was around that time when Joel started to injure himself. At first he would hit himself on his thighs using his fist, but later he escalated his SIV activities by using a hammer to hit himself. Although Joel has never broken a bone through this behavior, he does produce numerous serious bruises on his thighs.

Joel's thoughts are fairly predictable throughout his cycle of SIV. Initially, Joel's thoughts are very negative and pessimistic.

I can't do anything right.

I should be better than I am.

I'm such a loser.

No one wants to be with me.

I'll never feel any better.

The thoughts that occur before you injure yourself are largely responsible for your desire and decision to engage in SIV. Since these thoughts are so powerful, it is really important to break this cycle and change your thoughts before you hurt yourself. When you are able to change your negative thoughts, you will be much less likely to want to hurt yourself.

Challenging your thoughts. Like Joel, you probably have many negative thoughts immediately before injuring yourself, as you may have discovered in Activity 4.1, "The Cycle of My Thoughts." How you choose to handle these thoughts helps to determine your moods, physical sensations, and behaviors. While many of us unquestioningly accept the thoughts that pass through our minds as true, this is often not the case.

Let's take a look at the accuracy of Joel's thoughts. We know for certain that Joel's "I can't do anything right" thought is inaccurate. Joel is getting high grades in school and is successful in many extracurricular activities. Clearly, Joel is able to do at least some things right. It's probably safe to say that this thought is not true. Joel also believes that no one wants to be with him. However, he has a girlfriend and a fairly active social life. Again, Joel's thinking is a bit distorted.

One of the best ways to change negative thoughts is to challenge their accuracy. Typically, you'll find that many of your negative thoughts simply aren't true. It is necessary to question each negative thought that you can identify. Activity 7.5, which you will do shortly, will help you begin to do this.

When you do not assess the accuracy of your negative thoughts you typically act as though these thoughts are true, which can in turn actually make these thoughts come true. For example, Joel believed that his life would never get better. Without challenging this thought, Joel might have begun to behave as if his life would not improve, retreating from others and isolating himself and perhaps ceasing to engage in activities which once brought him pleasure. Had Joel acted in this manner for a substantial period of time, it is likely that he would have lost much of his support system and many of his friends. Joel could have easily trapped himself in this self-fulfilling prophecy.

The necessity to identify, challenge, and alter each negative thought that you have cannot be denied. Changing your thoughts will help you to change your behaviors, emotions, and physical sensations and will help to decrease your desires to hurt yourself.

Stopping your thoughts. Instead of permitting yourself to continue such negative and potentially dangerous styles of thought, it would be better for you to stop or change them.

Two ways of altering these types of thoughts seem to work particularly well for people who engage in SIV. One is to just stop negative thoughts as they occur. First, of course, you must be able to identify those thoughts. Once you can recognize them, you can stop these thoughts by simply saying *Stop!*—aloud or in your mind.

It takes some practice and much repetition to make this rather simple-sounding strategy actually work. However, if you are able to get the hang of it, you will find that it does cut off negative thoughts quite effectively. If you find this technique helpful, you might also try doing this before or during an episode of SIV.

Reframing your thoughts. The second method of altering negative thought patterns requires a bit less practice and actually, in my opinion, works somewhat better. In this process you change negative thoughts into positive ones. Just like the old saying "Every cloud has a silver lining," every negative thought has a positive counterpart. A few of the thoughts Joel has after he injures himself will demonstrate this technique.

Negative Thought	Positive Thought
I'm so dumb for hurting myself.	I did what I needed to do to take care of myself.

| I can't believe I let myself do this again. | I used the best method possible at that time to cope. |
| I have to keep this a secret. | I can decide who I would like to tell—and not tell—about this. |

Using this technique, Joel easily transforms his thoughts. While some of the changes in thinking may be fairly subtle, they all allow for a more positive and powerful view of the behavior. Thoughts that support beliefs about your strength, choice, and optimism provide a foundation for changes in your attitudes, mood, behaviors, and even physical sensations. Identifying and altering negative patterns of thought is an essential component in creating lasting change in a behavior. Thoughts can be modified through identification, evaluation of accuracy, elimination, and rephrasing. Each of these methods will aid in changing your thoughts and reducing the likelihood that you will injure yourself. Activity 7.5 will help you begin this process.

Activity 7.5: Changing My Thoughts

When we begin to question the truth of our thoughts, we become detectives investigating our own lives. Imagine that you are investigating a fascinating case, collecting evidence to support your beliefs and evidence to refute them.

1. Referring back to what you wrote in your journal for Activity 4.1, "The Cycle of My Thoughts," select one of your thoughts that precedes an episode of SIV. Write that thought at the top of a fresh page in your journal.

2. Beneath the thought, draw a vertical line down the center of the page, dividing it into two columns. Write the heading "Evidence For" at the top of the left column, and the heading "Evidence Against" at the top of the right.

3. Now find all the evidence you can to support that thought and write it in the left column.

4. Then find all the evidence you can to refute this thought, and list it in the right column.

5. Finally, keeping in mind the evidence against it, rephrase your original thought in a more powerful, positive light. Write your new phrase across the bottom of the page.

When you are finished, you should have something like what Joel came up with:

I Can't Do Anything Right

Evidence For	Evidence Against
I was late for work again.	*I was late because my coach needed to see me about a possible college scholarship.*
Karla hated the video I rented.	*I thought it was pretty good. We just have different taste in movies.*
I blew my race at the swim meet and our team lost.	*I didn't swim my best, but it takes a lot more than my individual performance to lose a meet.*

6. Repeat steps 1 through 5 for each of the thoughts you identified in Activity 4.1 as preceding an episode of SIV.

7. When you are finished with all those thoughts, look back over what you have written. The evidence you collected refuting your negative thoughts probably proves how inaccurate they are. And the rephrased thoughts at the bottom of the pages are likely to be more realistic than the ones you started out with. This may be one time in your life when you will be happy to be proven wrong.

When you become aware that you are engaging in this cycle of negative thoughts, you can review this exercise and change your style of thinking.

Changing Your Feelings

Suppose you are snorkeling in the ocean on a beautiful, warm spring day. Suddenly, about ten feet away from you, a large pointed fin cuts through the surface of the water. You're terrified; how do you react?

A. Do you tread water while you tell yourself that it's probably a dolphin and anyway sharks are usually harmless?

B. Or do you get the heck out of there as fast as your arms and flippers will carry you?

If you're like most people, you'd answer B. You'd wisely react to your fear and swim as quickly as possible to the safety of the shore. Emotions often have a purpose, and fear's purpose is usually survival. Accepting your fear of a shark as real and true can enable you to react in a way that saves your life.

Although this section focuses on changing your feelings, it is important to understand the distinction between change and denial. Failing to recognize the emotions that you feel or pretending that they do not exist is very dangerous. Trying to talk yourself out of a fear of sharks could make you a tasty snack for a hungry sea creature. Often expressing your emotions and acting on them is a far more effective way of dealing with feelings than trying to pretend that they don't exist or simply ignoring them.

Emotions are much like the wind. We can't really see them, but we know they exist and we are able to see the results of their presence—often in our behaviors. We can't always tell their source or direction, but we find it much easier to move with them than to resist. And, again, like the wind, no matter what we do, our feelings change or go away on their own.

Feelings have several characteristics that it will be helpful for you to know:

- Feelings often exist for a reason.

- Feelings are not always logical or easy to understand.

- Feelings are always transitory. Given enough time, they will change or disappear on their own.

Because of the nature of emotions, the goal of this section is not to show you how to escape or avoid emotions, but rather to give you some ideas for the best ways to express, accept, and honor your feelings. By respecting and expressing your emotions, you will begin to be able to enjoy and cultivate their richness. And expressing those feelings that are currently most troublesome, may allow allow you to feel other more satisfying emotions and pursue ways of living that don't require self-inflicted violence.

Identifying your emotions. The first step in learning how to alter your emotions is learning to identify what you are feeling. You may currently use self-inflicted violence as a means of expressing or regulating your feelings. However, you may often be unclear about what emotions generate these episodes of self-injury. Being able to identify specific feelings is a necessary prerequisite for attempting to change them.

Many people do not know the difference between thoughts and feelings. Feelings can usually be described with a word or two. Feelings also always fit into one of the following sentence formats: "I feel . . ." or "I am . . ." Often people think that they are describing feelings when they are really describing thoughts. When you hear the key phrases "I feel that . . ." or "I feel like . . ." you are hearing thoughts.

For example, say that you feel hurt. This is a feeling. But if you feel that your friend really let you down, that is a thought. As you can see, feelings take very little description or explanation. Whereas thoughts can be explained in great detail. Thoughts can also be challenged quite easily—for instance, your friend could say, "I did not let you down. What do you mean I let you down?" Feelings cannot be argued away in this manner. Feelings reveal your actual experience. They are all your own.

You may want to review in your journal activity 4.2, "The Cycle of My Emotions," to refresh your memory about your feelings during the cycle of

SIV. Activity 7.6, which appears shortly, will help you begin to identify your emotions.

Expressing your emotions. Once you've begun identifying your feelings, the simplest way to change them is by expressing them. Feelings are like little kids, they are difficult to ignore, particularly when they're screaming. But if you give them what they want or need, they will be satisfied and quiet down.

Each feeling you have will demand its own method of expression. For instance, if you feel angry, watching a dull movie may not be the best option. Instead, you may want to go to the batting cages for an hour. It takes a great deal of practice and patience to find the match between your feelings and the best way to express them.

Most of the feelings you have will require some sort of physical release. Crying is an example of such a release. Our bodies have built-in coping mechanisms that respond to our emotions. However, many of us have been conditioned not to use these physical outlets. It is important that you relearn how to identify and respond to your body's natural needs. Activity 7.6 will help you begin this process. Learning to identify and express your feelings will gradually cause your feelings to change. It is this change that will allow you to feel more content and resolved. In contrast, withholding, denying, or avoiding your feelings will make you more likely to want to hurt yourself.

You may have been using self-inflicted violence as a method of releasing your emotions. While this may have been effective and necessary in the past, you may find that other methods of expressing your feelings work equally well and have fewer negative consequences.

Activity 7.6: Expressing My Emotions

This exercise will help you identify your feelings and create some methods of expressing them. Since you probably use SIV as a way to release your emotions, knowing how to express these feelings in alternate, healthy ways will prevent you from hurting yourself.

Pages 144 and 145 list some common emotions (the left-hand column) and some responses (the right-hand column)—both instinctual and learned—that you may have used or may want to try using as ways to express your emotions.

In your journal, make a list, pairing emotions that you can identify as having felt in the past (even if you're not sure you have) with an activity that has or you think might work as a means of expressing that feeling. Whenever you are feeling overwhelmed emotionally, it will be helpful for you to return to the list in your journal or the ones here and try at least three ways to release your emotions before considering SIV as an option.

Feeling	Activity
Afraid	Boxing
Amused	Cleaning house
Angry	Climbing
Annoyed	Cooking
Anxious	Creating something
Bored	Crying
Confident	Cuddling
Confused	Cycling
Defeated	Dancing
Dejected	Diving
Delighted	Drawing
Depressed	Driving
Despairing	Exercise
Desperate	Fighting
Disappointed	Fixing something
Discouraged	Floating
Embarrassed	Flying
Enraged	Gardening
Excited	Getting a massage
Frustrated	Helping someone
Furious	Hiking
Grateful	Hugging someone
Guilty	Lifting weights
Happy	Listening to music
Helpless	Making music
Hopeless	Painting
Impatient	Petting an animal

Feeling	Activity
Irked	Playing
Irritated	Reading
Isolated	Rocking
Livid	Running
Lonely	Screaming
Loving	Sculpting
Miserable	Seeing a friend
Needy	Sex
Overwhelmed	Shopping
Panicky	Shouting
Pessimistic	Singing
Pleased	Skating
Proud	Sleeping
Relieved	Stretching
Resentful	Sunbathing
Threatened	Swimming
Thrilled	Taking a bath
Trapped	Taking a sauna
Resigned	Talking
Satisfied	Throwing things
Stuck	Venting
Unappreciated	Walking
Uneasy	Watching a movie
Unloved	Window shopping
Violated	Working out
Vulnerable	Writing
Worried	Yoga

Changing Your Physical Sensations

Free diving is perhaps one of the least well-known aquatic activities. In this sport, individuals dive to ocean depths of several hundred feet without the aid of any underwater breathing apparatus such as scuba gear. These individuals learn to train their minds and bodies to survive without oxygen for several minutes at a time. In some cases, these divers can reduce their heart rates to roughly twenty beats per minute and can divert the flow of blood to only the essential organs (such as the brain). Although these divers need to be in excellent physical shape to achieve such a feat, much of their training is mental.

There is no doubt that the mind and body can influence each other. It has been demonstrated time and time again that physical problems influence psychological problems. It also works in the other direction. It is not uncommon for psychological problems to cause or affect physical problems. Hostility, a psychological phenomenon has been linked to heart attacks, a physical phenomenon. The course of serious illnesses, such as cancer, AIDS, chronic fatigue syndrome, directly relate to the person's emotional state—a positive outlook versus depression, for example. How you treat your body affects your psychological health, so when you do things to hurt yourself physically, you are also damaging your emotional health. Likewise, if you take care of your body, your psychological health will benefit.

Just as free divers can train their bodies to produce different physical behaviors and sensations, so can you. When you engage in SIV you probably feel a state of great tension before injuring yourself. At the time it may seem like SIV is the best option for reducing this tension. However, many other options are less physically damaging and will produce a similar result.

The first step in changing physical sensations is to identify what you are feeling on a physical level. You need to do this before, during, and after hurting yourself. Try to identify not only the what you are feeling, but also where on your body you are feeling it. Activity 7.7 will help you do this.

Activity 7.7: My Physical Sensations During SIV

1. In your journal, on a left-hand page, draw a rough outline of your body, like the one shown on page 148.

2. Divide the opposite page into three columns. Down the left margin, make a numbered list of all the physical sensations you experience during SIV, leaving some space after each item, as shown below.

3. On the outline of the body, write the number corresponding to each sensation in the place where you feel it.

4. In the second column, list the emotions you have that are related to this physical sensation. For example, a feeling of physical ten-

sion in your stomach might correspond to anxiety. The physical sensation might be a result of your emotional experience, or it might be a cause of it. In other words, the tension in your stomach could be the way your anxiety manifests itself in your physical sensations, or you might have the sensation of tension first and that physical sensation leads to anxiety. Either way, record your emotions.

5. In the third column, list the thoughts that go along with these physical experiences. Tension in your stomach may relate to thoughts such as "I hate my life" or " I just can't cope." Again, the physical sensations you are experiencing may either lead to or result from these thoughts.

Physical Sensation	Emotion	Thought
1. *Tension*	1. *Anxiety*	1. *I can't cope*
2. _____	2. _____	2. _____
3. _____	3. _____	3. _____
4. _____	4. _____	4. _____

This activity should enable you to begin to see how strongly connected your body, mind, and emotions are. By altering any one of the three, you can change your patterns and decrease your desire to self-injure. The following sections will help you to explore some ways of changing your physical sensations. There are several good methods you can use.

Exercise. One of the easiest ways to change physical sensations is to exercise. In addition to the obvious effects of increasing your heart rate and changing other physical patterns such as respiration, digestion, and blood flow, exercise can alter the exchange of neurotransmitters in your brain. The chemical neurotransmitters in your brain affect your physical experience—causing you to feel sleepy, or energized or even to think more clearly.

As discussed in earlier chapters, during the process of self-inflicted violence, the brain releases endorphins, whose effects closely resemble those of morphine. Generally, endorphins are released to minimize feelings of pain. During SIV, endorphins are released so that you don't feel the pain associated with hurting yourself. They can also cause a very pleasant physical sensation.

Like SIV, exercise can also produce endorphins, and it is much less destructive. By engaging in vigorous exercise instead of hurting yourself, you can achieve similar psychological effects while simultaneously obtaining much more beneficial physical results.

Exercise is a very personal matter. Each of us has forms of physical activity that we enjoy more than others. Personally, I would rather die than jog a mile. However, I enjoy swimming and playing racquetball. It is impor-

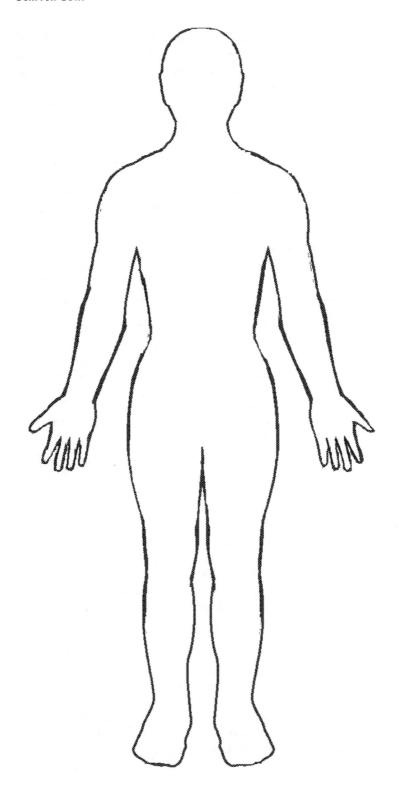

tant to identify the types of physical exercise that you enjoy as well as how convenient or accessible they are for you. For instance, in most parts of the United States, it is difficult to go snow skiing in July. It is also difficult to go sailing at 4:00 a.m. when you feel like hurting yourself. Think of as many options as possible that will allow you to exercise at those critical moments when you feel like hurting yourself. Activity 7.8 will help you get started.

Activity 7.8: Exploring Exercise Options

This exercise will help you identify various types of exercise that you can use at any time, but particularly when you feel like hurting yourself. Keep this list in a place where you can easily find it when you want or need to.

1. First, circle each of the forms of exercise listed below that you enjoy. Blank spaces have been provided so that you can add your own exercise preferences.

2. Next, using the following 1 to 10 scale, rate each of the circled activities for how likely are you to do it when you feel like hurting yourself.

1	2	3	4	5	6	7	8	9	10
Not at all likely				Somewhat likely					Very likely

_____ Walking	_____ Biking	_____ Swimming
_____ Running	_____ Sailing	_____ Lifting weights
_____ Aerobic dance	_____ Surfing	_____ Skating
_____ Tennis	_____ Racquetball	_____ Badminton
_____ Bowling	_____ Golfing	_____ Hockey
_____ Basketball	_____ Football	_____ Softball
_____ Baseball	_____ Soccer	_____ Shuffleboard
_____ Dancing	_____ Rowing	_____ Skateboarding
_____ Frisbee	_____ Skiing	_____ Gymnastics
_____ _____	_____ _____	_____ _____
_____ _____	_____ _____	_____ _____

When you feel like injuring yourself, review this list and try some of those ways of exercising that you gave a high number.

What Do I Do When I Feel Like Hurting Myself?

Much of this chapter has focused on methods of creating permanent change in SIV activity. Although these techniques will be helpful and will allow you to change your life in many respects, additional techniques may be more useful moment to moment, in times of stress or crisis, for example.

You may find that some of these strategies work better in some situations than in others. You will probably want to try several of these ways of trying to prevent an episode of SIV so that you can determine which strategy works best under which circumstances.

Relaxation Techniques

When you are feeling tense or anxious it can be very helpful to know how to relax and feel less stressed. Relaxation has both psychological and physical components that act to reduce physical stress. Because of the high degree of tension and anxiety associated with self-inflicted violence, knowing how to relax and using this knowledge at critical times is essential.

Each of the following methods of relaxation will help reduce tension and anxiety. By learning how to relax and discharge your tension in a healthy manner, you will find that your desire to hurt yourself decreases.

You will need to determine what works best for you with each of these techniques. Because dissociation, and sometimes dissociative identity disorder or multiple personality disorder, are related to self-inflicted violence, some of these methods (imagery, in particular) may produce an adverse or unwanted effect. If you are afraid that a particular technique might make you more likely to hurt yourself or feel worse in general, get more information. Talk to a friend, therapist, or significant other. Read a book on the subject. If this is not possible, try each method carefully and minimally at first, assessing its effects as you proceed. Finding the method that works best to let you relax may take a while.

Deep breathing. Several common techniques are used for relaxation. The first of these techniques involves altering your style of breathing. When you feel tense and anxious, you tend to breathe differently than usual, more rapidly and shallowly than when you feel relaxed. One of the ways to trick your body into feeling more relaxed is to act as if you are relaxed. Altering your breathing to resemble that of a normal relaxed state will produce this effect.

The first step in changing your breathing is to get comfortable. You may prefer to sit or lie down. Next place your hand (or a box of tissues, if you prefer) on your stomach. By doing this, you increase your awareness of your breathing; you can see and feel your hand rise and fall with each breath. Now close your eyes and breathe as slowly and as deeply as you can, letting your abdomen expand first, and then your chest. Feel your hand rise and fall as you breathe in and out. Breathe through your nose instead of your mouth—this also helps slow your breathing. Practice breathing deeply and slowly for at least five minutes.

When you are first learning this procedure, you will probably have to concentrate on your rate of breathing a great deal. It is very easy to slip back into a pattern of short, shallow breaths. However, after you develop this skill, you will be able to change your breathing with little thought or effort. You will find that taking long, deep breaths makes your body automatically relax and enables you to feel much less tense and anxious.

Visualization. A second method of enhancing relaxation involves the use of imagery. Although you can perform visualization techniques almost anywhere and under almost any circumstances, it works better if you are able to find a quiet, comfortable spot in which you feel safe and secure. You might prefer to sit or lie down, and you might also want to soften the lighting or turn off the lights. Once you have made yourself comfortable, you are ready to begin.

This technique can be used in two ways. First, imagery can be used simply to divert your attention. To use imagery in this manner, you just create an imaginary situation that you find pleasant. For instance, if you enjoy being at the beach, then imagine yourself there. Make this imaginary setting as specific and detailed as you can. Picture the color of the water and the sand; try to hear the sounds of the waves and the seagulls flying overhead. Breathe slowly and deeply, just as you would if you were really at the beach.

The other way imagery is used is a bit more specific. In this technique, you first identify the area in your body where you feel tension. Once you have found that place, you then try to imagine and describe what the tension looks like. For example, Jackie (who appeared in the early parts of this chapter) felt tension primarily in her abdomen. She imagines this tension to resemble a solid black ball, somewhat like a cannonball. She describes this ball as radiating heat and as being impenetrable. Using imagery, Jackie has created a picture of her physical sensation.

Once the sensation has been described as fully as possible, it can be changed. Jackie imagines the cannonball in her abdomen shrinking to the size of a pea and rolling out of her belly button. After she created this mental image, Jackie's tension had largely disappeared. Her use of imagery changed her physical sensations. Using imagery makes it possible to relieve stress and tension and enhance relaxation.

Directed attention. A third method of relaxation involves focusing your attention on each area of your body in turn. Although this method seems simple, because of the amount of concentration required, you may find this more difficult than you would expect.

Again, it is important that you be comfortable to perform this task. Then, starting at your toes and working your way up your body, ending at the top of your head, focus on each part of your body and simply notice the physical sensations that are present in each area. Be sure to stop at each area of your body and assess how it feels physically. Can you identify the texture of the surface on which your fingers are resting? Is one leg more relaxed than the other?

By selectively guiding your attention and concentration, you will find that you become more and more relaxed. Using this technique in combination with deep breathing and imagery will produce the best results.

Activity 7.9 will help you to develop your skills in relaxing.

Activity 7.9: Exploring Relaxation Techniques

Although having to learn to relax may sound strange, many people have great difficulty slowing down and releasing stress, tension, and energy in a healthy way. In this activity you will explore the three relaxation techniques presented in this section: deep breathing, visualization, and directed attention.

Part 1.

1. First, spend a minute or two rereading the preceding section on deep breathing.

2. Now get yourself into a comfortable position and try this technique for at least five minutes. Remember to take deep breaths into your abdomen rather than breathing from your chest.

3. Now, in your journal, describe your experience of this activity. Did you feel more relaxed when you were finished? More anxious? What did you notice about the changes in your body and your physical sensations as you did this activity? What about your thoughts and feelings, did they change as well? What difficulties did you experience in completing this activity? Are you likely to try it again?

Part 2.

1. Reread the paragraph on visualizing yourself in a pleasant setting.

2. In your journal, describe in as much detail as possible as many imaginary settings that you would like to visit as you can. These may be places which you've been to before and enjoyed, or they may be places you've created with your imagination.

3. Once you have written down these settings, close your eyes and try to imagine being there. Remember to breathe deeply as you do this.

4. When you are finished, write about your experiences and how helpful you found this activity.

Part 3. Now try the other type of visualization, in which you imagine your physical sensations as tangible objects and try to change them with your mind. You may want to reread the material on this presented above first. You may also need to repeat this exercise often until you further develop this skill.

1. Consider these questions as a guide: Where in your body is your tension located? What does it look like? Sound like? Feel like?

2. Draw an image of your tension in your journal.

3. If your tension were the physical object you have drawn, how could you change it? For example, if your tension looks like a fire, you might pour water on it or smother it to put it out. Try visualizing these methods and see how they work.

4. Now describe and draw your tension again. How has it changed? How useful was this technique for you?

Part 4.

1. Next, use the directed attention technique to help you relax. Remember, in this technique you are to get into a comfortable position and simply focus your attention on each part of your body. Begin at your toes and work your way up to the top of your head. Review the description of this procedure in the previous section if you need to.

2. Once you are finished, describe your experience in your journal. Was it difficult to focus on specific areas of your body? Which areas felt the most relaxed? The most tense? Do you feel any different after completing this exercise? Did you find directed attention to be useful?

You will probably find that you prefer one of these techniques to the others. That's just fine. Any way you are able to relax and to relieve some of the physical sensations you experience will also help prevent you from hurting yourself.

Quick Fixes

Several other techniques can be used to change physical sensations. Some of these methods are more extreme than others. Again, I suggest that you try some of these to find out if they might help you.

Changing sensations. Each of the following techniques will alter what you are feeling on a physical level:

- Splash water on your face. This is more fun if you use a squirt gun. No matter how you do it, this will help to alter your attention, concentration, and physical sensations.

- Take a bath or shower. Immersing your body in either warm or cold water will change your body's temperature, thus changing your physical sensations.

- Make your entire body as tense as you can. When you release yourself from this state of tension, your body will feel more relaxed.

- Change the temperature of your environment. Make your setting either really warm or really cold. Creating drastic changes such as these not only changes what you are feeling on a physical level but it can also help reduce or eliminate dissociation.

SIV substitutes. The following methods might be helpful for you if you are not ready to change your SIV behaviors and/or if you simply need a break from hurting yourself.

Some of these techniques have been suggested by other researchers and seem to be effective in reducing self-injury, at least temporarily.

- Instead of cutting, burning, or bruising yourself, color your body to resemble what would have happened if you did self-injure. For example, draw long red lines on your arms instead of cutting. Make sure to use nontoxic art supplies for this activity.

- Hold an ice cube in your hand. The pain from the ice will resemble pain from SIV. However, the result will not be as detrimental to your body.

- Plunge your arm into a bucket of ice water. Again, the shock of the cold and the resulting pain will somewhat resemble the pain from an act of SIV.

- Play an audiotape or videotape of yourself that you have previously recorded. In this tape, indicate all the reasons why you like yourself and shouldn't hurt yourself. This will not only raise your self-awareness but it will make you feel loved.

- Call, write, or visit a friend, family member, significant other, or therapist.

These are just a few ideas; you can probably come up with some methods of your own. The basic premise behind altering your physical sensations is that by doing so, you are changing your level of dissociation, your thoughts, feelings, and moods. By creating these changes, you also alter the strength of your desire to hurt yourself.

Reaching out. As humans, we all have the need for others. Research has shown that babies raised in isolation or with little human contact fail to thrive. When you are in pain—whether it is emotional, physical, or both—it is critical that you reach out to others. Connection and human contact are what we as humans rely on for survival. This is also what you need the most when you feel as though you want to hurt yourself.

It is essential that while you are trying to end or reduce SIV behaviors, you reach out to others. Having a network of friends, family, and others who will be there to support you when you are at your weakest is necessary in this process. Be sure to arrange this support system before deciding to stop hurting yourself. It is much easier to pick up the phone at 4:00 a.m. if you know that you will hear a friendly, supportive (although sleepy) voice on the other end of the line. Also, if your friends know that they might be hearing from you and indicate that they will be there to support you, you will feel cared for, connected and supported. Refer back to activity 7.4, "My Support System," to help you identify those individuals who might be helpful to you in times of need.

CHAPTER 8

After Self-Inflicted Violence

The changes you have begun to make in your life are something like the changes that take place in a garden over time. In gardens, flowers bloom, weeds thrive, and various insects come to visit. But things are constantly changing. Flowers wilt, weeds are removed, and insects can vanish as quickly as they appeared. The contents of a garden are recycled and used in differing forms. Decayed flowers and weeds return to the soil to enrich it and are later reborn, sprouting anew from the seeds of their past lives.

After changing your self-injurious behaviors, you are likely to feel similar to a newly turned garden. It may take a while before you see the results you expect. You have planted the seeds of your future, and you will need to wait for these seeds to germinate and grow before you can see something new and beautiful. And there is always the chance that not everything you planted will thrive.

What You Can Expect

How you will feel once you've changed your self-injurious behaviors is difficult to predict. Your feelings, thoughts, and behaviors are dependent on a great number of things beside your change in SIV activities. Much as uncontrollable and unpredictable weather affects a garden, life will affect you. Events that occur in your life will at least partially determine how you deal with and feel about hurting yourself.

There will be times when you want to hurt yourself, and there may even be times when you do hurt yourself. You may feel barren or empty without SIV to help you cope. Give yourself permission to be human and thus imperfect. You are your harshest critic. Allow yourself to experience the desire to hurt yourself and feel proud about how you handle these feelings. Feel proud even if you did hurt yourself—you survived! Simply by reading this book and exploring the role of self-inflicted violence within your life, you have shown yourself to be courageous and strong. Be proud of yourself.

Many people believe that once they conquer a problem, life will progress smoothly. Life is rarely smooth and almost never predictable. Whether or not you have changed your self-injurious behaviors, life will be difficult at times. You will be faced with challenges, conflicts, isolation, victories, and a variety of other events. You will experience a wide spectrum of emotions, ranging from extreme joy and happiness to extreme sorrow and rage. This is simply the nature of life. In changing your patterns of SIV, you have changed a behavior, not life itself. Expect the unexpected.

Gordon is a thirty-year-old professional who has spent the last sixteen years dealing with the issue of self-inflicted violence. When Gordon was fourteen he started cutting on himself with a razor blade, mostly injuring his arms and chest. Although Gordon hasn't hurt himself in the past four years, SIV continues to be an issue, creating strong urges to cut himself. Recently Gordon felt a very strong desire to hurt himself. Instead, he wrote this:

> What the hell is going on with me? I can't stop thinking about cutting. I want to cut so badly. I don't know where this is coming from or what these feelings are doing here. I just want them to go away. I haven't felt like this in so long. I just got back from visiting my neighbor. I thought if I went over there I wouldn't want to hurt myself so bad. I'm not sure if it helped at all. I was so close to cutting before I went to my neighbor's. I was way zoned out, losing track of time, place, and everything in between. I stood before the bathroom mirror and chose the place on my arm I would cut. I could imagine the blood and the heat and the cool, cool blade. It would have felt so good. But I chose not to cut. I *choose* not to cut.

Coming Out and Empowerment

Regardless of whether you have stopped hurting yourself or continue to engage in SIV, you may decide to "come out" about your self-injuries. This is to say, you may want to tell others that you used to, or still do, hurt yourself. Coming out about your self-injuries is an empowering act. It allows you to be more honest with others and increase your connection with these individuals. Coming out also delivers the message that SIV is not a disgusting or shameful activity. It means telling others about your SIV: that this behavior exists, that it helped you to cope and survive, and that you are not ashamed.

Coming out to others about your self-injuries also allows you to serve as a role model for others. You are not the only person who self-injures—you are just one of many. However, most individuals keep these behaviors hidden. By being out about your self-inflicted violence you are showing others that it's OK to talk about SIV. You are giving others permission to be as courageous as you are and to communicate openly about SIV. You will find that once you start talking about your self-injurious behaviors, others will approach you to tell you of their own struggles. By being open about self-inflicted violence, you demonstrate positive behaviors for others, and through this process become a role model.

Betsy, a twenty-one-year-old college student, used to pull out her hair. She would have large bald spots on her head, and would frequently cover them with hats and sometimes a wig. Betsy stopped pulling out her hair about two years ago. Once she stopped her SIV activities, she felt more at ease telling people what she used to do. As Betsy states,

> It was weird, you know. It's like once I stopped pulling out my hair, I felt OK telling people about it. It was like I felt proud that I quit and I wanted my friends to know and to feel proud of me. This one girl I know even told me about something similar that she used to do. It's like I feel really free or liberated or something. Telling my friends was definitely a good thing.

Shame is an incredibly powerful emotion that will keep you feeling negative about yourself and your behaviors. There is nothing shameful about injuring yourself. Through inflicting injuries upon yourself you were able to cope and survive. Your scars are testimonies to this survival. Shame and secrecy go hand in hand: openness and honesty are the antithesis of shame. Coming out about your SIV behaviors will enable you to dispel your feelings of shame and begin to foster feelings of pride and worth. Be proud of the courage it took for you to survive a difficult time in your life, and be proud of the courage it takes to talk about self-inflicted violence.

Guidelines for Coming Out About SIV

Coming out about your SIV activities can truly be empowering and healing. When you are ready, you will begin to tell others about your self-injurious activities. In telling others that you hurt yourself, there are some guidelines that can make this coming out experience a more positive one.

Understand your motives for coming out. Are you trying to shock others? Are you hoping to improve communication and increase honesty? Is coming out your own idea, or is someone else telling you to tell others that you hurt yourself?

Come out for yourself, by yourself. Don't tell others about SIV unless you are doing it with honest intentions. In other words, don't come out just to get others to react. Shocking others has limited value in your own growth.

Instead, come out for reasons that will improve your life and your connections with others. Tell others about your SIV so that you can be more honest with them, make a connection, and open up communication. Be aware of what you hope to achieve through disclosing your self-injurious activities. If you know why you're telling someone about your SIV and what you hope to achieve by doing so, you will be better able to direct the conversation and more likely to get what you want from this disclosure.

Only come out when you're ready. As the saying goes, timing is everything. Only you will know when you are ready to tell others about your self-injuries. Don't be pressured into coming out by the insistence or suggestions of others. Try not to pressure yourself into this action, either. Coming out will probably be difficult, and you may feel anxious, tense, scared, fearful, or a myriad of other emotions. These feelings are normal; it is unlikely that they will disappear. When you come out, you will feel scared and uncomfortable. Don't wait to feel relaxed before you tell others about your SIV. When you first begin to tell others of your self-injurious behaviors you won't feel calm or at ease, so don't wait for these feelings to occur. Coming out can be difficult. Don't let difficulty or fear stand in your way.

Present your self-inflicted violence without shame. Although SIV is not the most typical behavior, it helped you to cope and to survive. When you tell others about engaging in self-injurious behaviors, feel proud that you were able to cope and survive. Your emotions concerning SIV will greatly influence those around you. If you present SIV as a negative behavior or as a behavior of which you are ashamed, others will see SIV as a negative, shameful activity. If you present SIV as something you did in order to cope—as a functional behavior—others will see it that way as well.

Be direct when you tell others about your self-injurious behaviors. Being indirect makes it look as if you have something to hide or something of which you are ashamed. Talk about self-inflicted violence with pride. You are courageous and strong for being able to discuss these behaviors.

Have your support system ready. Regardless of how others react upon learning about your SIV behaviors, you will probably want your support system near you. You may simply want to relate the story to others. You may need more intense support if the reactions of those to whom you come out is not what you anticipated or hoped.

Although arranging your support network before telling others about your SIV is desirable, it may not be possible. If you are not able to get support when you need it, find other ways to nurture and take care of yourself. You probably listed many of these methods and particular supports in the activities in chapter 7. Review those activities, and create a list of people you can talk with and things you can do to take care of yourself after your coming out experiences.

Try it again. There is no question that coming out to others about your self-injurious behaviors is difficult. However, with practice it gets much easier to talk about SIV and to tell others about your experiences. Even if coming out didn't go so well the first time, try it again. By the fiftieth person you tell, it will be much, much easier and much more rewarding.

Activity 8.1 will help you make a plan to tell another individual about your SIV activities.

Activity 8.1: Planning to Come Out

Although you can never control the reactions of others, being prepared will help you feel more in control. In this exercise you will plan not only who, how, when, and where you will tell about your SIV behaviors, but also what you will do following this coming out experience to take care of yourself. The more prepared you are in your plans to tell someone else that you hurt yourself, the better.

In your journal, answer the following questions.

1. Who are you going to tell? It's best if you choose just one person to tell to begin with, instead of a group of people. You can better predict the reactions of one person than of several people or a group as a whole.

2. Why do you want this person to know you hurt yourself? What are your motives in telling this person?

3. When will you tell this person? Be as specific as you can, including both day and time.

4. Where will you be when you tell this person that you hurt yourself? Choosing a place where you feel comfortable will help you feel more at ease and relaxed when you break the big news.

5. How will you tell this person about your SIV? What exactly will you say? Sometimes it helps to write out what you will say in advance, almost like preparing for a speech.

6. How do you expect this person will react? If he or she does react in this way, how will that be for you? What other reactions might that person have? How might those reactions affect you?

7. What will you do to take care of yourself after this event? Who can you call or see for support? What can you do to make yourself feel better?

8. After you have come out about your SIV, write about how it went. What might you have done differently? Were there things you did or said that in retrospect were not helpful? What went well? What would you do again? Overall, how was the experience for you?

Since you undoubtedly will tell more people about your SIV behaviors, you might want to complete this activity after each coming out experience and review your responses before telling others. Eventually you'll feel much more comfortable revealing your SIV.

Healing Through Helping

As someone who has struggled with and survived self-inflicted violence, you have a great deal to offer others. You have knowledge, experience, and your own perspective to share with others. By sharing your experiences you can help others a great deal. Think of how helpful it would have been (or was) to have had someone to talk with who really understood self-inflicted violence.

Many philosophies and religions work on the premise that what you put out into the world by means of your actions, thoughts, and energies is what the world returns to you. Both the Golden Rule ("Do unto others . . .") and the concept of karma exemplify this belief. In dealing with psychological issues, this same premise seems to be true. When you help others, you help yourself.

Through helping others with their issues of self-inflicted violence, you also help yourself. When you help another deal with SIV, you can see more objectively the functions, actions, thoughts, and emotions associated with these behaviors. This objective view of SIV allows you to better understand the role of self-injury in your life.

When you help others deal with SIV, you also place yourself in a different role; you are acting as an active participant in healing. When you were dealing with your own issues of self-injury, you were coping and struggling and surviving. Through assisting others with this issue you take the next step and become an active part of the healing process.

How to Help Others with SIV

You may be able to help others with issues of self-inflicted violence in many ways. Some of these ways are very in-depth and time-consuming, while others are more peripheral and occasional.

Be a pen pal to someone who is injuring himself or herself. You might go about becoming a pen pal in many ways. Because SIV is so secretive, you aren't likely to be able to flip through the classified section of your local paper and find someone advertising for a pen pal to correspond about self-injury. However, since many people who hurt themselves also read the newspaper, you might do well to place your own advertisement for a pen pal.

There are several things to consider in placing this ad. First, you will want to find the newspaper that best suits your needs. Most cities and many towns have a weekly alternative type of paper, which might fit your purpose better than the local daily newspaper. You might also want to consider placing an ad in a magazine or newsletter.

Once you have figured out where to place the ad, begin thinking about what the ad will say. You might decide on something very simple and direct, like "Dealing with issues of self-inflicted violence? Me, too. Want to write?" Or perhaps you will want to take a less direct approach: "Looking for a friend to correspond with. Must be open-minded and willing to deal with difficult issues."

Once you've written your ad, you are ready to send it, and probably a check or money order, to the newspaper or magazine you've chosen. As a rule, the publication will receive the responses and forward them to you in batches. Once you have found someone—or more than one person—you want to write to, you'll need to decide whether to give him or her your home or work mailing address, or whether to rent and use a post office box or mail drop. The choice is yours, but it never hurts to be safe.

Start a group for individuals who are injuring themselves. You don't need to be a trained professional to begin a peer support group. However, if you are interested in beginning a group, it would probably be helpful to first speak with someone who has had experience starting a support group, even one for a different issue. You can learn a great deal—and save lots of time and energy—using the experience of others.

Offer individual support to someone you know is struggling with self-inflicted violence. You can provide help to someone who is having a difficult time with self-injury. The level and intensity of this support is totally up to you. You may simply offer to talk over the telephone, or you may wish to become more involved and devote your time and presence to helping this person. There are numerous ways of being supportive (see chapter 9 for more ideas).

Educate others. Give presentations, workshops, speeches, or informal talks on the issue of self-inflicted violence. As someone who has had personal experience with SIV, you have a great deal to offer in terms of education. SIV is greatly misunderstood, and the educational materials available on this topic are incredibly limited. Do something to change this by educating others.

Contribute to publications about self-inflicted violence. Write, draw, or otherwise relate your experiences of self-injury to publications that deal with this issue. By contributing to these publications you give your own perspective on this issue and add to the store of information on SIV. Several publications can be found on the Internet as well as in print; see the following section for details.

No matter how or to what extent you assist others with self-inflicted violence, you are really helping yourself. You are showing your courage, your strength, and your pride when you are able to act in ways that promote growth, change, and knowledge in others. Activity 8.2 will help you formulate a plan to help others deal with issues of SIV.

Activity 8.2: Planning to Help

Remember that you need to take care of yourself before you can take care of others, so only help to the extent that it meets your needs. If you find yourself becoming overinvolved or overwhelmed by helping others, pull back and take care of yourself first.

1. In your journal, make a list of all of the possible ways you could help others with SIV.

2. Now, choose one way from that list to try out.

3. Once you have chosen what you'll be doing, you need to figure out the best way to make it happen. Begin by listing, step by step, how you will actually engage in that behavior. For instance, if you want to give presentations on SIV, you might start by making an outline of what you would present. Or you might begin by contacting a mental health agency and asking if they would be interested in a presentation on this topic.

4. After you have listed as many steps as you can, start at the first step you've listed and give your plan a try. You will probably be apprehensive about doing this, but do it anyway. You'll find that the possible rewards greatly outweigh the risks.

Resources

Although self-inflicted violence affects a large number of individuals, few resources are available on the topic. Presented here is a list of what I consider to be some of the major written works and other resources available in this area. This list is by no means representative of all the literature and resources available on SIV. You will also find a more complete reference section at the end of this book, which includes all the sources used in the writing of this text.

Some of the writings identified here are geared toward professionals and may be difficult for many readers (including professionals) to understand. However, due to the scarcity of information on SIV, I have included these titles despite their difficulty.

In addition, many of the titles listed below present a rather condescending and pejorative view of self-inflicted violence and the people who engage in these actions. However, there may still be some information in these writings that you will find helpful or interesting. I suggest, as I hope you do with everything you read, that you consider the source, the content, and your own experiences before deciding to agree with or act on what has been presented—including what you have read in this book.

I consider several of the publications available on the topic of self-inflicted violence to be exceptional. These publications are identified with a star. The assessment of the quality and the accuracy of the contents of these publications is purely by my own opinion. I have found these writings to be helpful, accurate, and positive in their approach. I urge you to formulate your own opinions as to what you find helpful and of exceptional quality.

Newsletters

★ *The Cutting Edge*
P.O. Box 20819
Cleveland, Ohio 44120

Copies of this newsletter (and subscriptions) can be obtained from the address listed above. Contributions and donations are requested and are used for the production of the newsletter.

Books

★ *Bodies Under Siege: Self-Mutilation in Culture and Psychiatry*, by A. R. Favazza. Baltimore: Johns Hopkins University Press, 1987.

Self-Mutilation: Theory, Research and Practice, by B. Walsh and P. Rosen. New York: Guilford Press, 1988.

The Luckiest Girl in the World, by S. Levenkron. New York: Scribner, 1997.

Women Who Hurt Themselves, by D. Miller. New York: Basic Books, 1994.

Workbooks

★ *Understanding Self-Injury: A Workbook for Adults*, by K. Trautmann and R. Conners. Pittsburgh: Pittsburgh Action Against Rape, 1994. This workbook can be ordered through the Pittsburgh Action Against Rape, 81 South 19th Street, Pittsburgh, PA 15203. Please include a check or money order for $11 ($10 for the workbook and $1 for shipping).

Articles and Chapters of Books

"The Challenge of Self-Mutilation: A Review," by M. Feldman. *Acta Psychiatrica Scandinavica* 79 (1989), pp. 283–289.

★ *The Courage to Heal: A Guide for Women Survivors of Child Sexual Abuse*, 3d edition, by E. Bass and L. Davis. New York: Harper & Row, 1994 (pages 53 and 229–230).

"Self-Cutting: Can It Be Prevented?," by K. Hawton, in *Dilemmas and Difficulties in the Management of Psychiatric Patients*, K. Hawton and P. Cowen, editors. Oxford, England: Oxford University Press, 1990.

★ "Self-Injury in Trauma Survivors: 1. Functions and Meanings," by R. Conners. *American Journal of Orthopsychiatry* 66 (1996), pp. 197–206.

★ "Self-Injury in Trauma Survivors: 2. Levels of Clinical Response," by R. Conners. *American Journal of Orthopsychiatry* 66 (1996), pp. 207–216.

★ "Self-Mutilation" in *Treatment of Adult Survivors of Childhood Abuse,* by E. Gil. Walnut Creek, Calif: Launch Press, 1988.

★ "Self-Mutilation and Self-Blame in Incest Victims," by S. Shapiro. *American Journal of Psychotherapy* 41 (1987), pp. 46–54.

Internet Sites

Many excellent sources of information can be found on the Internet, and an Internet search is the best way to locate and access them. Possible search topics include self-injury, self-abuse, self-mutilation, self-inflicted violence, and trauma.

Information Lines

(800)366-8288 [(800)DONTCUT] sponsored by Hartgrove Hospital; sends out information and referrals to the hospital's inpatient treatment program upon request.

Treatment Programs

Hartgrove Hospital Program for the Treatment of Self-Injury. Call (800)366-8288 [(800)DONTCUT] for information.

PART III

For Others

CHAPTER 9

For Family and Friends

This chapter is intended to address the experiences of those close to someone who self-injures. You may be a friend, spouse, partner, sibling, parent, family member, teacher, or simply a concerned other—whatever part you play in the life of a person involved in SIV, this chapter can help. Experiences you probably have had and the resulting emotions, thoughts, and actions are presented in this chapter.

While the contents of this chapter will help you better deal with the SIV activities of those close to you, you should also read at least the first part of this book if you have not yet done so. Part I (chapters 1 through 5) covers general issues related to SIV and will provide you with a greater understanding of how and why self-inflicted violence occurs, along with other important related issues. You may also wish to read part II, "Ending Self-Inflicted Violence," to gain knowledge about some of the aspects of stopping SIV that your family member or friends will probably experience.

What You May Feel

A variety of feelings are common on learning of another person's SIV: shock and denial, anger and frustration, empathy and sadness, and guilt. These emotions are discussed below.

Shock and Denial

When Sara rolled up the sleeves of her shirt to reveal her badly scarred arms, her mother could not believe what she saw. Sara looked like a burn victim. The chemicals she had been using to burn her flesh had taken their toll. Although Sara always washed her arms before the burns got too severe, the frequency of her behaviors had left her arms raw and badly damaged. Sara's mother could not fathom what she saw, and stood facing her daughter in a silent state of shock.

Because self-inflicted violence is such a secretive behavior, you, like Sara's mother, may have been shocked to learn that a loved one is injuring himself or herself. You may not have noticed many of the signs of SIV, such as your friend's or family member's refusal to wear shorts or short-sleeved shirts. You probably gave no thought to his or her frequent "accidents" or the bruises and cuts on the arms and legs that were always logically accounted for. SIV lends itself to secrecy; the actions usually take place in isolation and the results can be concealed with relative ease. Also, however, friends and family members are often eager to ignore or deny many of the telltale signs. Thus, when you finally do find out about the self-injurious behavior, you feel shocked.

Closely related to the feeling of shock is the behavior of denial. It is impossible for human beings to take in the full extent of the misery that surrounds us. In order to survive we must deny the presence of a great deal of sadness and horror. If we were unable to deny or minimize the enormous amount of starvation, illness, devastation, poverty, and violence that exists on this planet, we would most likely be in a constant state of depression. So denial is sometimes appropriate, useful, and even necessary.

At other times, however, denial is detrimental—as in the case of self-inflicted violence. If you observe the level of emotional pain of someone close to you and then deny its presence, you do a disservice to those you love. Your friend or family member who is self-injuring is in a great deal of psychological distress. To deny this distress will only communicate that you are not interested, unwilling to try to help, or do not understand. Therefore, it is extremely important that as you are confronted with the self-injurious behaviors of someone you care for, you do your best not to deny the reality of the situation and its implications. Although this may be difficult, responding to the SIV, rather than denying its existence, is necessary to aid a person who is injuring him- or herself.

Anger and Frustration

Marge's eighteen-year-old son, Josh, has been intentionally injuring himself since he was fourteen. Marge remembers clearly the first time she learned of her son's SIV behaviors:

> About two years ago Josh had broken his arm playing football with some friends of his. At the time I was quite upset with him

for being so careless. But when he later confessed that he had done this to himself intentionally, and that he hadn't even been playing football that day, I was furious!

Marge's reaction is not unique. Anger is a common response to learning of someone's self-injurious behaviors.

There are many reasons to respond to self-injurious acts with anger. First, anger may stem from the deception that often surrounds SIV. Like Josh, who originally told his mother that he had injured himself playing football, many people who hurt themselves do not present the truth about the causes of their injuries. Deception is used to reduce feelings of shame and ward off others' possible reactions of anger, disgust, or rejection. However, the deception, when discovered, often produces those very same feared reactions. You may feel angry or disgusted by having been betrayed or lied to. You may not understand the necessity for the deception and feel even more irate as a result. The need for deception indicates distrustfulness, and this implied lack of trust and openness between you and the self-injurer may hurt or anger you.

In addition, believing that the self-inflicted violence was unnecessary may also anger you. Watching someone do things that physically damage themselves is very frustrating. You may feel yourself wanting to scold the person or force him or her to stop self-injuring. The frustration stems from this inability to control the behaviors of others. But as much as you may not like what they do, and no matter how much you try to control what they do, you cannot.

Self-injury, as opposed to many other self-destructive behaviors, usually produces visible evidence. This physical evidence of the SIV activities forces you to realize the extent of your helplessness in changing the person's behaviors. Realization of your own helplessness in controlling the behaviors of someone you care about can cause you to feel frustrated and angry.

Empathy, Sympathy, and Sadness

Understanding the extent of someone's suffering is often a mixed blessing. On one hand, it allows you to be of more help to that individual. On the other, it can also penetrate you deeply, causing you to feel sadness and psychological pain like that of the person with whom you are dealing.

Empathy refers to this ability to understand the perspective and situation of another. When you are empathic, you are able to enter the emotional world of another. You take the perspective and see the world through the eyes of that person. Of course, it is impossible to take someone else's perspective entirely or completely accurately, but through empathy a general understanding of the individual's situation evolves.

People who engage in self-inflicted violence experience enormous amounts of psychological distress. To be able to understand the immense nature of this distress is helpful when you are providing support and assistance to those people. However, one negative side effect of empathy is the loss of detachment or separate perspective. When we empathize, we see into the inner world of another. And by doing so we run the risk of allowing that person's inner world to seep into us. As feeling and caring human beings, we are unable to guard completely against this infiltration. The result is that we may feel some of the sadness and pain of our friends. Thus, sadness is sometimes the result of empathy.

We may also feel sad for the person who self-injures. When we feel sad for another, we are generally feeling sympathy. When we feel sympathetic toward others, we are seeing them as figures worthy of our pity, which in many ways is a condescending view. While empathy is a helpful emotion, sympathy is not. Sympathy keeps others in an inferior position. When we feel sympathy, we presume to know how the other person is perceiving the situation. Someone who hurts him- or herself may view SIV as a positive action, an action that helped him or her to survive. Whereas from our sympathetic stance his or her SIV looks like a negative, pitiful behavior, an act of desperation. Thus, sympathy and any sadness it evokes is not particularly useful; it blocks understanding and to some extent objectifies the person for whom you feel pity.

Guilt

Throughout history, people have struggled with issues of morals and conscience. Often the result of these struggles is guilt, a feeling of remorse stemming from a perceived wrongdoing. When we do something that goes against our morals and values, our conscience supplies us with adequate measures of guilt.

Self-inflicted violence often provokes feelings of guilt in those close to the people engaging in these behaviors. You, for example may feel as if you did something to cause your friend or relative to purposefully injure him- or herself. Perhaps you're afraid you weren't the best parent, partner, or friend. Maybe you feel as if you didn't provide enough love, affection, or attention. It could be you're worried that it was because you weren't supportive enough or didn't listen well enough or weren't around enough. Guilt is a useful emotion, in that it signals that you have done something to compromise your morals and values. However, in the case of SIV you will often experience guilt that is not appropriate, necessary, or useful.

You cannot make anyone do anything. Your behaviors, or lack thereof, certainly influence the perceptions, beliefs, behaviors, and emotions of another, but influence is far from force. No matter what you did or did not do, you did not make anyone injure him- or herself. Even under the most extreme circumstances, people always have choice in their actions.

The guilt you feel, although a normal reaction to learning of a loved one's self-injurious behaviors, is not particularly helpful. It will be more helpful for you to surpass these feelings of remorse and regret and focus your energy in a more positive and useful direction. Talk with your friend or family member and find out how you can be of help. Wallowing in your own guilt will only keep you immobilized and probably depressed. To act in a manner more congruent with your morals, you need to be an active participant, offering assistance instead of apologies.

Activity 9.1 will help you assess your feelings about your loved one's self-injurious behaviors.

Activity 9.1: My Feelings About Another's SIV

In this exercise you are asked to rate the intensity of your emotions when you first learned of your loved one's SIV and now. Looking at the change over time in your emotions will enable you to see your progression through this experience. The more exposure you have to SIV, the less strongly you will feel about these behaviors. Your initial feelings will weaken over time, and once you realize that your reactions will subside, you will be better able to help those around you who are hurting themselves.

1. Use the following scale to assist you in determining how strongly you experience each of the listed feelings. Add additional feelings in the blank spaces and rate them as well.

1	2	3	4	5
Not at all		Moderately		Very strongly

Emotion	Initial Strength	Present Strength
Guilt		
Anger		
Frustration		
Sadness		
Fear		
Guilt		
Helplessness		
Shock		
Confusion		
_____		
_____		

2. Once you have finished with this list, review it, looking at how the strength of your emotions has changed. Your emotional reactions now are almost certainly far less intense than they were at first.

What You May Think

Consider an analogy. A baseball game usually has two components: players, who hit the ball and run, strike out, score runs, field and throw the ball; and fans, who are up in the stands cheering, booing, doing the wave, and occasionally giving an umpire a bit of grief. Teams usually play better at home, in part because of the fans urging them on. The players in the game are like feelings, and the fans are the thoughts that accompany these feelings. Feelings seldom play without a large, noisy audience of thoughts, which in turn influence the feelings' presence and strength.

Like athletes and fans, thoughts and feelings play off each other. If your team is performing well, you will continue to provide support. If your team begins to play badly, you might change your cheers to jeers or you might just leave the ballpark. The same is true of emotions and thoughts. For example, when you feel helpless, your thoughts might support this emotion. You might think to yourself that there is nothing that you can do, and you may believe that because you are stuck in a given situation, that you have no choice. These thoughts strengthen the feeling of helplessness. Similarly, when your feelings change, so will your thoughts, and vice versa.

A variety of thoughts commonly accompany the knowledge that someone you love is performing SIV, among them:

- *It's all my fault.*

- *I can fix this.*

- *You're nuts.*

- *This changes our whole relationship.*

- *You're not who I thought you were.*

- *You're doing this to manipulate me.*

Considered objectively, many or all of these thoughts are erroneous, and could easily influence your feelings in negative ways. It is important to be aware of your thoughts so that you can prevent them from contributing to or exacerbating negative emotional responses that could damage your relationship with the person who is self-injuring.

Activity 9.2 will help you examine the ways that your thoughts influence your feelings.

Activity 9.2: My Thoughts About Another's SIV

Part 1. On the left side of the chart on the following page, list each of the thoughts you have regarding your loved one's SIV behaviors. On the right side, identify the emotion that is most closely linked with this thought. An example has been provided.

Thought	Feeling
You're doing this to manipulate me.	*Anger*
_____	_____
_____	_____
_____	_____
_____	_____
_____	_____
_____	_____
_____	_____

Part 2. Once you have completed this list, take some time to think about how your thoughts and feelings influence your behaviors. In a journal or on a piece of paper, write about how your thoughts and feelings affect your behaviors in regard to SIV. Do you refuse to discuss SIV with your loved one because you feel too uncomfortable? Do your thoughts lead to feelings of anger that cause you to be irritated with the person who is hurting him- or herself? Do you feel so guilty that you overcompensate and overnurture the person?

Understanding how your thoughts and feelings combine to influence your behaviors will be important when you are trying to help someone close to you who is self-injuring.

What to Do and Not Do

As humans, we don't like to see others in pain. It is almost instinctual to try to end another's misery. When we see friends or family injuring themselves, we begin to understand the enormity of their psychological pain, and it is only natural that we want to help. However, without the proper education and training, our "helping" could end up doing more harm than good. This section offers some ideas of what you can do and what you should not do in trying to assist someone who is self-injuring.

Do Talk About SIV

As mentioned previously, SIV is surrounded by shame and secrecy. But SIV exists whether you talk about it or not. As you know, ignoring something does not make it disappear. The same is true with self-inflicted violence: It will not go away because you pretend it doesn't exist.

Not discussing SIV has several negative effects. First, ignoring the obvious helps to reinforce and strengthen the feelings of shame attached to this behavior. People who engage in SIV may get the idea that the behavior is so shameful that even talking about it is taboo. Thus, the secrecy and feelings of shame surrounding self-inflicted violence are strengthened.

Additionally, not discussing SIV can exacerbate the factors leading to these behaviors. When communication is lacking, feelings of isolation and alienation—the same feelings that often precede an act of self-injury—are increased. Consequently, by not talking about SIV, you may be actually increasing the likelihood that your friend or family member will self-injure again. Silence makes a very powerful statement.

Dylan is a fourteen-year-old high-school freshman who repeatedly bangs his head against walls, doors, or other hard objects when he gets upset. About a year ago, Dylan's mother walked into his room and observed this SIV activity. Instead of asking what he was doing or interrupting this process, she simply said "Excuse me" and left his room. They have never discussed this incident with each other and have never talked openly about SIV. Dylan continues to bang his head on a frequent basis.

Talking about self-inflicted violence is essential. Only through open discussion of SIV will you be able to help someone who is hurting him- or herself. By addressing the issues of self-injury, you remove the secrecy and reduce the shame attached to self-inflicted violence. And you encourage connection between you and your friend. You are helping create change just by the mere fact of being willing to discuss SIV.

You may not know what to say to someone who is performing acts of SIV. Fortunately, you don't have to know what to say. Simply by acknowledging that you want to talk, even though you're not sure how to proceed, you are opening the channels of communication. The following are some questions and topics you might want to address when discussing SIV:

- How long have you been hurting yourself?

- Why do you hurt yourself?

- How do you hurt yourself?

- When and where do you usually injure yourself?

- How often do you injure yourself?

- How did you learn to hurt yourself?

- What is it like for you to talk with me about hurting yourself?

- Does it hurt when you injure yourself?

- How open are you about your self-injurious behaviors?

- Do you want to change your SIV behaviors?

- How can I help you with your SIV?

Only through open dialogue can these issues be discussed. It is necessary to talk about SIV so that the person who is engaging in these activities feels more supported, less isolated, and more connected. Simply talking about SIV will help to decrease his or her need for self-injurious behaviors.

Do Be Supportive

Talking is one way to provide support; however, there are numerous other ways to show your support to another. One of the most helpful ways to determine how you could offer support is to ask directly. In doing so, you might find that your idea of support is vastly different from another's. Knowing what kind of support to offer, and when, is essential to truly being helpful.

A key component of being supportive is the ability to keep your negative reactions to yourself. Judgments and negative responses conflict with support. To help another individual, you need to put these feelings aside for the time being. You can only provide support when you act supportively. Your ability to separate your feelings, thoughts, and behaviors will be a crucial part of your assistance to your friend or family member. This is not to say that you should not or will not have judgments or negative reactions to SIV. However, you must conceal these beliefs and feelings when you are providing support. Later, when you are not offering assistance, is the time to release and express these thoughts and emotions.

Do Be Available—Within Limits

Most people who injure themselves will not do so in the presence of others. Therefore, the more time you spend with your friend, the less opportunity he or she will have to inflict self-harm. By offering your company and your support, you actively decrease the likelihood of SIV.

Many people who hurt themselves have difficulty recognizing or stating their own needs. Therefore, it is helpful for you to volunteer the ways in which you are willing to help. This will allow your friend to know when and in what ways he or she can rely on you.

As discussed in chapter 5, some people who injure themselves often have difficulty with boundaries. Boundaries are the limits you place on yourself and others in interpersonal relationships—ground rules, in effect. They help you know what you can expect from others and what others can expect from you. Your ability and desire to set and maintain these limits, or rules, will partially dictate the nature of the relationship. An inability to maintain or form consistent, healthy boundaries frequently results from having endured events such as trauma or abuse, that modeled poor boundaries. The result of this is that your friend who self-injures may try to impinge on your boundaries. Because of this, you will need to set and maintain clear and consistent limits with these individuals. In doing so, you are actually modeling appropriate forms of behavior. So if you are not willing to take crisis calls after nine o'clock at night, then say this to your friend. If you can only offer support over the telephone, rather than in person, be clear about that. When people need support around issues of SIV, they need to know who is available to help them and in what way that person can offer help. While what you do for your friend is important, establishing and maintaining appropriate boundaries is equally necessary to the relationship.

Activity 9.3 is aimed at helping you become more aware of the ways you can help someone who is self-injuring and will assist you in determining your availability to offer help.

Activity 9.3: How and When I Can Help

Through this exercise you will begin to develop clear and consistent ideas about when you are willing to help.

1. Working with the person in your life who is self-injuring, identify at least five ways in which you can be a support.

2. On this schedule below (or another sheet of paper), indicate what type of assistance you are willing to give (for example, telephone calls, personal contact) and when you are willing to provide it. Be sure also to include when you are absolutely *not* available. You may want to develop a color code or some other key to help you in this process; for instance, pink might mean you're willing to talk on the telephone, black could mean you're unavailable.

Time	Monday	Tuesday	Wednesday	Thursday	Friday	Saturday	Sunday
6:00 a.m.							
8:00 a.m.							
10:00 a.m.							
Noon							
2:00 p.m.							
4:00 p.m.							
6:00 p.m.							
8:00 p.m.							
10:00 p.m.							

The more clearly you define the ways in which you are willing to help and support your friend or family member, the more helpful and consistent you will be. You will also find that maintaining clear, consistent, and predictable boundaries in terms of your availability will enable you to avoid feeling overwhelmed or manipulated.

Don't Discourage Self-Injury

Around the age of two, children begin to encounter and comprehend the words *no* and *don't*. At this time, we begin our lifelong resentment of those words and the meanings which they carry. No, you can't leave the table until you eat your peas. No, you can't sit in first class with a coach ticket. No, you can't drive fifty in a thirty-mile-per-hour zone. Our lives are greatly limited and defined by these small, but powerful words.

Typically, when we are told that we can't or shouldn't engage in a given behavior, it is for a good reason (although I still question the logic of eating peas). However, these reasons take on much more meaning and relevance if we can determine them for ourselves. The consequences of our behaviors help us to determine what we should and should not do. For example, last year after going to the movies and eating popcorn along with Hot Tamales candy, I became terribly nauseated. That was the last time I mixed Hot Tamales with popcorn. However, if someone had told me that I would be sickened by this mixture and prohibited me from eating it, I would have been skeptical and resentful.

Rules, shoulds, shouldn'ts, dos, and don'ts all limit us and restrict our freedom. When we maintain the right to choose, our choices are much more powerful and effective.

Telling an individual to not injure him- or herself is both aversive and condescending. As mentioned previously, SIV is used as a way of coping and is often used as a final attempt to relieve emotional distress when other methods have failed. Most people would choose not to hurt themselves if they could. Although SIV produces feelings of shame, secrecy, guilt, and isolation, it continues to be used for coping. That people will engage in self-injurious behaviors despite the many negative effects is a clear indication of the necessity of this action to their survival.

When you tell someone to stop something, you are erecting a barrier to communication. This barrier will probably increase the secrecy around self-inflicted violence. Several years ago I had a close friend who began to use crystal methamphetamine (speed). She was quite open with me about her crystal use and would tell me when she was under the influence, although it wasn't very difficult to figure out. When she was on this drug, like most people who take it, she was overly talkative, paranoid, and quite restless. I felt that it was my duty to tell her to stop using this substance. I wanted her to get clean so that she could avoid the numerous possible physical, psychological, and legal ramifications of her drug use. I also wanted her to stop using crystal so that she would be more tolerable to be around. These were my needs. She was using this drug as a way to feel better. This was her need.

Ignoring her needs, I told my friend to stop using drugs because I didn't want to see her destroy her life. Although I thought I was communicating a sense of caring and support, she took my statement as judgmental and demanding. The result of this statement was that my friend became more and more secretive about her drug use, at times even lying about her continued use of drugs. She began to withdraw from me, and from others, and, as I came to find out later, heavily increased her use of crystal. My comment helped to sever the communication and connection she desperately needed at that time.

Even by making a casual comment indicating that your friend or relative should stop self-injuring, you run the risk of damaging your relationship and existing channels of communication. Your friend or relative will continue to injure him- or herself as long as he or she needs to—your directives will not change this. However, the amount of secrecy and shame resulting from these actions might change significantly.

Additionally, some people who injure themselves may react adversely to demands of cessation. By imposing your limits on another, you create the potential for failure. Thus, some who self-injure will increase their SIV behaviors in order to feel as if they have a choice about and control over these actions.

Ann is a forty-year-old carpenter who used to burn herself with cigarettes. She began this activity when she was about sixteen and stopped when she was thirty-two. Ann can't recall why or how she began to hurt herself. However, she is able to remember a specific incident involving her mother when she was about seventeen:

> My mom finally noticed the scars on my arm and asked what they were from. I didn't feel like screwing with her, so I 'fessed up. I told her I burned myself with cigarettes. Know what she said? She said I should stop smoking. I knew what she meant, but, God, was I pissed off! I remember that same night, I must have burned half a dozen holes in my skin. God, was I mad.

Although it may be incredibly difficult to witness a loved one's fresh wounds, it is really important that you offer support, not ultimatums.

Do Recognize the Severity of the Person's Distress

Most people don't self-injure because they're curious and wonder what it would be like to hurt themselves. Instead, most SIV is the result of high levels of emotional distress with few available means of coping. Although it may be difficult for you to recognize and tolerate, it is important that you realize the extreme level of emotional pain that gives rise to SIV activities.

Open wounds are a fairly direct expression of emotional pain. One of the reasons people injure themselves is to transform internal pain into something more tangible, external, and treatable. The wound becomes a symbol of both intense suffering and of survival. It is important to acknowledge the messages sent by these scars and injuries.

Your ability to understand the severity of your friend's distress and empathize appropriately will enhance your communication and connection. Don't be afraid to raise the subject of emotional pain. Allow your friend to speak about his or her inner turmoil, rather than having to express this chaos through self-damaging methods.

Do Get Help with Your Own Reactions

Imagine the following situation: You are on an airplane, waiting on the runway ready for takeoff. A flight attendant stands in the aisle, demonstrating the correct use of the seat belt and doing a two-finger point toward each of the exit doors. As the flight attendant reaches for another safety device to demonstrate, you actually begin to listen to the muffled voice emanating from the ancient sound system of the airplane. You hear an unseen flight attendant saying, "In the result of loss of cabin pressure, an oxygen mask will fall from the overhead compartment. Place the mask over your nose and mouth and pull on the ends of the string to tighten. If you are traveling with an infant or someone who needs your assistance, put your own mask on first, then offer assistance."

The concept of taking care of yourself before trying to assist another, is not intuitively obvious. Many of us were taught to think of others first. Yet, in general we cannot be of much use to anyone else if we ourselves are in a state of need. When trying to help a friend or family member who is self-injuring, this point becomes even more critical.

Most of us have had the experience at some point in our lives of feeling distressed by our reaction to someone else's behavior. Al Anon and similar self-help groups were created to help the friends and families of people dealing with problems of addiction and similar behaviors. At this point, no such organizations exist for those coping with a loved one's SIV. However, the basic premise of these groups clearly applies to the issue of self-inflicted violence. Sometimes the behavior of others affects us in such a profound manner that we need help in dealing with our reactions. Entering psychotherapy to deal with your responses to SIV is one way to handle reactions you find to be disturbing or overwhelming.

You might find the idea of seeking help for someone else's problem strange. However, the behaviors of others can have a profound effect on you. This effect is further strengthened by the mysteriousness, secrecy, and misconceptions about self-inflicted violence. Thus, entering psychotherapy with a knowledgeable clinician can educate you about SIV as well as assist you in understanding and altering your own reactions. When you learn that a friend or family member is injuring him- or herself, you are likely to have an intense emotional reaction; psychotherapy can help you deal with these reactions.

Sometimes asking for help is very difficult. The person who has come to you about his or her SIV and asking for your help is highly aware of this. Follow your friend's lead. If you need or want help, get it. Seek a trained professional. Ask some other friends for support. Speak with a religious counselor if that's helpful. Chapter 6 offers some helpful suggestions for finding and interviewing a therapist.

Tom is the father of a sixteen-year-old girl who cuts herself. He recently discovered his daughter's SIV when she came home from school with blood on the sleeve of her shirt. After checking the fresh wound, he noticed that she had many other scars on her arm. Both Tom and his daughter began psychotherapy the following week. Tom describes his experience:

> I couldn't believe how scared I was. Learning that my daughter would do something like that to herself was bad enough, but having to say that to a stranger was really difficult. I felt like I'd be judged or labeled a bad parent. I can only imagine how my daughter felt. The therapist was OK. She helped me understand what the cutting was about and how I could help. I still haven't told many people about my daughter's cutting. I pretend I'm keeping quiet to protect my daughter's privacy, but I know it's really my own privacy I'm protecting.

The bottom line is that your reactions are likely to be upsetting to you and getting support will make your life easier. The better you are able to handle your own reactions, the more you will be able to help your friend who is injuring him- or herself. If you begin to forget this, simply hop on an airplane. A very kind (if unseen) flight attendant will remind you that you need to take care of yourself before you can care for others.

CHAPTER 10

For the Therapist

While this chapter is written specifically for therapists working with clients who self-inflict violence, others may also find this chapter to be interesting and helpful. Clients who are engaging in SIV may wish to read this chapter and perhaps discuss aspects of it with their therapists.

Similarly, therapists reading this chapter in an effort to better help their clients would be well served to use this book as a whole, reading the entire text and using some of the activities with their clients as tools for therapy. Although this chapter will provide therapists with greater knowledge of psychotherapeutic issues as they relate to SIV, the previous chapters of this book lay the groundwork for a more comprhensive understanding of this complex topic. Thus, if you have not yet done so, I strongly recommend that you read the preceding chapters of this book.

Types of SIV

As mentioned in chapter 1, self-inflicted violence is generally divided into three categories: Psychotic, Organic, and Typical. The majority of this book has focused on Typical forms of SIV, those acts of SIV that occur due to emotional or psychological reasons, and not from Psychotic (hallucinations or delusions) or Organic (physical) factors. Most of the people who engage in SIV fall into the Typical category. Typical forms of SIV generally stem from distressing psychological states and are used as methods of coping and easing psychological distress (see chapter 2 for a discussion of the rationales and reasons for self-inflicted violence).

Although most of this text has addressed issues relating to Typical forms of SIV, as a clinician you may also encounter acts of self-injury that fall into the psychotic or organic category. The following section discusses SIV in individuals with Psychotic or Organic disorders.

SIV and Psychotic Behavior

Some of the most severe forms of self-inflicted violence have a psychotic origin. Conceptually, the term *psychotic* refers to a severe disturbance in an individual's sense of reality. Psychotic behavior is behavior that corresponds to this distortion of reality. Although there are a variety of specific disorders within the realm of psychoses (such as schizophrenia, delusional disorder, and schizoaffective disorder) each involves abnormal patterns of thought, perception, or belief in reality.

Many individuals who experience psychotic thoughts and behaviors also have hallucinations or delusions. In simple language, hallucinations are false perceptions. These perceptions may take the form of any type of sensory input (taste, sight, sound, touch, or smell), but typically are auditory. Feeling the sensation of bugs crawling up your arms (when in reality this is not the case) is an example of a hallucination. Hearing things or seeing things that are not there is also considered an hallucination. Delusions, false or distorted beliefs, are commonly associated with psychotic states. For example, believing that you are Amelia Earhart is a delusion. Many people who have delusions believe themselves to be God or to possess supernatural powers, such as the ability to read others' thoughts or control people. Psychotic states can originate from a number of sources, including certain psychological disorders, chemical or neurological imbalances, injuries, or the use of certain substances.

Individuals who experience psychotic states occasionally engage in SIV. Due to the loss of contact with reality, self-inflicted violent activities that occur during a psychotic state have the potential to be extreme. Amputation of one's own body parts or eyes (eye enucleation), castration, and eating one's own flesh (autocannibalism) are examples of some of the more severe forms of SIV. Not all SIV behaviors stemming from a psychotic source are this extreme. However, psychotic incidents of self-injury are in general potentially more dangerous than acts of SIV with nonpsychotic origins.

Self-inflicted violence does not serve the same purpose for individuals experiencing psychotic states as it does for nonpsychotic individuals. For most people, SIV is used as a method of coping with overwhelming internal pain, and although a high amount of dissociation often occurs, contact with reality is not lost. In contrast, individuals experiencing psychotic states clearly experience a disturbance of their sense of reality. Those with psychotic behaviors use self-injury as a way of responding to hallucinations or delusions. For example, an auditory hallucination may tell you that you need to sever your ear lobe (as did van Gogh) to appease some higher power. This hallucination may be so convincing that you respond to it and cut off your ear. Although in a sense this self-injurious act is helping to lessen an intense psychological experience, the primary motivation for this behavior stems from the presence of these false perceptions or beliefs.

Treatment of self-inflicted violence in individuals experiencing psychotic states generally focuses on the reduction or elimination of the psychosis rather than the self-injury. Because the self-harm stems from these abnormal thought processes, changing these processes typically alters self-injurious behaviors. Psychopharmacological methods (medications) are generally recommended for treating most forms of psychosis.

Organic SIV

Psychology as a field rarely concludes that there is any one cause for a behavior. However, mental retardation and autism are generally believed to stem from organic, genetic, or other physical factors. Although these disorders are quite distinct from one another, it is relatively common that individuals with these disorders engage in self-injurious activities, and the specific forms of SIV used, as well as the functions these behaviors serve, are similar. For these reasons, I have combined these two groups in this discussion.

Mental retardation describes a condition of significant limitations in intellectual abilities along with significant difficulties in social relations, communication skills, employment, and/or self-care. Individuals who are mentally retarded span the spectrum in terms of ability to function within society. Many mentally retarded individuals are able to adapt to the demands of society and lead reasonably normal lives, while others are unable to care for themselves at all and must remain under constant supervision.

Individuals with autism have great difficulty relating to others in a typical manner; often their communication skills are greatly impaired. Many times it seems as if autistic individuals are in their own world because they don't respond to external cues in a typical manner. For instance, you might need to stand in front of an autistic person and repeat his or her name for several minutes to get a response, and even then you may not get one. Autistic individuals sometimes have strange and narrow interests and behaviors, as portrayed by Dustin Hoffman's character, Raymond, in *Rain Man*. In the film, Raymond was unable to care for himself or communicate effectively with others. However, he could remember numbers and perform complex mathematical equations in his head, which worked very well in the Las Vegas casinos. Like Raymond, some autistic individuals are quite skilled in particular areas. Some may be excellent at math; some at music. Although autism is relatively widespread, there is still much to learn about this mysterious disorder.

Self-inflicted violence is a relatively common behavior in both mentally retarded and autistic individuals. However, the form and the rationale for the behavior are quite different than they are for SIV in the general population. For example, in these populations SIV is not ordinarily related to dissociation, rituals, previous trauma, substance use, and many similar factors.

Individuals with these disorders tend to injure themselves in particular ways. Head banging and lip biting are two common methods of self-injury. Hitting, slapping, and biting are also relatively common forms. These types of SIV are much more basic than those in the general population. That is, using a knife to injure yourself is a more complex behavior than simply hitting your head against a wall.

In addition, the frequency of self-injurious behaviors in mentally retarded and autistic populations is much greater than in the general population. These individuals often abuse themselves many times a day, frequently in the presence of others. In the general population, in contrast, SIV is kept secret for the most part and does not usually occur when others are present. But autistic and mentally retarded individuals frequently hurt themselves even when others are physically trying to restrain them from doing so.

Among these populations, self-inflicted violence serves two primary functions. First, self-abuse may provide stimulation that is lacking from their lives. This lack of stimulation is not usually due to the enviroment, but is part of the disorder itself. In other words, there may be plenty of stimulation going on around these individuals, but they are unable to sense and respond to it in a typical way. By using the body to increase sensory input, autistic and mentally retarded individuals may be finding an important and useful way of experiencing the world. To better understand how this might be helpful, imagine that you are suspended in a large tank of Jello (you choose the flavor). You cannot feel anything but the rubbery, slick, cool gel surrounding you. Occasionally someone is able to penetrate the gelatin and actually connect with you. But this is rare. Usually you spend your time just floating, experiencing little change in your sensations. You can probably imagine how dull this would get after only a short time. Now imagine you can't leave. What will you do to entertain yourself? How will you show yourself that you still exist, that you still have a body, that you have not become one with the Jello? Self-inflicted violence provides stimulation, disrupting boredom and helping one to maintain a sense of self.

A second reason for self-injury among mentally retarded and autistic individuals is reinforcement. In chapter 4, I explained how behaviors that are reinforced tend to be strengthened. Receiving a reward or something desired following a behavior is positive reinforcement. In these populations, positive reinforcement often comes in the form of attention. After an episode of self-injury, the autistic or mentally retarded individual often receives some type of reinforcing response. Whether it is someone caring for the injuries or delivering a scolding, the outcome may be desired and thus positively reinforcing.

Negative reinforcement can also result from self-inflicted violence. The autistic or mentally retarded individual may avoid something unpleasant or undesired through the use of SIV. For example, several years ago I was working with a twelve-year-old autistic girl in a school setting. This girl loved to sit on the floor and rock back and forth (another type of self-stimulating activity). When the teacher would make her sit at a desk, she would scream and cry. The tears and shrieks of the girl were not enough for the teacher to give in and allow her to sit on the floor. However, when she would begin to bang her head on the desk, the teacher would quickly remove her from the seat and allow her to return to the floor. This girl learned through negative reinforcement that banging her head would release her from having to sit at the desk. Thus, negative reinforcement served to increase the frequency of her self-injurious activities. In this situation, communication was also accomplished through SIV.

The treatment of self-inflicted violence in these populations also differs from that in the general population. One of the major differences in terms of treatment has to do with the issue of consent. Most individuals within the general population who self-inflict injuries will seek treatment (or not) by their own choice. This is not the case for most mentally retarded and autistic individuals. SIV tends to be more problematic for the caretakers than for these individuals, so mentally retarded and autistic people are often forced to reduce or eliminate this behavior, even though it may serve several important purposes for them.

Treatment in these populations generally includes some form of operant conditioning (when the consequences of an action determine the likelihood of the recurrence of that action). Elimination of a behavior involves removing all reinforcers from its consequences. In other words, self-injurious activities are simply ignored until they disappear. Since they no longer yield a positive result, they are no longer useful. Additionally, providing positive reinforcement (candy, for example) for appropriate behaviors, such as sitting at a desk without head banging, will help to promote these desired activities. Ignoring undesired behaviors and reinforcing desired behaviors is the most effective way to shape behavior.

This method sometimes works well, when several conditions are met. First, great patience and consistency is necessary on the part of the caretaker; this method can take a long time for success. However, since many reinforcers stem from internal sources, such as providing stimulation in an otherwise dull world, this method is not always effective. As long as the individual is receiving reinforcement from a behavior, the behavior will continue.

Therefore, when operant conditioning treatment is not effective or is inappropriate, other treatments may be necessary. The use of medication in these populations has had mixed results. Sometimes it has been helpful, other times it has either not been helpful or has had serious side effects. While I personally do not advocate the use of psychopharmacology as a method of changing behaviors—particularly behaviors that seem to serve some purpose—this is an option. If you feel that treatment is a necessity, I strongly recommend the use of operant conditioning techniques, even though they require much more time, effort, and consistency on the parts of those involved.

As you can see, SIV has many differences between the general population and the mentally retarded and autistic populations. Forms, frequency, cause, and purpose of self-injury are distinct in these populations.

Prevalence of SIV

Although the prevalence of self-inflicted violence is difficult to determine exactly, it has been estimated that approximately 960,000 to 1.8 million individuals in the United States engage in these behaviors. An estimate of everyone affected by self-inflicted violence (family, friends, significant others, care-service providers, etc.) would double or triple those numbers, at a minimum. Self-inflicted violence is clearly a widespread phenomenon with far-reaching significance.

In discussing the prevalence of self-inflicted violence, it is important to take into account the secrecy and shame linked with these behaviors. Self-inflicted violence may be grossly underreported due to its clandestine nature. Many individuals who hurt themselves are reluctant to tell others for fear of being rejected, ostracized, physically confined, or simply misunderstood. Most SIV activities do not necessitate medical attention. In those situations where medical attention is needed, many individuals distort the cause of the injury, indicating accidental rather than intentional injury. Thus, accurate measurement of the prevalence of SIV is probably impossible. In short, estimated numbers of 1 to 2 million individuals engaging in self-injurious behaviors is likely to be a vast understatement of the actual prevalence of SIV.

SIV by Population

Because self-inflicted violence is often used as a method of coping, it would follow that there is a negative relationship between opportunities for typical coping and self-inflicted violence. This is to say that when fewer opportunities for more typical coping methods exist—crying, talking, exercising—the likelihood that someone would use SIV to cope would increase. Therefore, it makes some sense that certain environments would have a higher incidence of SIV than the general population. Environments that restrict an individual's freedom of expression are likely to foster self-inflicted violence.

Prisons are one such setting. There is a significantly higher frequency of self-inflicted violence in prison than in the general population, and a great number of prison inmates demonstrate SIV behavior, often cutting, burning, or hitting themselves.

In addition to its use as a coping mechanism, SIV is used by inmates to manipulate their environment or obtain some type of desired attention or reinforcement. Recently, I heard of a case in which a prisoner was going to be transferred from one prison to another one farther from his family and friends. This inmate didn't want to go to this new setting but was unable to prevent the transfer through appropriate channels, such as convincing prison staff that it would be in his best interest to remain where he was. On the morning of his transfer, guards found him sitting in a pool of his own blood. He had used a piece of broken mirror to repeatedly slash his arms. Because of his physical condition, the inmate could not be transferred to the new prison on that day and instead spent several days in the prison infirmary. Thus, in some environments SIV can effectively produce secondary gains as well as help with coping.

A high level of self-inflicted violence is also found in inpatient psychiatric settings. Contagion of SIV behaviors is a frequently reported problem in these institutions. *Contagion* refers to the spread of a particular behavior or activity throughout the environment. In other words, when one individual in an inpatient setting begins to practice SIV, others begin to mimic these behaviors. Often SIV behaviors in these settings produce desired secondary gains, such as increased personal attention, medication, or simply communication. Individuals observing these self-injurious behaviors are likely to notice some of its reinforcing qualities, which increases the likelihood that they too will engage in an act of SIV.

Higher-than-expected frequencies of SIV behaviors have also been noted in specific groups of individuals, including people with eating disorders and substance abuse difficulties and adults who were abused as children. The relationship of SIV with each of these groups is discussed in chapter 5.

SIV by Gender

Given the difficulty estimating the prevalence of self-inflicted violence, it is not surprising that gender differences for this behavior are equally in question. Some researchers believe that roughly equal numbers of men and women engage in SIV activities. In emergency departments of hospitals there appear to be no significant gender differences with regard to self-inflicted injuries. However, because the majority of individuals seeking psychotherapeutic treatment are women, and because much of what we know about any type of psychological disorder stems from that setting, women may be identified more often than men as engaging in SIV. Similarly, because men make up the majority of prison inmates, SIV is noted more for men than for women in these settings. It seems apparent that the setting in which the SIV behavior is identified plays a primary role in any observed gender differences. Overall, however, it appears as though men and women engage in self-injurious behaviors with similar frequency.

SIV and Psychotherapy

This section focuses on issues related to self-inflicted violence within the therapeutic process. While some individuals engaging in SIV activities may avoid entering into a psychotherapeutic relationship due to shame or fear (or finances), a large number of people who engage in SIV do seek psychotherapy to deal with these and related issues. It is important that therapists attempting to provide assistance be aware of their own limitations and that they educate themselves about SIV and particular therapeutic issues and techniques.

Although this section is designed to help clinicians explore and enhance their understanding of self-inflicted violence in a clinical context, clients may also benefit from reading this section and discussing these issues with their therapists.

Limitations of the Therapist

As a therapist, it is essential to understand your own limitations in dealing with SIV and related issues. The following sections explore several areas that can limit your effectiveness.

Lack of knowledge. Therapists are well trained in many areas, but self-inflicted violence is generally not one of them. While most therapists encounter clients who hurt themselves, few receive any formal training on this behavior. Moreover, although SIV is a relatively common phenomenon, the information available to therapists is limited both in quantity and usefulness. If you are a therapist, you may have read an article or two on SIV, but it is unlikely that you have attended a workshop or seminar on the subject. (One of the goals of this book is to provide an additional source of information on this topic that therapists and the general public will find useful and informative.)

One of the primary causes of therapists' lack of knowledge in this field is the secrecy surrounding self-inflicted violence. Most clients do not enter therapy for the purpose of dealing with SIV issues. Instead, they begin working on other areas, and only later, after establishing trust, reveal their self-injurious behaviors. Thus, because SIV is typically not a presenting issue, the prevalence of this behavior is underestimated. This view of SIV as an infrequent behavior or secondary issue can lead clinicians to believe that a great deal of knowledge in this area is unnecessary, but that belief would be grossly incorrect. It is essential that, if you are to treat clients who engage in SIV, you acquire as much knowledge and understanding of the phenomenon as possible.

Lack of awareness. Because of the lack of available material on self-inflicted violence and the secrecy associated with these behaviors, most therapists have a limited awareness of this issue. For example, it may not have occurred to you to consider whether clients were engaging in self-injurious activities until a client raised this issue and brought it to your attention.

When taking a client's history, you probably address specific topics, such as drug and alcohol use, history of trauma, and previous suicidal thoughts or behaviors. You probably don't ask about self-injurious behaviors.

By inquiring about these actions, you open the door for your clients who do injure themselves to admit or discuss this topic. Unless you raise the issue of SIV, your clients may be too shy, ashamed, embarrassed, or scared to bring up the topic themselves. Asking about SIV during an intake assessment will serve you well in all phases of treatment.

Lack of awareness of SIV can also cause you to miss important clues in subsequent stages of the therapeutic process. Often clients will come to therapy with bruises, scrapes, cuts, and other physical ailments. Unless you suspect that your client is being abused by another, such as a spouse or parent, it is likely that you will not inquire about the source of these injuries. Only after you notice a pattern of injury (in either frequency or location) will you be more apt to ask about the wounds. By being aware of the possibility of SIV, you can better attend to and help your clients.

To heighten your awareness about SIV, it may help to recall all the clients you have seen who have self-injured. How long did it take each of them after entering therapy to reveal this behavior? How did you learn that SIV was an issue? Was it related to their initial reasons for entering therapy? Were there signs of SIV, such as fresh wounds on a consistent basis or the wearing of concealing clothing? Did you ask your clients about SIV or did they tell you directly?

You have probably noticed that there is no one specific time or method by which SIV is revealed. By raising the issue of SIV in your initial interview with a client you will most likely find that the time it takes for your client to reveal SIV behaviors is shortened and the manner in which these behaviors are exposed becomes much more direct.

Your Feelings About SIV

Within the psychotherapeutic environment, feelings come in many forms and from many sources; they are shaped by past, current, and anticipated events. *Countertransference* refers to therapists' feelings toward and about their clients that stem from previous relationships that the current therapeutic relationship may mimic in some sense. These feelings are not based in the reality of the therapeutic relationship. For example, I might develop feelings of fondness for a client because she reminds me of my sister. That I feel fond for my client may have little to do with her actual personality. Rather, these feelings may have been transferred to my client from the positive feelings I have for my sister.

Not all feelings are based in countertransference, however. The therapeutic process also lends itself to production of emotions based in the reality of the present relationship between therapist and client. I could enjoy working with a client because she has a great sense of humor. Although my feelings for this client might be tied to past events (as anything can), I would probably not view this as countertransference.

Whether they stem from issues of countertransference or from the present dynamics of the actual psychotherapeutic relationship, learning of a client's self-injurious behavior is likely to produce strong emotions and reactions. I can clearly remember the first client I worked with who engaged in SIV. She was an adolescent I had been working with during a predoctoral internship.

Although I had been studying the area of self-injury for some time, seeing the fresh jagged wounds on her arms and legs had a major impact on me. I felt as if *I* had been wounded. I imagined the great amount of pain this girl must have felt in order to cut herself, and I felt quite sad. I wanted her to talk to me about the pain, to tell me about what she was going through when she hurt herself. I wanted her to promise she would never injure herself again. I wanted to make her stop. And, as commonly experienced in any therapeutic relationship, what I wanted and what the client wanted were two different things. She continued to injure herself. I continued to want her to stop. Eventually, I became discouraged and frustrated because she wouldn't do what I wanted.

Treating this adolescent was admittedly not one of my finer therapeutic moments. I had great difficulty keeping my own feelings and desires out of the therapy. Fortunately, I had excellent supervision and was able to recognize my own limitations and refer this girl to another therapist. And, although this case did not go exactly as I had hoped, I did learn a great deal from the experience. One of the things that became obvious to me was the effect self-inflicted violence can have upon the therapist. (I also learned the great value of supervision and referral sources.)

It is extremely important to recognize how strongly you can be affected by the experiences of your clients. It may be useful for you to review your own earlier experiences with self-injuring clients, in particular your reactions and responses to your clients. Some questions to consider are:

- What were your first reactions? What went though your mind? What did you feel emotionally and physically? What did you do?

- How did your reactions affect your client? Do you even think that the client was aware of your reactions?

- How did you respond to the client? What did you say or do? Did you talk about SIV? Did you ignore this revelation? Did you hospitalize your client? Did you express concern or empathy?

- In retrospect, do you think your responses were appropriate and/or effective? How would you change your responses? What would you have done differently?

- In what ways have your reactions and responses to your self-injurious clients changed since that time?

Self-inflicted violence can affect clinicians very strongly, in part because of the lack of exposure and training in the area of self-injury. SIV can also affect therapists quite intensely because of its style of presence—the real, tangible and observable wounds. Most of the behaviors of your clients do not produce observable results. You know your clients use drugs, yet you are unlikely to see them under the influence. You are not able to observe the effects of the drugs, although you may be able to see the long-term effects on the brain. You deal with clients with gambling problems and know they are suffering financially, yet you do not actually see the results (unless they can't pay for a session). Your clients who engage in acts of SIV present you with concrete evidence of their pain. You can see the scars and wounds they inflict on themselves. Your clients, through SIV, bring you into their inner experience. Being confronted with the intensity of your client's suffering is likely to produce strong reactions.

Empathy.   You may feel a great deal of empathy for your self-injurious clients, recognizing and understanding the intense inner turmoil that leads to SIV. While empathy is a useful response, it also has the potential to create a barrier to good and effective therapy: Too much empathy and you may lose your objectivity and become overinvested in your client's progress. You may find yourself trying to solve the client's problems and ease his or her suffering instead of helping the client to solve his or her own problems. The therapist's ability to empathize with a client is essential; you must be able to understand and relate to the experiences of your clients. However, you also need to maintain your professional role and distance and use your empathic experiences effectively.

You also will need to distinguish between empathy (emotionally understanding and relating to your client's situation) and sympathy (feeling bad for your clients). When you respond to your clients with sympathy, you are viewing them pessimisticly and you may be underestimating their potential. Sympathy assumes that a negative event, situation, or emotional state exists. However, the sympathy you experience as a therapist is your own reaction. It may not correspond to the client's experience at all.

Imagine the following scenario: During a session, a client rolls up his pant leg to expose several new burns made from a lit cigarette. He tells you that he burned himself last night after being dumped by his girlfriend of six months. You might react with sympathy, thinking that the loss of his girlfriend is a horrible thing and feeling sad for his inability to deal with the world in a more typical way, instead of burning himself. If you express this to him, either overtly or covertly, he is likely to see himself as being wounded, and possibly as abnormal. However, if you allow him to express his perception of these events, you might learn that he feels proud to have coped with this event without doing anything worse than giving himself a few small burns. By understanding his perspective, you are able to feel empathic. By forcing your sympathetic perspective on him, you restrict his ability to express his own emotions and thoughts surrounding this event.

To gain a better understanding of SIV and your clients' experiences, try an experiment. Spend one full day with red streaks drawn on your arms. Try to make the streaks look like self-inflicted cuts. Or, if you prefer to appear bruised or burned instead, feel free to color yourself creatively. (Be sure to use nontoxic paint or markers.) Then observe your own reactions and the reactions of others. You might want to keep a small notebook handy so you can jot down your experiences. At the end of the day, write about your experiences in detail. Did you try to cover the marks after a while? How did people respond to you? What were you aware of thinking or doing? What emotions did you experience? Did you feel any different physically because of these markings? How did you change your behaviors? Did you actually last an entire day with these false wounds? Did you gain a better understanding of what your clients have to deal with on a daily basis?

Disgust. On some level, you will probably react to your clients' wounds with disgust. The mere thought of blood may result in a feeling of nausea or squeamishness. When I go to horror movies, I frequently watch the audience during the violent scenes. (This is a great excuse for averting my attention from the screen.) A great number of people are peeking at the screen from behind their hands. Some slump in their seats or utter noises of disgust. Some even leave the theater. Disgust is a normal, innate reaction to particular types of experiences. Seeing your clients' injuries may produce feelings of disgust simply because of the condition of the wound.

Although this feeling might be normal and adaptive in some ways, it will not serve your clients well if you let your feelings overwhelm you. You can walk out of a movie without any serious repercussions, but you cannot walk out on your client without the possibility of inflicting psychological damage. Thus, it is extremely important that you learn your own level of tolerance for viewing injuries. Once you know how you might react to seeing the damaged flesh of a client, you can decide whether it is in the client's best interest to begin a psychotherapeutic relationship with you (another reason SIV should be addressed during an intake assessment as opposed to later in the therapeutic process).

There are a number of ways to desensitize yourself to the sight of the wounds, or at least to assess how you are likely to react to seeing the newly inflicted wounds of a client, among them:

- Watch a surgical operation being performed (in addition to surgeries occurring within hospital settings, many cable companies have stations which regularly air television shows such as these).

- Visit the burn unit of a local hospital.

- Watch a movie or video that contains graphic violence and/or surgical procedures.

- Have each of your friends tell you of a particularly painful or serious injury sustained.

After one of these activities, record your initial responses and reactions. Be as detailed as you can. What did you feel emotionally and physically? What did you do? What thoughts went through your mind? Then complete the activity at least four more times. And, again, write about your reactions. You will find that continued exposure to experiences such as these will make you feel less uncomfortable or disgusted by self-inflicted violence. Your ability to be comfortable discussing and observing the results of SIV is invaluable to your clients.

Frustration and control. Frustration is another emotion commonly experienced by therapists who work with clients who injure themselves. Working with these individuals can be trying at times, and you may find yourself feeling frustrated because a client just won't stop self-injuring. You cannot make anyone do anything, and cannot make your clients stop injuring themselves—nor can you make them want to stop injuring themselves. All that you can do is provide an atmosphere in which change is possible. While this may seem like a very basic idea in therapy, it's amazing how easily and quickly we can forget this.

Control is an essential component in our lives. We like to view the world as predictable and malleable. When we think we do not have control, we tend to feel helpless, hopeless, angry, or frustrated. As much as we may try to leave this need for control outside the psychotherapeutic realm, we can only do so with limited success.

Most of us don't realize the extent to which we do control what occurs within the therapeutic session, regardless of our chosen psychotherapeutic orientation—humanistic, self-psychology, psychodynamic. For instance, we determine where the sessions will be held. (Have you ever said to a client, Your place or mine?) We decide when the sessions will be held. We control the length of the session (the fifty-minute "hour"). We even control things like who sits in which seat in the office, where clients are allowed to park their cars, and whether the clients are permitted to bring food, drinks, pets, gifts, or small appliances into the session. With all the control we already exert, it is only natural to want to control the client's goals and progress.

Although control is necessary and helpful in many ways, if we try to control the course of the client's therapy we will often be disappointed. This disappointment manifests itself in frustration. We may become frustrated with ourselves for our own shortcomings in helping our clients, and we may also become frustrated with our clients for not progressing in the ways or as quickly as we desire.

Because self-inflicted violence is such a difficult behavior to extinguish, and because clients often do not wish to rid themselves of this behavior (remember, it does serve many functions), you are likely to find yourself dealing with your own frustration. It is important that you find ways of doing so that do not harm your clients.

These feelings of frustration may appear in many forms, in subtle or obvious ways. Subtle clues of frustration become evident in your thoughts or feelings about the client. You may have negative thoughts about your client. You may find yourself being grouchy before a session with this client.

You may catch yourself hoping that the client will call and cancel the session. You may realize that you are having difficulty concentrating or focusing on the client during the session. While these subtle forms of frustration may not interfere with the client's treatment or progress, it is important to recognize their occurrence before they become more severe and more harmful.

Sometimes frustration will take a more obvious and intrusive form. When your clients continue to hurt themselves no matter what you do, it is only natural to become frustrated. However, it does not serve your client for you to act out of this frustration. Threatening clients with hospitalization in order to stop their self-injurious behaviors is one example of how your own frustration may manifest itself. Informing clients that you will terminate therapy unless they stop injuring themselves is another demonstration of your own feelings and desires. Sometimes therapists who are frustrated with their SIV clients will simply get angry with the clients about this behavior. Occasionally, therapists will refuse to listen to SIV-related stories or issues. Learning to recognize and manage your level of frustration will help you to avoid acting in similar ways.

The first step is to acknowledge the ways you experience or express your frustrations when working with these clients. The following is a partial list; your experiences may differ:

- Consistently beginning your session late

- Dreading seeing client

- Feeling tired before seeing client

- Double-booking client

- Feeling grouchy or angry before session

- Forgetting a scheduled session

- Having difficulty concentrating in session

- Hoping that client will cancel the session

- Frequently arguing with client

- Thinking negative thoughts about client

- Frequently scolding client

- Making judgmental statements to client

- Refusing to work with client

- Forcing client to promise not to injure herself or himself

- Forcing client to sign a no-SIV contract

- Threatening hospitalization

- Refusing to listen to SIV-related issues

- Raising fees of client

When you recognize signs of frustration in your dealings with a client, you need to create a plan for dealing with your emotions. Write down your plan so you can refer to it later when you actually need it. How will you cope with your feelings? How will you release your frustration in ways that will not affect your client? You may want to look at Activity 2.3, "Exploring My Coping Techniques," for some ideas.

As a therapist, it is essential that you not fall victim to your own unfiltered emotions. This is not to say that you shouldn't have feelings, but rather that you need to be able to recognize and control your emotions in order to use them more productively. You can always use your reactions and emotions to influence therapeutic discussions. The relationship which you have with your client is a real relationship—albeit very different from many other types of relationships. If you feel disgusted, frustrated, helpless, hopeless, or sad, chances are your client has also experienced these emotions. Many of your client's friends or family may also respond in these ways, which can help you use your feelings as a therapeutic tool. The following very brief excerpt from a session may help illustrate this point.

Client: I cut myself again last night. (*Client pulls up the sleeve of her shirt to reveal three fresh wounds on her forearm.*) I can't believe I did this to myself again.

Therapist (feeling frustrated by the client's continued self-injurious behaviors): I wonder if you're feeling frustrated about this.

Client: Yeah, it's like I really want to stop, but something happens and I just can't. God, it's driving me crazy!

By using your own feelings to guide your responses to the client, you demonstrate empathy and understanding. Your awareness of your own emotions can help you become more aware of clients' inner experiences. In this way, recognizing and acting on your feelings can be quite helpful.

Fear and overreaction. Most of our emotions serve a valid function within our lives, and fear is no exception. Fear is a response to perceived danger, and helps us react in ways that keep us safe. However, we can also overreact to situations because of our own fear, which can have effects far more damaging than those of the originally feared situation.

The following story may help demonstrate this point. Late one cold February afternoon in central New York state, I was driving home on country roads content and tired, after a long day of skiing. At sixteen, I had had my driver's license for just seven weeks. The Rolling Stones were blaring from the radio, insisting that you can't always get what you want, and the defroster was on full blast, battling the icy film on the windshield. Suddenly, my car seemed to be gliding just a bit more smoothly than I expected.

The stretch of road I was driving—or skidding—on was pure ice. Remembering my driver's education training films (or so I thought), I quickly jerked the steering wheel to the left while slamming on the brakes—creating my own private Tilt-A-Whirl on ice. After several circles at what felt like pretty high speed, the car eventually stopped, facing the wrong direction. I stepped out unharmed but shaken and humiliated. Later, when I related this story to my parents, they told me that had I simply kept the wheels aligned in the direction of the skid and continued without braking, I would have reached the other side of the icy section safely and without incident. Instead, my overreaction had nearly caused an accident.

Obviously, the point here is not driving tips for severe weather but is that fear can lead to dangerous overreactions. In dealing with clients who hurt themselves, you will probably feel fear. You might fear for their safety—that they will hurt themselves more than they intend. You might fear for your own safety—that self-inflicted violence is related to violence toward others. You might fear the intensity of emotions that lead to self-injurious behaviors. You might fear your potential ineffectiveness in treating this activity. You might even fear legal and ethical issues that could arise from working with a client who engages in SIV. For whatever reason, your clients' self-injurious behaviors will probably make you wary, and you are likely to overreact to the fear.

As in my driving incident, the ways we overreact to our clients' behaviors can be potentially damaging. Hospitalizing clients for self-inflicted violence is one such form of overreaction. Many therapists, because they do not possess an adequate understanding of SIV, will use extreme measures to assure (they think) their clients' best interests. However, few people who self-injure need to be hospitalized or institutionalized. The vast majority of self-inflicted wounds are neither life threatening nor require medical treatment. Hospitalizing a client involuntarily for these issues can be damaging in several ways. Because SIV is closely related to feelings of lack of control and overwhelming emotional states, placing someone in a setting that by its nature evokes these feelings is very likely to make matters worse, and may lead to an incident of SIV. In addition, involuntary hospitalization often affects the therapeutic relationship in negative ways, eroding trust, communication, rapport, and honesty.

Caution should be used when assessing a client's level of threat to self or others. In most cases, SIV is not life threatening. Far more individuals are treated in the emergency rooms of hospitals for substance-related problems than for injuries stemming from self-inflicted violence. However, you would not usually recommend involuntary inpatient treatment for clients using drugs. Because SIV is so misunderstood, clinicians often overreact and provide treatment that is contraindicated.

It might be useful to come up with a list of ways to deal with clients' self-injurious behaviors to have on hand when the need for them arises. This way, your first, possibly overreactive response won't be your only option.

Begin by listing every possibility you can think of, without censoring yourself. Include hospitalization, refusal to treat, no-SIV contract, but strive to think of alternatives, such as medication and extra sessions. When you've thought of as many alternatives as you can for the time being, go back over the list and mark with a Ø symbol those options that in most cases are likely to be an overreaction. Mark with a star or a plus sign the alternatives that seem especially promising and worth trying. Keep the list handy, and continue to add to it any new ideas you have for treating your self-injuring clients.

Fear, frustration, and disgust are the main emotional reactions to working with issues of SIV. It is important for you to monitor your own emotions and handle these feelings appropriately. As clinicians, we are always concerned with the welfare of our clients. Because SIV tends to elicit such strong emotions, we need to guard against allowing our own responses to interfere with the treatment of our clients.

Specific Psychotherapeutic Issues

This section is designed to help you explore and understand many of the common issues you are likely to encounter when working with clients who hurt themselves. While these issues are not specific to SIV clients (resistance, boundaries, and ethics apply in all psychotherapeutic settings), some of the implications and dynamics of these issues are unique to self-injury. This section will address the ways that resistance, boundaries, and ethical concerns may appear within the context of self-inflicted violence.

Resistance

When a client does not adhere to the prescribed course of psychotherapy treatment or does not act in ways consistent with the recommended treatment, we call it *resistance*. With self-inflicted violence, clients may demonstrate resistance in a number of ways, including concealing self-injurious behaviors, refusal to address issues of SIV, or being unwilling to decrease or alter the course of SIV.

Resistance generally stems from one of two sources. The first source is related to the client's fear. Change is difficult and frightening for most people, and the issues dealt with in psychotherapy often require alterations in fundamental patterns of thought and behavior. Change on such a deep level will often be met with apprehension, anxiety, or hesitancy. Clients may reject the treatment you suggest because of these feelings. Working through these fears and apprehensions is a way to conquer resistance.

You may find that your clients are particularly resistant to changing their patterns of self-injury. Again, this may stem from their fear of change. It is important to remember that SIV serves many functions for your clients; it can be a method of coping, a way to relieve tension, a means to control dissociation, and a form of communication, among other things. Your clients are going to be afraid to eliminate a behavior that is so important and powerful.

Say you use exercise as a way of coping with stress, and then someone tells you that you can never exercise again and asks you to discard your Stairmaster. In response, you might suggest that this person take up bungee jumping—sans bungee—but you wouldn't stop your workouts.

Now imagine the same situation, but before asking you to retire your sweatsuit, the person shows you a great new way to handle stress. You try this new method a few times, and you become convinced of its effectiveness. Now when asked to stop exercising and use this new method to deal with your stress you would be far more likely to do so (or taper off) because you now have a new behavior that serves the same purpose.

As a therapist, you have a duty to try to help your clients find alternatives to SIV before asking them to stop hurting themselves. Resistance stems from fear. Once your clients have tried other ways to cope and found them effective, they will be less frightened and less resistant to giving up old behaviors.

Clients may also be resistant to treatment that does not suit their needs. Your client may not want to eliminate or reduce self-injurious behavior. By suggesting that he or she do so, you may be placing your desires ahead of your client's.

Several years ago I went to a physician because I was having bad stomach aches and nausea. The doctor looked in my throat and informed me that I might have strep throat and that was the source of my complaints. I gave her a puzzled look and mentioned that it was my stomach and not my throat that hurt. She wrote out a prescription for an antibiotic and reasserted that it was indeed my throat that hurt and that I had strep throat. I am the first to admit my ignorance of medicine, but I do know the difference between my stomach and my throat. My throat did not hurt. I felt as though I had received medical treatment that did not suit my needs, and I threw away the prescription. You could say that I was resistant to the prescribed treatment. However, seeking a second opinion yielded a much more accurate diagnosis.

As therapists, it is easy for us to fall into a mindset of thinking we know what is best for our clients. With our objectivity and training, sometimes we do know what is best for them, but not always. Resistance can be an indication that we are not meeting the client's needs. We may be basing our treatments on our own desires or experiences without considering those of the client. Thus, resistance can be helpful, in that it signals to us that our treatment may not be appropriate for the client at that moment.

While there are many ways to deal with resistance, the direct approach allows you to more fully understand the dynamics of the situation. Questioning clients about their apparent resistance generally gives you a better sense of the source of this problem. You may find that the client simply fears change and changing behaviors. When this is the case, it is best to use techniques designed to reduce fear and explore perceptions of how changing SIV behaviors might influence other areas of the client's life. These techniques will allow you and your client to better understand the cognitive and emotional dynamics relating to self-injury. Through inquiry about possible resistance, you may also discover that your goals are significantly different from your client's. If this is the case, reassessment and clarification of therapeutic goals are necessary.

Boundaries

Formation and maintenance of appropriate boundaries is a necessity for clinicians working with any type of population. Boundaries become particularly important when you are working with clients who injure themselves. Regardless of psychological diagnosis, issues of boundaries will come up more frequently when dealing with these individuals than with people who do not injure themselves. Because clients who hurt themselves are generally very secretive about their self-injurious behaviors, in many cases, you may be the only person who your client has told about the SIV. Thus, you could easily become the client's sole source of support around these activities and be called upon frequently for support, guidance, or assistance. These greater demands on your attention will no doubt raise boundary issues.

It is important for both your peace of mind and the welfare of the client to be clear and consistent regarding your boundaries. Informing the client about your availability (and unavailability) is essential. If you do not answer pages or telephone calls after 10:00 p.m., tell the client this and offer some suggestions for other places he or she can get assistance. If you do not work on weekends, let the client know this in advance, before any emergency arises. If you charge for the time you spend on the telephone with clients, again, inform the client of this before the situation occurs.

It may be useful to make a checklist of the boundaries you have established, and be sure you directly express each of these boundaries with each of your clients, either verbally or in writing. You may also want to keep track of how often you make exceptions for a client in regard to one or more boundaries.

Directly expressing your boundaries to your clients will help avoid confusion should a client begin to test these boundaries. Keeping track of exceptions you have made can help you head off potential problems. For instance, you may see that there are areas you really haven't addressed specifically. Once you are aware of them, you may choose to speak with your clients about these particular issues.

Whatever your boundaries are, be consistent with them. Clients will be confused if you are not, and will not know what to expect from you. For example, say you receive a page from a client at eleven o'clock on a Friday night. You're awake, so you decide to return the call, although you typically do not return calls at this hour. You and your client talk for twenty minutes, and you help her through the crisis at hand which is all well and good. But your client may now believe that you will always be available if she calls at that hour, so the next night she decides to test this theory and you receive a page. You cannot blame your client for pushing your boundaries, as you previously compromised them. When your boundaries are inconsistent or changeable they might as well not exist.

The importance of the role you play in the lives of your self-injurious clients makes it even more essential that you establish and maintain clear and ethical boundaries. You are not required to meet all the needs of each of your clients; however, you should inform your clients of what they can expect from you in terms of your services, support, and availability.

Ethical Issues

Whenever the welfare of our clients is at stake, we must raise questions of ethics. While each licensing agency has its own set of ethical standards, practices, rules, and laws, most postulate that as clinicians we are bound to act in ways that support the welfare of our clients. When our clients are intentionally injuring themselves, and they find this behavior to be helpful, we are left with a great deal of confusion with regard to ethical issues.

Unfortunately, there is no clear-cut ethical standard for dealing with issues of self-inflicted violence. How we choose to treat this issue will be based on our own perception of the risk-benefit ratio. In other words, do the risks of our actions surpass the benefits that may derive from these actions? For instance, if I determine that a client's frequency or severity of self-injury is endangering her welfare, I may decide that hospitalization is necessary. However, in proceeding with hospitalization, I will most likely have to break confidentiality, which may damage the client's level of trust. Also, by placing this client in an inpatient setting, I am decreasing her control, choice, and sense of autonomy and increasing her feelings of alienation, shame, and isolation—all of which could lead to an increase in SIV. As you can see, the benefits of this action may or may not outweigh the possible risks, and the best course of action is difficult to determine.

Whenever you are confronted with issues of SIV, it may be useful for you to consider a series of questions in deciding whether to take action and, if so, what action to take:

- What is the ethical issue?

- What are the laws, rules, or codes governing this issue? (Your answers to this question will vary based upon your license and the state where you work.)

- Are you mandated by law to take any action, such as in cases of suspected child abuse?

- What are your options?

- What are the benefits of each option?
- What are the risks of each option?
- What information do you need to make this decision?
- What is the probable effect of this decision on clinical matters?
- How will you go about implementing this decision?
- How do you think the client will respond to this decision?

Typically, injuries inflicted through SIV are not life threatening. Most often, these injuries do not even require professional medical attention. However, without a clear understanding of self-inflicted violence and its functions, it would be easy to jump to an erroneous conclusion and assume that our clients were at great risk. Thus, the best way to protect the welfare of our clients is to be knowledgeable and stay informed about issues of SIV. There may be times when we have to take extreme actions to protect the well-being of a client. Nevertheless, only through education will we be able to differentiate these times from others.

Therapeutic Strategies

Many specific techniques that are useful in the therapeutic setting are presented in chapter 7, which focuses on the treatment of self-inflicted violence. This section discusses some general strategies that are often employed in the therapeutic setting.

Rapport

For therapy to be effective, rapport must be established. Rapport involves building a relationship with the client, generally one of trust, respect, and some degree of affinity. There are many ways to establish rapport, and you undoubtedly have your own distinct style. Yet there are some basic ingredients for fostering rapport in a therapeutic relationship. First, being attentive is a necessary component of rapport. Your clients need to know that you are listening to them and will know this by your responses to what they present.

In addition, being able to attend to your clients in a nonjudgmental manner is extremely important when dealing with issues of self-inflicted violence. For instance, you wouldn't want to respond to a client's telling you about an incident of self-injury by showing your disgust and making statements such as "That's gross!" or "You're nuts!" As mentioned earlier, you may think or feel these things, but it is important that you don't share these thoughts or emotions with your clients.

The ability to stay connected with a client is also an essential component of rapport. This is even more true when treating clients who hurt themselves. Often their experience of lack of connection influences their desire to injure themselves, and although it may sometimes be difficult to listen to clients describe the trauma they have endured (whether self-inflicted or perpetrated by another), it is necessary that you do so. In some respects, you become your client's anchor to reality and sanity. Your ability to connect with your client and remain present during difficult moments will greatly influence his or her therapeutic progress.

Contracts

Contracts in the therapeutic arena may be written or verbal agreements made between a therapist and a client. Typically, contracts are used as a way of decreasing the likelihood that a client will engage in a dangerous or detrimental behavior. Generally the contracts stipulate that the client will perform some action (such as calling the therapist) before engaging in the detrimental activity.

With clients who engage in SIV, contracts are generally not recommended (of course, there are always exceptions). As discussed, because SIV is not normally life threatening and because it serves an important role in coping, it would be unwise to request that the client simply stop this behavior. Contracts in which clients pledge not to hurt themselves tend to produce negative therapeutic effects. They may feel a lack of control or choice within the therapeutic setting if you require them to agree to a contract such as this, and this lack of control will increase the likelihood of self-injurious behaviors as well as foster shame and dishonesty within the therapeutic alliance. In sum, contracts are generally made to meet the needs or fears of the therapist, rather than the client.

Nonetheless, a contract can be useful, provided the agreement specifies a proactive behavior rather than just the nonuse of self-injury. For example, a contract could stipulate that the client call at least one person before self-injuring. This agreement does not take away any of the client's choices regarding SIV; rather it presents a behavior that would, hopefully, decrease the likelihood of an SIV episode.

The following is an example of a contract that could be used in the therapeutic setting.

I, ____*client's name*____ , agree to contact at least one person before I go through with hurting myself. This person need not be ____*therapist's name*____ ; however I may contact ___*her/him*___ if I desire. This contract will be effective for a period of ___*one week*___ , beginning on the date indicated at the bottom of this page.

____*client's signature*____   _____*date*_____

____*therapist's signature*____   _____*date*_____

As you can see, this contract does not demand the cessation of SIV behaviors. Rather, it specifies the inclusion of behaviors that lessen the likelihood of self-injury.

Paradox

Like contracts, the use of paradox with self-injurious clients is not recommended. *Paradox* means prescribing a treatment that is in opposition to the desired outcome. For example, one of the more common uses of paradox occurred in an episode of *The Brady Bunch*. Bobby, the youngest son, was planning on running away. Instead of trying to convince Bobby not to run away, Mike, his father, helped him to pack his suitcase. Mike was using an intervention that seemed to oppose the desired goal. And, like most interventions within that television series, it worked. Bobby decided that he would not run away from home.

Although paradox can be an effective technique in therapy, as in television shows, it presents a certain degree of danger when used with self-injurious clients. Using paradox might encourage clients to dramatically increase the frequency or severity of their injuries. Personally, I would never advise a client to increase the frequency of self-injury. This is not to say that paradox would never work as a therapeutic technique. However, to my mind, the risks outweigh the potential benefits.

Medication

The role of medication in treatment of self-injurious behaviors continues to be a source of some speculation. Due to the scarcity of quality research on SIV and its treatment, the effectiveness of medication has not been adequately determined. However, it appears that medication for treatment of self-injurious behaviors is limited in its usefulness.

Medication may be of use with clients who exhibit obsessive or compulsive symptoms. Some medications can decrease obsessional styles of thought, and consequently decrease the compulsive behaviors (including SIV). For others, however, medication may cause an increase in feelings of loss of control. Remember that SIV is frequently used as a method of gaining control. Therefore, for these clients medication that decreases a sense of control may serve to increase the frequency of self-injurious behaviors.

Additionally, medication, a psychoactive substance, may not be appropriate for clients with substance-abuse issues. Many clients who are in recovery from the abuse of substances are likely to refuse to take nonessential medications. Many medications also have side effects or addicting qualities that would deter some clients from adherence to the recommended treatment.

On the other hand, for some clients medication does have the positive effect of helping them feel nurtured. Medical treatment symbolizes special attention or treatment of the client's symptoms. Some clients may be more likely to adhere to recommended treatment and remain in therapy when they believe they are receiving additional care. However, it is important to note that it is not necessarily the medication itself that is beneficial to treatment. Rather, it is the perception of being cared for and viewed as special that positively influences the treatment of self-inflicted injuries. I would like to think that, as clinicians, we would be able to make our clients feel supported, cared for, and unique without the use of pharmaceutical intervention.

Treating the Problem, Not the Symptom

As mentioned previously, most clients do not enter therapy for reasons of self-injury. Rather, most enter psychotherapy to work on the emotional reactions to issues related to self-injury—trauma, abuse, stress, and so on. Self-injury is typically a symptom of a more serious or deeply rooted problem, and finding ways to help your clients work though and resolve those issues needs to be a primary goal of the therapy. Exploring issues of abuse and trauma, helping your client form a more definitive and rich sense of self, teaching skills in assertion, independence, and autonomy may all be long-term goals of therapy. You will find that as you progress toward your distant therapeutic goals, your clients will no longer need to use self-inflicted violence as a method of coping, communicating, or managing their lives. Instead, they will be able to use skills that are more effective and less detrimental, such as expressing their emotions directly.

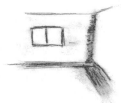

References

Chapter1 — What Is Self-Inflicted Violence?

Conn, L., and J. Lion. 1983. Self-mutilation: A review. *Psychiatric Medicine* 1:21–33.

Conners, R. 1996. Self-injury in trauma survivors: 1. Functions and meanings. *American Journal of Orthopsychiatry* 66:197–206.

Dycian, A., G. Fishman, and A. Bleich. 1994. Suicide and self-inflicted injuries. *Aggressive Behavior* 20:9–16.

Favazza, A. R. 1987. *Bodies Under Siege: Self-Mutilation in Culture and Psychiatry*. Baltimore: Johns Hopkins University Press.

Favazza, A. R., and K. Conterio. 1989. Female habitual self-mutilators. *Acta Psychiatrica Scandinavica* 79:283–289.

Favazza, A. R., and K. Conterio. 1988. The plight of chronic self-mutilators. *Community Mental Health Journal* 24, no. 1: 22–30.

Favazza, A. R., L. DeRosear, and K. Conterio. 1989. Self-mutilation and eating disorders. *Suicide and Life-Threatening Behavior* 19, no. 4: 352–361.

Favazza, A. R., and R. Rosenthal. 1993. Diagnostic issues in self-mutilation. *Hospital and Community Psychiatry* 44, no. 2: 134–140.

Figueroa, M. 1988. A dynamic taxonomy of self-destructive behavior. *Psychotherapy* 25, no. 2: 280–287.

Haines, J., C. Williams, K. Brain, and G. Wilson. 1995. The psychophysiology of self-mutilation. *Journal of Abnormal Psychology* 104, no. 3: 471–489.

Hawton, K. 1990. "Self-Cutting: Can It Be Prevented?" In *Dilemmas and Difficulties in the Management of Psychiatric Patients*, K. Hawton and P. Cowen eds. Oxford, England: Oxford University Press.

Hillbrand, M., J. Krystal, K. Sharpe, and H. Foster. 1994. Clinical predictors of self-mutilation in hospitalized forensic patients. *Journal of Nervous and Mental Disease* 182, no. 1: 9–13.

Langbehn, D., and B. Pfohl. 1993. Clinical correlates of self-mutilation among psychiatric inpatients. *Annals of Clinical Psychiatry* 5, no. 1: 45–51.

Mazelis, R. (ed.). 1990—1997. *The Cutting Edge: A Newsletter for Women Living with Self-Inflicted Violence.* (Available from The Cutting Edge, P.O. Box 20819, Cleveland, Ohio 44120.)

Menninger, K. 1935. A psychoanalytic study of the significance of self-mutilation. *Psychoanalytic Quarterly* 4:408–466.

Miller, D. 1994. *Women Who Hurt Themselves.* New York: Basic Books.

Morgan, H., C. Burns-Cox, H. Pocock, and S. Pottle. 1975. Deliberate self-harm: Clinical and socioeconomic characteristics of 368 patients. *British Journal of Psychiatry* 127:564–574.

Novotny, P. 1972. Self-cutting. *Bulletin of the Menninger Clinic* 36:505–514.

Ross, R. R., and H. B. McKay. 1979. *Self-mutilation.* Lexington, Mass: Lexington Books.

Trautmann, K., and R. Conners. 1994. *Understanding Self-Injury: A Workbook for Adults.* Pittsburgh: Pittsburgh Action Against Rape.

Vela, J., J. Harris, J. K. Wright, et al. 1983. Self-mutilation. *Journal of Trauma* 23:165–167.

Walsh, B., and P. Rosen. 1988. *Self-Mutilation: Theory, Research and Practice.* New York: Guilford Press.

Winchel, R., and M. Stanley. 1991. Self-injurious behavior: A review of the behavior and biology of self-mutilation. *American Journal of Psychiatry* 148:306–317.

Chapter 2—Why Do People Engage in Self-Inflicted Violence?

Conn, L., and J. Lion. 1983. Self-mutilation: A review. *Psychiatric Medicine* 1:21–33.

Conners, R. 1996. Self-injury in trauma survivors: 1. Functions and meanings. *American Journal of Orthopsychiatry* 66:197–206.

Conners, R. 1996. Self-injury in trauma survivors: 2. Levels of clinical response. *American Journal of Orthopsychiatry* 66:207–216.

Coons, P., and V. Milstein. 1990. Self-mutilation associated with dissociative disorders. *Dissociation 3*, no. 2: 81–87.

deYoung, M. 1982. Self-injurious behavior in incest victims: A research note. *Child Welfare* 61:577–584.

Favazza, A. R. 1987. *Bodies Under Siege: Self-Mutilation in Culture and Psychiatry*. Baltimore: Johns Hopkins University Press.

Favazza, A. R. 1989. Why patients mutilate themselves. *Hospital Community Psychiatry* 40:137–145.

Favazza, A. R., and K. Conterio. 1989. Female habitual self-mutilators. *Acta Psychiatrica Scandinavica* 79:283–289.

Favazza, A. R., and K. Conterio. 1988. The plight of chronic self-mutilators. *Community Mental Health Journal* 24, no. 1: 22–30.

Favazza, A. R., and R. Rosenthal. 1993. Diagnostic issues in self-mutilation. *Hospital and Community Psychiatry* 44, no. 2: 134–140.

Haines, J., C. Williams, K. Brain, and G. Wilson. 1995. The psychophysiology of self-mutilation. *Journal of Abnormal Psychology* 104, no. 3: 471–489.

Hawton, K. 1990. "Self-Cutting: Can It Be Prevented?" In *Dilemmas and Difficulties in the Management of Psychiatric Patients*, K. Hawton and P. Cowen eds. Oxford, England: Oxford University Press.

Mazelis, R. (ed.) 1990–1997. *The Cutting Edge: A Newsletter for Women Living with Self-Inflicted Violence*. (Available from The Cutting Edge, P.O. Box 20819, Cleveland, Ohio 44120.)

Miller, D. 1994. *Women Who Hurt Themselves*. New York: Basic Books.

Rosenthal, R. J., C. Rinzler, R. Walsh, and E. Klausner. 1972. Wrist-cutting syndrome: The meaning of a gesture. *American Journal of Psychiatry* 128:1363–1368.

Ross, R. R., and H. B. McKay. 1979. *Self-mutilation*. Lexington, Mass: Lexington Books.

Stone, M. 1987. A psychodynamic approach: Some thoughts on the dynamics and therapy of self-mutilating borderline patients. *Journal of Personality Disorders* 1, no. 4: 347–349.

Trautmann, K., and R. Conners. 1994. *Understanding Self-Injury: A Workbook for Adults*. Pittsburgh: Pittsburgh Action Against Rape.

Van Moffaert, M. 1989. Management of self-mutilation: Confrontation and integration of psychotherapy and psychotropic drug treatment. *Psychotherapy and Psychosomatics* 51:180–186.

Vela, J., J. Harris, J. K. Wright, et al. 1983. Self-mutilation. *Journal of Trauma* 23:165–167.

Walsh, B., and P. Rosen. 1988. *Self-Mutilation: Theory, Research and Practice.* New York: Guilford Press.

Winchel, R., and M. Stanley. 1991. Self-injurious behavior: A review of the behavior and biology of self-mutilation. *American Journal of Psychiatry* 148:306–317.

Chapter 3 — The Nature of Self-Inflicted Violence

Conners, R. 1996. Self-injury in trauma survivors: 1. Functions and meanings. *American Journal of Orthopsychiatry* 66:197–206.

Conners, R. 1996. Self-injury in trauma survivors: 2. Levels of clinical response. *American Journal of Orthopsychiatry* 66:207–216.

Favazza, A. R. 1987. *Bodies Under Siege: Self-Mutilation in Culture and Psychiatry.* Baltimore: Johns Hopkins University Press.

Favazza, A. R., and K. Conterio. 1989. Female habitual self-mutilators. *Acta Psychiatrica Scandinavica* 79:283–289.

Favazza, A. R., and K. Conterio. 1988. The plight of chronic self-mutilators. *Community Mental Health Journal* 24, no. 1: 22–30.

Favazza, A. R., and D. Simeon. 1995. "Self-Mutilation." In *Impulsivity and Aggression*, eds. E. Hollander and D. J. Stein. New York: John Wiley & Sons.

Feldman, M. 1989. The challenge of self-mutilation: A review. *Acta Psychiatrica Scandinavica* 79, no. 3: 283–289.

Figueroa, M. 1988. A dynamic taxonomy of self-destructive behavior. *Psychotherapy* 25, no. 2: 280–287.

Hawton, K. 1990. "Self-Cutting: Can It Be Prevented?" In *Dilemmas and Difficulties in the Management of Psychiatric Patients*, K. Hawton and P. Cowen eds. Oxford, England: Oxford University Press.

Herpertz, S. 1995. Self-injurious behaviour: Psychopathological and nosological characteristics in subtypes of self-injurers. *Acta Psychiatica Scandinavica* 91:57–68.

Leibenluft, E., D. Gardner, and R. Cowdry. 1987. The inner experience of the borderline self-mutilator. *Journal of Personality Disorders* 1, no. 4: 317–324.

Mazelis, R. (ed.) 1990–1997. *The Cutting Edge: A Newsletter for Women Living with Self-Inflicted Violence.* (Available from The Cutting Edge, P.O. Box 20819, Cleveland, Ohio 44120.)

Miller, D. 1994. *Women Who Hurt Themselves.* New York: Basic Books.

Shapiro, S. 1987. Self-mutilation and self-blame in incest victims. *American Journal of Psychotherapy* 41:46–54.

Siomopoulos, V. 1974. Repeated self-cutting: An impulse neurosis. *American Journal of Psychotherapy* 28:85–94.

Trautmann, K., and R. Conners. 1994. *Understanding Self-Injury: A Workbook for Adults*. Pittsburgh: Pittsburgh Action Against Rape.

Van Moffaert, M. 1990. Self-mutilation: Diagnosis and practical treatment. *International Journal of Psychiatry in Medicine* 20, no. 4: 373–382.

Vela, J., J. Harris, J. K. Wright, et al. 1983. Self-mutilation. *Journal of Trauma* 23:165–167.

Walsh, B., and P. Rosen. 1988. *Self-Mutilation: Theory, Research and Practice*. New York: Guilford Press.

Winchel, R., and M. Stanley. 1991. Self-injurious behavior: A review of the behavior and biology of self-mutilation. *American Journal of Psychiatry* 148:306–317.

Chapter 4 — The Cycle of Self-Inflicted Violence

Conners, R. 1996. Self-injury in trauma survivors: 1. Functions and meanings. *American Journal of Orthopsychiatry* 66:197–206.

Coons, P., and V. Milstein. 1990. Self-mutilation associated with dissociative disorders. *Dissociation Progress in the Dissociation Disorders* 3, no. 2: 81–87.

Favazza, A. R. 1989. Why patients mutilate themselves. *Hospital Community Psychiatry* 40:137–145.

Haines, J., C. Williams, K. Brain, and G. Wilson. 1995. The psychophysiology of self-mutilation. *Journal of Abnormal Psychology* 104, no. 3: 471–489.

Hawton, K. 1990. "Self-Cutting: Can It Be Prevented?" In *Dilemmas and Difficulties in the Management of Psychiatric Patients*, K. Hawton and P. Cowen eds. Oxford, England: Oxford University Press.

Menninger, K. 1935. A psychoanalytic study of the significance of self-mutilation. *Psychoanalytic Quarterly* 4:408–466.

Miller, D. 1994. *Women Who Hurt Themselves*. New York: Basic Books.

Pattison, E., and J. Kahan. 1983. The deliberate self-harm syndrome. *British Journal of Medical Psychology* 140:867–872.

Ross, R. R., and H. B. McKay. 1979. *Self-mutilation*. Lexington, Mass: Lexington Books.

Shapiro, S. 1987. Self-mutilation and self-blame in incest victims. *American Journal of Psychotherapy* 41:46–54.

Stone, M. 1987. A psychodynamic approach: Some thoughts on the dynamics and therapy of self-mutilating borderline patients. *Journal of Personality Disorders* 1, no. 4: 347–349.

Trautmann, K., and R. Conners. 1994. *Understanding Self-Injury: A Workbook for Adults*. Pittsburgh: Pittsburgh Action Against Rape.

Vela, J., J. Harris, J. K. Wright, et al. 1983. Self-mutilation. *Journal of Trauma* 23:165–167.

Walsh, B., and P. Rosen. 1988. *Self-Mutilation: Theory, Research and Practice*. New York: Guilford Press.

Chapter 5 — Self-Inflicted Violence and Other Psychological Factors

Conners, R. 1996. Self-injury in trauma survivors: 1. Functions and meanings. *American Journal of Orthopsychiatry* 66:197–206.

Conners, R. 1996. Self-injury in trauma survivors: 2. Levels of clinical response. *American Journal of Orthopsychiatry* 66:207–216.

Coons, P., and V. Milstein. 1990. Self-mutilation associated with dissociative disorders. *Dissociation Progress in the Dissociation Disorders* 3, no. 2: 81–87.

Cross, L. 1993. Body and self in feminine development: Implications for eating disorders and delicate self-mutilation. *Bulletin of the Menninger Clinic* 57, no. 1: 41–67.

Demitrack, M., F. Putnam, T. Brewerton, H. Brandt, and P. Gold. 1990. Relation of clinical variables to dissociative phenomena in eating disorders. *American Journal of Psychiatry* 147, no. 9: 1184–1188.

deYoung, M. 1982. Self-injurious behavior in incest victims: A research note. *Child Welfare* 61:577–584.

Dulit, R., M. Fyer, A. Leon, B. Brodsky, and A. Frances. 1994. Clinical correlates of self-mutilation in borderline personality disorder. *American Journal of Psychiatry* 151, no. 9: 1305–1311.

Dycian, A., G. Fishman, and A. Bleich. 1994. Suicide and self-inflicted injuries. *Aggressive Behavior* 20:9–16.

Favazza, A. R. 1987. *Bodies Under Siege: Self-Mutilation in Culture and Psychiatry*. Baltimore: Johns Hopkins University Press.

Favazza, A. R., L. DeRosear, and K. Conterio. 1989. Self-mutilation and eating disorders. *Suicide and Life-Threatening Behavior* 19, no. 4: 352–361.

Favazza, A. R., and R. Rosenthal. 1993. Diagnostic issues in self-mutilation. *Hospital and Community Psychiatry* 44, no. 2: 134–140.

Herpertz, S. 1995. Self-injurious behaviour: Psychopathological and nosological characteristics in subtypes of self-injurers. *Acta Psychiatica Scandinavica* 91:57–68.

Leibenluft, E., D. Gardner, and R. Cowdry. 1987. The inner experience of the borderline self-mutilator. *Journal of Personality Disorders* 1, no. 4: 317–324.

Mazelis, R. (ed.) 1990—1997. *The Cutting Edge: A Newsletter for Women Living with Self-Inflicted Violence.* (Available from The Cutting Edge, P.O. Box 20819, Cleveland, Ohio 44120.)

Miller, D. 1994. *Women Who Hurt Themselves.* New York: Basic Books.

Morgan, H., C. Burns-Cox, H. Pocock, and S. Pottle. 1975. Deliberate self-harm: Clinical and socioeconomic characteristics of 368 patients. *British Journal of Psychiatry* 127:564–574.

Parry-Jones, B., and W. L. Parry-Jones. 1993. Self-mutilation in four historical cases of bulimia. *British Journal of Psychiatry* 163:394–402.

Shapiro, S. 1987. Self-mutilation and self-blame in incest victims. *American Journal of Psychotherapy* 41:46–54.

Simeon, D., B. Stanley, A. Frances, J. J. Mann, R. Winchel, and M. Stanley. 1992. Self-mutilation in personality disorders: Psychological and biological correlates. *American Journal of Psychiatry* 149:221–228.

Trautmann, K., and R. Conners. 1994. *Understanding Self-Injury: A Workbook for Adults.* Pittsburgh: Pittsburgh Action Against Rape.

Vela, J., J. Harris, J. K. Wright, et al. 1983. Self-mutilation. *Journal of Trauma* 23:165–167.

Walsh, B., and P. Rosen. 1988. *Self-Mutilation: Theory, Research and Practice.* New York: Guilford Press.

Zweig-Frank, H., J. Paris, and J. Guzder. 1994. Psychological risk factors and self-mutilation in male patients with bpd. *Canadian Journal of Psychiatry* 39:266–268.

Zweig-Frank, H., J. Paris, and J. Guzder. 1994. Psychological risk factors for dissociation and self-mutilation in female patients with borderline personality disorder. *Canadian Journal of Psychiatry* 39:259–264.

Chapter 6 — Talking to Others About Self-Inflicted Violence

Bass, E., and L. Davis. 1988. *The Courage to Heal: A Guide for Woman Survivors of Child Sexual Abuse.* New York: Harper & Row.

Conners, R. 1996. Self-injury in trauma survivors: 2. Levels of clinical response. *American Journal of Orthopsychiatry* 66:207–216.

Hawton, K. 1990. "Self-Cutting: Can It Be Prevented?" In *Dilemmas and Difficulties in the Management of Psychiatric Patients*, K. Hawton and P. Cowen eds. Oxford, England: Oxford University Press.

Mazelis, R. (ed.) 1990–1997. *The Cutting Edge: A Newsletter for Women Living with Self-Inflicted Violence.* (Available from The Cutting Edge, P.O. Box 20819, Cleveland, Ohio 44120.)

Shapiro, S. 1987. Self-mutilation and self-blame in incest victims. *American Journal of Psychotherapy* 41:46–54.

Stone, M. 1987. A psychodynamic approach: Some thoughts on the dynamics and therapy of self-mutilating borderline patients. *Journal of Personality Disorders* 1, no. 4: 347–349.

Trautmann, K., and R. Conners. 1994. *Understanding Self-Injury: A Workbook for Adults.* Pittsburgh: Pittsburgh Action Against Rape.

Van Moffaert, M. 1989. Management of self-mutilation: Confrontation and integration of psychotherapy and psychotropic drug treatment. *Psychotherapy and Psychosomatics* 51:180–186.

Van Moffaert, M. 1990. Self-mutilation: Diagnosis and practical treatment. *International Journal of Psychiatry in Medicine* 20, no. 4: 373–382.

Walsh, B., and P. Rosen. 1988. *Self-Mutilation: Theory, Research and Practice.* New York: Guilford Press.

Chapter 7—Deciding to Stop Self-Inflicted Violence

Bass, E., and L. Davis. 1988. *The Courage to Heal: A Guide for Woman Survivors of Child Sexual Abuse.* New York: Harper & Row.

Conners, R. 1996. Self-injury in trauma survivors: 2. Levels of clinical response. *American Journal of Orthopsychiatry* 66:207–216.

Gil, E. 1988. *Treatment of Adult Survivors of Childhood Abuse.* Walnut Creek, Calif: Lauch Press.

Hawton, K. 1990. "Self-Cutting: Can It Be Prevented?" In *Dilemmas and Difficulties in the Management of Psychiatric Patients*, K. Hawton and P. Cowen eds. Oxford, England: Oxford University Press.

Mazelis, R. (ed.) 1990–1997. *The Cutting Edge: A Newsletter for Women Living with Self-Inflicted Violence.* (Available from The Cutting Edge, P.O. Box 20819, Cleveland, Ohio 44120.)

Stone, M. 1987. A psychodynamic approach: Some thoughts on the dynamics and therapy of self-mutilating borderline patients. *Journal of Personality Disorders* 1, no. 4: 347–349.

Trautmann, K., and R. Conners. 1994. *Understanding Self-Injury: A Workbook for Adults.* Pittsburgh: Pittsburgh Action Against Rape.

Van Moffaert, M. 1989. Management of self-mutilation: Confrontation and integration of psychotherapy and psychotropic drug treatment. *Psychotherapy and Psychosomatics* 51:180–186.

Van Moffaert, M. 1990. Self-mutilation: Diagnosis and practical treatment. *International Journal of Psychiatry in Medicine* 20, no. 4: 373–382.

Walsh, B., and P. Rosen. 1988. *Self-Mutilation: Theory, Research and Practice.* New York: Guilford Press.

Chapter 8—After Self-Inflicted Violence

Conners, R. 1996. Self-injury in trauma survivors: 2. Levels of clinical response. *American Journal of Orthopsychiatry* 66:207–216.

Hawton, K. 1990. "Self-Cutting: Can It Be Prevented?" In *Dilemmas and Difficulties in the Management of Psychiatric Patients,* K. Hawton and P. Cowen eds. Oxford, England: Oxford University Press.

Mazelis, R. (ed.) 1990–1997. *The Cutting Edge: A Newsletter for Women Living with Self-Inflicted Violence.* (Available from The Cutting Edge, P.O. Box 20819, Cleveland, Ohio 44120.)

Trautmann, K., and R. Conners. 1994. *Understanding Self-Injury: A Workbook for Adults.* Pittsburgh: Pittsburgh Action Against Rape.

Van Moffaert, M. 1989. Management of self-mutilation: Confrontation and integration of psychotherapy and psychotropic drug treatment. *Psychotherapy and Psychosomatics* 51:180–186.

Van Moffaert, M. 1990. Self-mutilation: Diagnosis and practical treatment. *International Journal of Psychiatry in Medicine* 20, no. 4: 373–382.

Walsh, B., and P. Rosen. 1988. *Self-Mutilation: Theory, Research and Practice.* New York: Guilford Press.

Chapter 9—For Family and Friends

Conners, R. 1996. Self-injury in trauma survivors: 2. Levels of clinical response. *American Journal of Orthopsychiatry* 66:207–216.

Hawton, K. 1990. "Self-Cutting: Can It Be Prevented?" In *Dilemmas and Difficulties in the Management of Psychiatric Patients,* K. Hawton and P. Cowen eds. Oxford, England: Oxford University Press.

Mazelis, R. (ed.) 1990–1997. *The Cutting Edge: A Newsletter for Women Living with Self-Inflicted Violence.* (Available from The Cutting Edge, P.O. Box 20819, Cleveland, Ohio 44120.)

Trautmann, K., and R. Conners. 1994. *Understanding Self-Injury: A Workbook for Adults.* Pittsburgh: Pittsburgh Action Against Rape.

Van Moffaert, M. 1989. Management of self-mutilation: Confrontation and integration of psychotherapy and psychotropic drug treatment. *Psychotherapy and Psychosomatics* 51:180–186.

Walsh, B., and P. Rosen. 1988. *Self-Mutilation: Theory, Research and Practice.* New York: Guilford Press.

Chapter 10 — For the Therapist

Conners, R. 1996. Self-injury in trauma survivors: 2. Levels of clinical response. *American Journal of Orthopsychiatry* 66:207–216.

Gil, E. 1988. *Treatment of Adult Survivors of Childhood Abuse.* Walnut Creek, Calif: Lauch Press.

Hawton, K. 1990. "Self-Cutting: Can It Be Prevented?" In *Dilemmas and Difficulties in the Management of Psychiatric Patients,* K. Hawton and P. Cowen eds. Oxford, England: Oxford University Press.

Mazelis, R. (ed.) 1990–1997. *The Cutting Edge: A Newsletter for Women Living with Self-Inflicted Violence.* (Available from The Cutting Edge, P.O. Box 20819, Cleveland, Ohio 44120.)

Shea, S. 1993. Personality characteristics of self-mutilating male prisoners. *Journal of Clinical Psychology* 49, no. 4: 576–585.

Van Moffaert, M. 1989. Management of self-mutilation: Confrontation and integration of psychotherapy and psychotropic drug treatment. *Psychotherapy and Psychosomatics* 51:180–186.

Van Moffaert, M. 1990. Self-mutilation: Diagnosis and practical treatment. *International Journal of Psychiatry in Medicine* 20, no. 4: 373–382.

Walsh, B., and P. Rosen. 1988. *Self-Mutilation: Theory, Research and Practice.* New York: Guilford Press.